nderground
Out
of
Holland

S.E. HANSON

Underground Out of Holland

LONDON

IAN ALLAN LTD

ACKNOWLEDGEMENTS

My grateful thanks are due to the following for the invaluable help afforded in the preparation of this book:

Messrs A. F. Christie, H. J. A. Hulshof, M.A. Garbett, H.W. Lensink, B.W.C. van Albeslo, Mr and Mrs L.L.A. Trethewey, Colonel J.S.O. Haslewood, Major S.G.B. Blewitt, Major P.L. Mercer, Mr J.F. Allen, Mr W.G. Beddows.

S.E. HANSON
Quinton,
Birmingham.
January 1975.

First published 1977

ISBN 0 7110 0631 8

Published by Ian Allan Ltd, Shepperton, Surrey, and printed in the United Kingdom by Picton Print, Chippenham, Wilts.

Contents

Dedication

To the men and women of the Dutch Resistance, who during the years 1940/45 did so much at so great a risk for the Allied cause.
And in particular to the memory of Mr and Mrs D.H. te Lindert, of Barlo, Gelderland, whose example of humanity and cool courage I was privileged to see and shall never forget.

Foreword

by W. ALLISTON, ESQ.,
Chairman Royal Air Forces Escaping Society

This story is indicative of many which can be told by members of the Royal Air Forces Escaping Society, in that it lays emphasis upon the wonderful work carried out by members of the Resistance organisations, who took such enormous risks to rescue, feed, hide from the enemy, and tend the wounds of airmen who were shot down during World War II.

The author of this book has been moved to write his story because of the memory of those who in spite of the enemy and collaborators in their midst, carried on, year in and year out, rescuing and getting back home numerous airmen who would have otherwise finished up in a German prison camp.

The Royal Air Forces Escaping Society was founded in 1946 by the late Viscount Portal of Hungerford, who felt that those who had been saved by resistance organisations, would owe to these people an everlasting debt.

The Helpers are now getting old and the Society exists to this day to help in a practical way any Helper who now finds him or herself ill, needy, or in distress, and to continue the friendships forged under such difficult circumstances.

1

Operation Dortmund - Ems

"Bomb doors open!"

The bomb-aimer's voice came flatly but insistently over the intercom as he took effective command of the aircraft during its bombing run.

The pilot complied and acknowledged that the doors were, in fact, locked fully open. The acknowledgement was largely superfluous so far as I was concerned. The Lancaster was a bomber built round its bomb-bays, and when those huge doors were open, the slipstream caught the leading edges and caused the aircraft to vibrate and shudder in its flight. It was a moment which invariably presaged the buffeting that came from exploding flak; it was a moment in which I was repeatedly aware of the sweat that comes from fear standing on my forehead and lining the edges of my oxygen mask. Always, during the actual run in to the target, I was acutely aware that I sat immediately above several tons of high explosives.

The bomber approached its target. The time was two minutes before midnight on the night of February 7th, 1945; the target was the Dortmund-Ems Canal; the objective to knock a hole in its banks at this, its weak spot, and so breach it.

Ron Young's patter droned on, seemingly interminable and with increasing slowness. The target gradually came down the grid of his bomb-sight. "Right, right, hold her there, left a touch, hold her there, hold her — bombs gone!"

Fourteen 1000lb General Purpose bombs, each with a half hour delayed action fuse fitted, nosed their way rapidly earthwards. The aircraft, relieved of its six and a half ton payload, heaved momentarily and sped more easily on into the night. The flak had been considerable but not particularly violent; of night fighters there had been no sign. We were strictly on time. Things had gone very well. My turn on the intercom now. Let's get home!

"Navigator to pilot. Fly course 245 degrees, height 10,000 feet, airspeed 175 mph, indicated."

"OK Nav"

I watched the duplicate set of the main instruments as 'Chuck' Fowler brought the aircraft round on to its homeward course. I really need not have bothered. He was, as ever, smack-on. I could afford to relax, for the rest was, navigationally, easy. I reached for my flask of coffee, sat back and poured myself a cup.

The Dortmund-Ems Canal had become something of a pet bunny for the squadrons of No 5 Group, Bomber Command. The canal bore little relationship to the British conception of an artificial waterway. If the average British canal might be compared in width with a trout stream, then the Dortmund-Ems resembled the lower reaches of the Thames. In fact it was a broad, deep waterway, capable of accommodating barges almost as large as a small destroyer and with a capacity equal to a fleet of our traditional longboats. Its importance as a communications artery to the German war effort was immense. Germany had little reserves of iron ore within her own borders, but neutral Sweden possessed vast quantities of ore of a high grade. Although nominally neutral, Sweden had no option but to ship this most vital of commodities to Germany, and the canal was the final means by which it reached the blast furnaces of the Ruhr, for it linked the navigable section of the River Ems with the industrial city of Dortmund. The equation was simple. Drain a section of the canal, and the last link in the chain which provided the raw material for the tanks and guns which had their birth in Krupps and similar factories of the Ruhr was broken.

The military importance of the canal had been realised since the beginning of the war, but attempts to breach it had not proved very successful until September 1944. Since then it had been breached repeatedly. Its value to the enemy was demonstrated by the fact that loaded barges were held in readiness to drop ballast into the gaps caused by bombing. There was therefore little point, once the water had drained away in a section, in bombing again until the Germans had restored the water to its normal level. It had thus become a four or five weekly chore. There had, for example, been an extremely successful daylight raid on the first day of January 1945, as a kind of New Year present to the Hun.

The raid from which we were returning was the follow-up now that the Germans had, with Teutonic thoroughness, restored the canal's viability. Always the point of attack was near the village of Ladbergen, some fifteen miles north of Münster. For a few kilometres here the canal ran between high earthen parapets above the level of the surrounding fields. This was the weak spot, a place where successful breaching was possible. But the Germans knew it and the area was heavily defended. Equally, the target was a difficult one to hit, for the parapets themselves were mere ribbons ten yards broad, and a bomb twenty yards short or even in the canal itself was not of much use. Our bombing height had, therefore, been a low one of 10,000 feet, which put us outside the effective limit of the light flak but well within the range of the heavy guns. Even at that height the probability of sinking any one bomb into the parapets was no greater than the likelihood of sinking a dart into the bull's eye of a dartboard from twenty feet. However, fourteen half ton bombs from each of some 180 Lancasters ought to produce results. We should not see the results until the reconnaissance photographs came in the next day, for the bombs were fused to explode half an hour after we had gone in order to obtain maximum penetration and, by obviating flashes, to present the bomb aimers with the best possible view of the target. We had expected a hot reception from the enemy but somehow the flak had seemed relatively spiritless. We were slipping quietly and steadily towards the Dutch border on our way home. The thought of the bacon and egg flying-breakfast awaiting us at our base at Spilsby, in Lincolnshire, had begun to assume a comforting place in my mind.

In the rear gun turret Norman Levick scanned the night sky behind the aircraft. He revolved his turret continually, watching the area between the port and starboard quarters of the aircraft, above, level and below. The Lancaster, even at this late stage of the war, was lightly armed. It had no cannon but carried for its defence a mere eight .303 Browning machine guns. Of these, four were in the rear turret as fighter attacks usually came from behind, and the Lanc's sting (such as it was) was therefore in the tail. At nineteen Levick was the baby of the crew and, when flying, its loneliest member. The so-called 'tail-end Charlie' position was not one usually envied by other members of the crew. He was physically separated from the rest of us by half the length of the aircraft but, locked away behind those turret doors, the psychological gap was greater. He spent all his flying hours facing backwards, and usually had a view of the firework display that characterised a target and the glow of the fires of a burning oil refinery or marshalling yards for miles on the return journey. Tonight, as we turned homeward, he had seen below him the broad band of the Dortmund-Ems Canal cutting like a gash across the flat Westphalian plain, the red cricket-like balls and black puffs of bursting flak, and then merely the last light of the flares and the red glow of a target indicator to indicate the point of attack. It was a period of no moon, but the target area was clear and, in the starlight, the small red glow on the canal bank remained visible for a time and then was gone. There were no bomb bursts and no firework display. It was singularly undramatic.

Norman had a speed of reaction and an equability of temperament that made him ideal as a rear gunner. But his outstanding quality was his night vision. He was a country lad from Nottinghamshire, fair of hair and solid of build, and he had a countryman's eyes. Most of us believed that no cat that walked could see better in the dark than Norman. Tonight, however, he saw nothing that disturbed him, except a thin layer of stratus cloud in broken patches which had begun to appear a thousand feet below the aircraft as we droned on westwards.

At the other end of the aircraft Leo Fowler sat at the controls accurately flying the course, height and airspeed I had provided. Meticulous attention to detail was his characteristic. He approached each operation with method and dedication. He was determined to complete an operational tour of thirty trips successfully and he intended to do it 'by the book'. He insisted on absolute formality in the use of the intercom, and was not favourably disposed towards chat when airborne. On the ground, however, he kept his crew well together and scarcely a non-flying night passed without a visit to some local pub by all or most of us in a group. From the first he had maintained that we should succeed only as a team and, to his credit, he had welded a happy crew together in his almost prim sort of way. At twenty-six he was the oldest member of the crew flying that night and had seen service first in the army, then as an engine fitter in the RAAF before finally remustering to aircrew. He was untypical of the boisterous Australian, but was dark, of relatively slight build and had an inclination towards dapperness which found its ultimate realisation in a neat moustache. The epithet 'Chuck' had, by virtue of his surname, been bestowed upon him by the real old man of the crew, Stan New, the mid-upper gunner. He had fallen sick a few days previously, immediately after celebrating his fortieth birthday on the squadron and was, no doubt, at this very moment safely tucked away in bed at Spilsby.

Chuck always flew in a concentrated, exact sort of way, and possessed a knowledge of aircraft engines superior to that of nine pilots out of ten. He had also shown that he was a cool hand in a crisis when, in a protracted and sticky situation in the recent past, he had, by persistently good piloting, wrought a successful issue out of a seemingly lost cause. Night vision was not, however, one of his strong points, and Ron Young tended to remain permanently in the discomfort of the bomb-aiming compartment, where he could look forward, instead of his enjoying spells in the relative comfort of the navigator's cabin working part of the radar. At all events, Leo Fowler flew contentedly enough during the first few minutes of February 8th, 1945. It was another target bombed; another op' towards his thirty. The trip had gone like clockwork and we were on our way home without apparent hindrance. He saw nothing untoward.

I, for my part, had done precisely nothing except drink a cup of coffee since leaving Ladbergen. There was no earthly reason why I should. The approach to the target had called for two quick course changes to confuse the enemy as to the exact point of attack. The return route, however, involved first one long straight westerly leg to a point just south of Arnhem, from where we should turn southwards over Allied occupied southern Holland and Belgium and so over the North Sea to base. That first leg of a hundred miles would take a little more than half an hour's flying time; that priceless piece of radar equipment known as the Gee box had been effectively jammed by the Germans as we came out over eastern Holland and was at the moment useless. But the windspeed and direction had proved very constant over this part of Europe. Therefore a dead-reckoning course could be relied upon until we came back into Gee range when I could check our position. Until that time, unless Ron Young with a set of maps in the nose of the aircraft came up with a pinpoint (improbable enough over this featureless stretch of Westphalia), there was nothing I could do or wanted to do. I was glad of a rest. I merely sat at my table in the light provided by an angle-poise lamp, occasionally glanced at the instruments which faced me on the left hand wall of the aircraft, and waited for someone to break the silence — for not a word had been said since we left the target.

The Lancaster was not a particularly comfortable aircraft in which to fly. It had a lifting power well in excess of any other bomber flying and it had manoeuvrability and dependability. But big bomb loads meant big bomb bays, and the crew's quarters were correspondingly restricted and compared unfavourably in this respect with the spacious Short Stirling on which we had finished our training. Such comfort as there was, was shared by the navigator and wireless operator. They at least had lighted, blacked-out cabins in which to work. Unless they came out of their nooks they saw nothing except the equipment of their trade, the walls of the aircraft and the black drapes which confined the light.

Johnny Eaton, the wireless operator, sat in his cabin astern of mine and waited for the next broadcast from base. It was due in about five minutes time, he reckoned. His job was to listen and relay messages to the rest of the crew. He was our link with home, but never, except in dire emergency, did he transmit; for transmissions could be monitored by the enemy and give away the position of the aircraft. He, too, was an Australian but some five years younger than his compatriot who sat at the pointed end of the bomber. Where Chuck had, in civvy street, worked in a Melbourne theatre, Johnny had been a bank clerk in his home town of Renmark, near Adelaide.

He was quick and ultra-efficient in his job, and sometimes a fraction intolerant toward people who did not know theirs. In addition to his main task, he could perform in emergency a fair job with the twin Browning guns in the mid-upper turret, and operated a device known as Fishpond, which gave early warning of fighter attacks. As, however, the Fishpond transmitted pulses (a possible give away of the aircraft's position) its use was curtailed. It was not scheduled to be used tonight, so Johnny merely sat and waited for the next broadcast. There were times when John Eaton found flying in a blacked-out cabin dull. At the moment the lack of activity left him, if anything, a touch bored.

Eric Copley, the flight engineer, had a different view. He was a qualified electrical engineer and had moved heaven and earth to get into aircrew because he loved flying. He had been in a reserved occupation from which he could not escape. In the end, because of his incessant applications and because of the temporary drying up of a job on which he was working, the powers that be had relented and he had got his way some years later than he wished. As a youth he had been a member of the No 1 Foundation Squadron of the ATC at Leicester and had done some gliding before the war. Now, at twenty-four, Eric stood to the right of the pilot on the darkened flight deck and gazed alternately at the luminous glow of the various instruments and gauges for which he was responsible and at the night sky from the starboard beam to the starboard bow. His urge to fly was sharpened by the fact that his flying hours were so few. The flight engineer's training course at St Athan included only a modicum of flying, and he had become operational with little more than a handful of flying hours to his name.

The Lancaster was a noisy aircraft. The din of those four superb Rolls Royce Merlin engines was ear shattering, and, in a Stirling, Copley would have had his own compartment amidships and the chance to sit down instead of spending virtually all his time standing — there was a tip-up seat fixed to the starboard wall of the aircraft, so small and uncomfortable that he rarely used it — here on the flight deck. But none but an idiot, he mused, would swap the comfort and room of the big, unmanoeuvrable, quiet Stirling with its very limited service ceiling and undependability for the noisy, cramped but highly efficient Lancaster. We had never flown this particular Lanc before but he was satisfied with its performance and very happy with the trip to date. However, at ten minutes past midnight, he did comment to his pilot that the stratus cloud beneath us was increasing and half suggest a descent to cloud top height.

It was Geoff Cheeseman, the substitute mid-upper gunner, who gave the first warning. Swinging his turret forward he spotted trouble.

"Mid-upper here skip. Fighter flares going down ahead and slightly to port. Do you see them?"

"I see them mid-upper. I'll steer round them to the north," responded

Fowler. "Where are we exactly navigator? Can you say?"

"Pretty close to the Dutch border. Give me two minutes and I'll see if I can get any joy out of this bloody Gee box."

Things were warming up. The leading aircraft of the bomber stream had been located. We, who were close behind them sitting clearly outlined above a thickening belt of layer cloud, were probably in for trouble.

Even as I turned to work on the radar set my mind flicked back to the briefing room, and the doubt which had plagued the minds of not a few of the navigators there, reasserted itself. It was true that we had bombed the canal near Ladbergen at midnight and were returning via virtually the same route by which we came. But the intention had not originally been so. Initially the raid had been scheduled for 2100 hrs and the return a direct one over the Zuyder Zee to Lincolnshire. Unfortunately heavy icing cloud had persisted off the Dutch coast, the raid was put back hourly until midnight in the hope of a clearance, and a return route over Belgium finally adopted. That would have been fair enough, but for one thing. The Canadian 1st Army with the British Armoured Corps attached to it had spent the winter sitting on the left bank of the river Maas at the northern end of the Allied line. The time had come for action. And, since the redoubtable XXX Corps, of Caen fame, were lined up with the Canadians, there was no doubt in anybody's mind where the action was going to be. The prize was the Ruhr with all its industries. In the early hours of this very morning the assault from the Maas towards the Rhine would be unleashed and, as a curtain-raiser, Main Force, Bomber Command, were, at this precise moment, blasting the three medium sized towns of Goch, Kalkar and Cleve which formed the northernmost bastions of the Siegfried Line into near obliteration with a mixed bag of 800 Lancasters and Halifaxes.

In any briefing room the routes to and from the targets were marked by red cord wound over the pins which marked the tactical turning points. In its original form the cord depicting the return route of 5 Group's strategic raid on the Dortmund-Ems ran well clear of the mass attack on the three towns: and indeed, we should have been landing just as that raid was commencing. But now we were journeying westward towards an area which had been under saturation attack for a quarter of an hour and was, no doubt, now glowing like a gigantic three-headed torch. The odds were that the night fighters ahead were on their way down from the large German air base at Rheine or one of its satellites to combat the bombers attacking the Siegfried Line to their south and had stumbled on our return by accident. The picture was not rosy.

Five pairs of eyes scanned their various allotted sectors of the night sky with the absolute of vigilance; I peered into the luminous green glow of the cathode ray tube, which was the guts of the Gee box, like a non-clairvoyant seeking to snatch a picture from a crystal ball. The screen was covered with the wisps of the so-called 'grass' with which the Germans were jamming it. Instead of five recognisable and translatable pulses there were myriads of wisps and pseudo pulses all over it. But, by the grace of God, and sooner than I could have hoped, the true pulses were just discernible beneath the muck. Rapidly I took the readings and began to transcribe them into a ground fix on my chart. Chuck Fowler, I noticed as I glanced automatically at the compass, had merely edged away to the north, and that made sense. The last thing we wanted at this point in time was to be isolated from the stream of bombers in which we flew. The altimeter showed a fractional descent toward the cloud top. The first position line traced by my pencil looked useful; the second one intersected it within a couple of miles of our desired track and within a whisker of the Dutch border. So close to the border were we that the amusing thought struck me that Chuck, for the first time that I could remember, would now have no chance to perform his operational ritual. There was an Elsan lavatory in the rear of the fuselage opposite the entrance door, and some pilots, when the need arose and the time was right, left the flight engineer to fly straight and level for a bit while they went back and performed. Fowler would have none of this. He refused to leave his pilot's seat, but was, at the same time, no stronger of bladder than the average man. He carried always a tin can, urinated into it invariably when we were over Germany itself, and passed it to Eric who tipped the contents down a chute used for releasing bundles of anti-radar silver paper strips known as Window. His form of words as he passed the can was always the same. It had become ritualistic. "There," he would say when he had finished, "tip that on the Third Reich, engineer!" Regrettably he had not performed tonight, and the Third Reich remained in that respect unscathed. That thought apart, I timed the fix at 0017 hrs and drew breath to announce our position.

In that very instant it happened. There was a sudden, violent explosion amidships that crashed on the ear, even above the roar of the engines, like a single, vicious thunderclap. The bomber bounced and bucked like an irritated bronco. There followed immediately over the intercom a gasping drawn-out groan as of a man in severe pain — the sound was muted but distinctly audible. "Christ Almighty!" I thought, "we're hit and one of the lads has had it!" But hit by what? There had been no warning from either of the gunners of a fighter attack. There was a chance of flak at this low altitude, for several of the small towns on the German side of the border were defended, but, unless my fix was wrong, we were past them. Collision with another bomber in the stream as we weaved to the north? That was possible but in clear starlight should not have happened. I glanced instinctively over my left shoulder towards the rear of the aircraft but saw nothing more dramatic than the funereal black of the curtain which separated me from Johnny Eaton.

My instinct was to dash through that curtain and see how Johnny and Geoff Cheeseman were faring, for it was there, amidships, that I felt the explosion had occurred. My intention was thwarted by a rapid, sotto-voce interchange between pilot and engineer.

"Take a quick close look at that fire on the port wing, engineer!", ordered Fowler, formal to the last. "I'm having a hell of a job to hold this bloody kite at the moment."

Copley's opinion was only seconds in coming.

"Hopeless! That's no piddling engine fire, it's a conflagration. A great chunk of the wing's gone and the sodding petrol tanks are ablaze. She's had it. She won't last many minutes. Wing'll burn off or she'll explode."

"Sod it!", I heard Chuck mutter between clenched teeth. "If we could only hold on to her for ten minutes we'd be over our own lines. But I agree. We can't. Jump! jump! jump!"

The last three words were snapped out. They constituted an order to abandon aircraft as fast as the proverbial bat out of hell.

I grabbed for the parachute pack that stood against the leg of my table, bawled over the intercom, "We're over Holland, chaps", and had begun to remove my flying-helmet when my attention was again arrested momentarily.

"Ron Young's sprawled out over the escape hatch. I think he's unconscious". Copley's voice came rapidly and anxiously over my half discarded headset.

"Get him out!" snapped Fowler.

I waited no more. That explained the groan. Ron Young was a big chap, more than six feet tall. My duty was to help Eric Copley get Ron's parachute fixed to his chest, put his right hand round the D-ring that operated the ripcord, get the hatch open and get him out. It was the only chance he had.

I slammed the rings on the back of the parachute pack into the clips on the harness on my chest, moved forward through the black-out curtain and on to the flight deck. Instead of a darkness relieved merely by the phosphorescent green of the instruments there was light in abundance. In fact it was as light as a summer's day. Chuck sat there grimly holding on to his stricken aircraft, his face clearly outlined against the lurid glare of the red and yellow flames which shot back, streamer-like, parallel with the fuselage. As I passed his right shoulder I glanced compulsively at the port wing. Eric was right; it *was* a conflagration and completely hopeless. The trailing half of the wing had been shot away over a distance extending from near the fuselage to the port outer engine, the petrol tanks were open to the air, spilling burning petrol backwards into the slipstream and blazing like Dante's Inferno.

Copley was half in and half out of the bomb aiming compartment when I arrived behind him. A single deep step led down from the flight deck into Ron Young's sanctum, and Eric had one foot down and was crouched with his head inside the aperture shouting and gesticulating. I bent down and peered round him as best I might. The light inside the compartment was vividly intense and I smelt heat. I saw Ron Young scrambling up from where he had lain prone with his head beneath the twin front guns. He shuffled towards us on his knees, deathly pale and obviously dazed. He caught the meaning of Copley's gesticulations, grabbed his parachute, fixed it to his chest and began to fiddle with the hatch. Fiddle was the operative word. His dazed reactions were slow and ineffectual; the hatch, a mere two foot square panel in the floor of the aircraft's nose, jammed. Copley began to edge into the cramped confines and I was at his very heels. There was no time to waste.

"For Christ's sake get that bloody hatch open, Young!" Eric had by nature a booming sort of voice and he used it to the last decibel now.

Ron ceased his efforts with the unyielding hatch. Not endowed by nature with a surfeit of patience and driven now by desperation he took the direct course. He stood crouching back from it, jumped on to the middle with all his force and disappeared feet first into the night taking the hatch with him. The abrupt mode of his departure held a touch of bizarre comedy.

Eric was down the step and positioned over the gap in the floor within a second; I followed down the step. My view of the compartment had, up to that point, been restricted, but now I saw the unpleasant truth. In the left hand rear corner the F 24 camera which took the automatic photo-flash of our bombing had been hit and was blazing furiously. It was mounted in the floor within a foot or so of the hatch, the fire was being driven inwards by the slipstream, and swirling gusts of flame were beginning to lick along the floor and up the port wall of the nose.

Copley let go and vanished from view. With those tongues of flame writhing about like demented yellow snakes and the danger of a burnt parachute pack to goad me on I needed no bidding to the night outside.

I paused for a moment leaning with my hands outstretched on either side of the hole and stared into the black void. I had, it was true, been brought up in a rather devout C of E family, but I could not claim to be highly religious, or in any way given to praying, which I had never really understood. I remembered afterwards, though, that in the instant before I plunged I did call instinctively and fervently upon my Maker. Then I fell headlong into the blackness below.

The night air tore at me. I felt it plucking and snatching at the pack on my chest and at the bottom of the parachute harness round my rump as if it were a demon intent upon divesting me of the very things whose perfect functioning meant the difference between life and imminent bone-crunching death. I saw alternately stars and a black void as I somersaulted in the sky two miles above the earth. I was plummeting towards the ground at more than a hundred miles an hour and yet, strangely, having nothing to relate my fall to, I had absolutely no feeling of headlong descent. Rather I felt as if I were floating in space. It was, in point of fact, a rather pleasureable sensation: but that did not prevent me, after what I judged rather than counted to be five seconds, from pulling hard on the ripcord. Time seemed to stand still, seconds to be hours. For a moment that expanded mentally into an age nothing happened. And then, with a slowness that jarred on the nerves, I saw against the starlight the small pilot 'chute start its upward journey dragging the main parachute with it. There was a colossal roaring of aircraft engines as a bomber passed close above me. I saw, as I looked upward, the shrouds and the unopened 'chute wavering and quivering in the undertow of the bomber's slipstream as they rose above me. "Open you bastard!", I shouted to the 'chute as if it could hear me. The whole thing could not have taken more than a second or so, but, as I twisted earthwards and lost sight of those upward mounting guy ropes and shrouds, I was despondently convinced that I had had it; that the air had won; that the slender threads by which I hoped to hang on to life would collapse round me as the canopy failed to open. A moment more, an almighty jolt under the armpits and in the crutch as the straps of the harness gripped and held me tight; and then I was floating gently downwards like a spider hanging beneath a huge nylon web.

Perhaps six or seven seconds had elapsed since I jumped. Not more than two minutes ago I had been seated comfortably in an aircraft going home. Now, as I hung above the dark and invisible earth, I gradually gathered my wits together. I must have come out of the dive facing westwards because I was immediately aware of our Lancaster ahead of and slightly below me. It was streaking on like a flaming meteor and losing height fast. As I hung there I watched the spreading flames with horror. It was all very well for me hanging safely beneath an opened parachute. But I knew only that Young and Copley, apart from myself, were out. What of the rest of the crew? As I watched, the aircraft's dive became steeper. She accelerated towards the earth, and then, inevitably, came the final death throes. Into a left hand spin she went. Three broad circular and yet downward passes she made. The flames had engulfed her. They took on a two-fold aspect as they licked their way along the wings; the impression was of a flaming cross spinning gyroscopically in the dark bowl of night. She was no more now than an incinerator: a white hot coffin for anyone left inside. And I could do no more than hang there and hope like hell that all the crew were out. The end was not long in coming. Midway through the third turn of the spin she hit the earth and lay there, a scattered mass of burning petrol, aluminium, canvas and rubber. She had not lasted more than five minutes after being hit. Lancaster X X-ray of No 207 Squadron had gone to her grave on the flat fields of eastern Holland three or four miles to the west of me.

She had one final word to say. Distantly but distinctly, like the sound of a saluting gun, two dull, resonant booms reverberated upwards in the stillness of the night as the petrol tanks in the starboard wing exploded. Those explosions jolted me back to a pitch of sharp awareness. Up to that point I had moved fast, acted by discipline, and finally watched, horrified and irresistibly fascinated, the death of an aircraft. There had been no time really to think and, therefore, no time for the fears that beset the unoccupied brain. Now that the aircraft was merely a glowing mass in the darkness below I knew fear once more. The patchy, fitful stratus above had almost vanished and I could see the parachute above me outlined clearly against the canopy of stars. That was fine; but I could not see the earth below. Into what should I fall? Discipline took over. With my right hand I checked the oxygen bottle tucked away in the bottom of my Mae West. If I fell into water the drill was to release the parachute immediately before entry and break the neck of that bottle by a swift downward blow of the hand to inflate the life jacket. But then, I ought not to fall into water. The area for miles on either side of the Dutch/German border was marshy but it contained no major rivers.

I began to use the fire below as a kind of marker. At the moment I knew that I was looking downward at a considerable angle on to it. Gradually, as I neared the earth, the angle must lessen and the fire finally disappear. Then would be the moment to prepare for impact. To such a practical purpose I set myself and drifted downwards with an attentive and reasonably composed mind. Vaguely, as in a dream, I knew that a mass of aircraft was roaring homeward above me. But I paid them no heed. I kept my eyes firmly fixed on the fire below.

I was aware quite suddenly that there was another parachute between me and that fire. I must have shifted my attention for a moment because I caught sight of the canopy slightly above me and not more than fifty or sixty yards distant.

"Hoy!" I hollered into the night. "Stick together when we land!"

There came no answer. I could see the parachutist with his legs drawn slightly up under him sailing downwards faster than I. He was now on my level and we were converging. I repeated my call. He heard me this time all right. "Hoy!" came back the answer. "We'll try - - -"

But it was no good. By some freak of the wind he was drifting away underneath me, and in the darkness below I lost both answer and him. For the first time I had had a chance to relate my fall to something visible and close. But it was not very encouraging. In fact I had the distinct impression that he was falling and I going up again. I was annoyed at the quick disappearance of a prospective mate. But air, I reflected, was like that. If it were merely a simple homogeneous mass blowing fixedly and evenly from one point of the compass navigation would be child's play. It was, in reality, full of updraughts and downdraughts, eddies and currents. That I was caught in an updraught on this boisterous night did not help matters at all. However, one problem was solved. It was Johnny Eaton's voice with its Australian overtones that had answered. He was another one who was safely out.

No matter how hard I tried I failed to detect any sign of the earth beneath me. When I looked downward the answer was a black nothing, and I became convinced that I should not see the ground until I hit it. The gradual descent seemed interminable. Slowly, though, the beacon that gave me a fixed mark in a pitch black sea took on a horizontal aspect and began to fade from view. That meant that I was nearing the earth, and the fact was reinforced by the realisation that I was beginning to swing backwards and forwards, pendulum like, on my parachute. There was a lively south-westerly wind blowing that stratus across the sky, and the eddying effect near the earth as it swept over woods and undulations of the ground caused the swinging. It had to be stopped. The force with which one landed by parachute was said to be equivalent to jumping from a fifteen foot wall. A vertical landing was, to put it mildly, greatly to be desired. I had no wish to make contact with an earth I could not see whilst on a forward or, particularly, backward swing. A broken leg or a twisted back was hardly calculated to help any. I began to correct by alternately pulling and releasing the guy ropes above my head. This had the effect of partially emptying the 'chute as one pulled and was reckoned to have a steadying effect. The drill worked. I saw momentarily the tops of a line of bare Lombardy poplars whipping by a few yards from my nose. I was amazed at the sudden sense of downward speed. This was it. I clamped my knees and ankles hard together and waited for the bump.

The time was half past midnight. Fifty miles away across that dreary Westphalian plain the first bombs were beginning to explode. The raid was a success and the water was already beginning to seep into the low lying fields surrounding the Dortmund-Ems Canal. Soon the trickle was destined to become a flood which emptied the canal for miles. But I knew nothing of that and certainly gave it no thought as my feet hit the wet earth of Holland.

2

Gelderland by Night

Wet was an understatement. My landing site had been ideal: I might have landed on a concrete road, or worse, on the roof of a building; I might even now have been suspended by my harness from the uppermost boughs of one of those nearby poplars waiting for daylight. Instead, Fate had placed me neatly in a soft, wet, level field and, apart from being heavily winded as I pitched forward, I had suffered not the slightest harm. I lay there for a moment on my stomach gasping for breath and blessing my good fortune. But, God, that field was wet. I realised as I rose that my flying boots were ankle deep in soft mud. Marsh? The idea of floundering about in a quagmire was not exactly appealing. I tested the ground, first with one foot and then the other. I felt uncertain. The top few inches had a consistency resembling treacle, but underneath it felt firm enough. I was inclined to the view that it was just a supremely wet field into which I had fallen.

In a way the very wetness of the field was an advantage. I was supposed, in theory, to bury my parachute in order to avoid giving the Germans notice of my landing. I had sat during escape lectures and listened to instructors (some of whom were experts at the game) prattling merrily on about the necessity of destroying the evidence of one's landing by burying the 'chute. Too idle, or perhaps too blasé to bother to pose the question, I had let it pass. But how the hell, I had always thought, do you bury a parachute with your bare hands? On a normally hard grass land I reckoned that to be an impossibility; but here, in the wet, I felt I had a fair chance of performing a badger-like operation and of thus at least beginning in the classic manner. First, though, I had another more pressing little burying job to do.

There were in the English Channel and in the North Sea two rectangular stretches of water known as the 'jettison areas'. It sometimes happened that, due to technical failure or because for some reason a raid was aborted, aircraft were returning to England with bombs still aboard. If the bombs were the normal thick-walled, low-capacity type there was no problem. Unfused they presented no particular danger and, on the 'waste not, want not' principle one simply brought them back and landed with them provided the aircraft was in good shape. The so-called 'Cookie' or 'Block Buster' was a different matter. These 4,000 lb or 8,000 lb high-capacity bombs had casings no thicker than those of large oil drums (which they resembled) and were designed to burst on impact in order to achieve maximum blast effect. To land on them was tantamount to an act of suicide. Therefore they were jettisoned, either over Germany itself or in one of the two 'jettison areas', which Allied shipping naturally avoided like the plague. I remembered vividly a night in early January when a raid in support of American troops engaged in the dying phases of the 'Battle of the Bulge' had been largely aborted because of heavy cloud over the target and the confused nature of the ground fighting, and from which Lancasters returning with a mixed load of General Purpose bombs and 'Cookies' were spattering the latter in the appropriate area of the Channel. Having given the order to jettison ours I had had a turn on the flight deck to see the show. The incandescent, blinding effect of those bursting 'Cookies' on the still, dark waters was impressive; but it made one think. Navigators were supposed to keep the precise latitude and longitude of those zones in their heads on the score of secrecy but, since mine would again have been the word which sent one of those sensitive, lethal canisters hurtling towards the unsuspecting fish which surround our shores, I preferred to have an aide-memoire rather than be responsible, through a memory lapse, for blowing up a battleship.

I had, then, in the pocket of my battledress a little note book which contained information of a secret nature, and I had a clear first duty to bury that. Without releasing my parachute I squatted down on my haunches and proceeded to scoop a hole in the slime and bury the book. That done I turned my attention to the canopy which had borne me safely earthwards and lay now under the stars, a crumpled patch of white fluttering and tugging at me in the brisk south-west wind. I turned the release mechanism on my midriff to the right, gave it a bang in the approved manner and began to haul the parachute into a compact bundle. As I did so I became acutely conscious of the roar of aircraft engines as the last few of our bomber stream droned their way home. It was a moment pregnant with envy; I felt desperately alone. The song of those motors burned in my brain and aroused, momentarily, combined feelings of jealousy and homesickness of an intensity I had never before known. For a full minute I stood there with the shrouds of the parachute in my hands, a prey to the emotive thought that in three hours time the fortunate would be eating bacon and eggs at base in England while I floundered about in this wretched marshland. The feeling was traumatic; but it passed. There was no time for moping.

I resumed my work. The parachute was within an ace of being drawn together into a manageable bundle when two unsavoury facts impressed themselves almost simultaneously upon my senses. I had, until that moment, had my back to the line of tall poplars which some beneficent type had been so kind as to plant a few yards clear of my point of impact. Now, as I turned, I was uncomfortably aware of the loom of a sizeable building amid the trees, distant only a few yards, immediately in front of me and with coiled barbed-wire stretching across the field in front of it. Instinct told me that this was a dangerous place to be near. In the same instant I realised that I was not alone. To my left the open field ended in a small belt of trees, and in that dark patch someone was moving. There was no stealth about his movements. I could hear him stumbling about amid the trees quite audibly although he was distant at least thirty yards. For a moment I entertained the hope that it was Johnny Eaton who, by chance, had fallen within a stone's throw. The juxtaposition of the barbed-wire surrounded building and this so unfurtive man moving around in the middle of the night made me doubt it. Coiled barbed-wire suggested a military post of some kind. The broken stratus, as if to mock me, had cleared entirely. I stood there like a goon, bathed in full starlight, surrounded by what seemed to be an acre of white nylon and with an enemy post in front and, presumably, an active enemy on my left. I dropped my parachute and fell flat on my face in the ooze.

I lay there on my stomach, outstretched across the shrouds of the 'chute watching intently the dark loom of the copse. I looked at the navigation watch on my wrist. That, thank God, was still working. By holding it near my face I could hear it ticking and could just discern that the time was twenty minutes to one. My night-walking companion in the trees continued his perambulations. Suddenly he began to hammer. What he was doing was utterly beyond me but, in the still of the night, the sound of metal clanging against metal wafted stridently across the field. No question remained in my mind now. That certainly was not Johnny Eaton! Imagination did not help. In my mind's eye I saw at least a platoon of German infantry ensconced in that nearby building. And, with at least one of their number hammering and banging about beside me, I failed entirely to see how my descent could have been missed. The fluttering of the parachute in the bright light of the stars was no comfort. Surely he must see it. Mental conflict reigned. Should I run for it or not? Caution bade me stay. Perhaps the Kraut was shortsighted. But he might react to sudden movement. I felt as naked as a new-born babe lying in that open field, but I stayed. The dream of a classic beginning to a life of evasion by burying my parachute faded. It was stalemate. He continued hammering; I lay on my face in the mud and wished devoutly for a return of the covering cloud.

For a time the fear of imminent discovery disguised from me the facts that the February night was bitter and the ground I lay on sopping wet. Then the cold and damp bit into my bones and I began involuntarily to shudder.

A grain of native sense told me that to stay long like this was to court pneumonia. Move soon I must. Propped up on my elbows I started methodically to assess the situation. The field was long and narrow. It ended in the line of tall poplars near me and stretched away in the opposite direction further than I could see. With my back to the copse I could discern what appeared to me to be a hedgerow marking the boundary of the field on that side, and I had a fancy — it was no more than that — that I should find a ditch running alongside it. There lay the opening gambit. If I could not bury my parachute I could drown it. On reflection it occurred to me that my industrious enemy hammering away there must have a light to effect his maintenance job. Yet I could see none. I was probably better screened by the trees than I reckoned. Wild horses would not drag me either towards the copse or the building. But then, I had no need to venture near either. The constellation of The Plough stood boldly in the sky pointing, faithfully as ever, to the North Star. The star was over the copse: therefore the long field ran due east-west, I was at the eastern end, and a move to the westward (which I wanted) open to me.

The fitful stratus reappeared and covered half the sky. At roughly the same time the banging stopped and quiet descended on the field. I rose cautiously, gathered my parachute together and stole stealthily across to the hedgerow. There *was* a ditch. Into it I gently dropped the parachute, then discarded both harness and Mae West and shoved them in after it. It was perhaps foolish to imagine that a life-jacket designed to bear a man up in the water would sink: but then, I could do no more.

I began my westerly walk keeping more or less to the centre of the field. It was hard work, for the mud frequently came over my ankles, but the exercise was stimulating after lying shuddering on the marshy ground. The field seemed of interminable length and broadened the further one went. Westwards I had set my course, and to that end I commenced to shade over toward a fringe of single trees extending in a line to the right as I walked. I thought the field would never end and I rejoiced in the fact because it presented no real obstacle, other than hard going, and led steadily on in the right direction. But end it did, quite suddenly. There was a gentle shelving of the earth, and then I stood beside a small, bare willow tree upon the bank of a stream running directly athwart my track. I stopped and considered my best course of action. I was acutely sensible of the fact that a lot of deviation round woods and along rivers could lead to my walking virtually in a circle. I was intent upon pursuing a straight course. The stream was, however, too broad to jump and I had no fancy to try its depth by wading. I continued for a moment to think. One thing I could do was to relieve myself. I had lain overlong on the cold, swampy ground and that function was overdue. I stood, then, obeying the call of nature against a stunted willow tree when a sixth sense, rather than anything I saw or heard, warned me of danger. I stood stock-still against the tree and glanced to my right. In the starlight I could clearly see a small bridge across the stream no more than twenty yards away casting a pale shadow on the water. A moment more, a footfall, and then a figure emerged from the line of trees, clumped heavily across the bridge and strode imperviously and obliviously on. I stood there astonished and relieved both physically and mentally as I watched his silhouette disappear silently into the night. I had not consciously heard him until he stepped on to the bridge, nor could I hear him the moment he stepped off it. There had been a phase during my walk to date when I had laughed at myself for being over dramatic by lying prone just because some clot was banging away in a wood. It was probably, I thought then, some Dutch farmer working late. But it was no Dutch farmer. It was a great, tall, erect type dressed in army uniform with forage cap on head and the tip of a rifle barrel projecting above the shoulder of his service greatcoat whose jackboots had thumped over that bridge. And there was little doubt that it was my noisy, nocturnal, German companion of the copse who must have been walking along a path on the far side of the fringe of trees whilst I walked down the centre of the field opposite him.

A sudden feeling of elation surged through my mind. I experienced the certain conviction that I was not going to be caught. It was illogical, with the Rhine and a whole German army separating me from freedom. And yet things had started so well that I felt convinced that Luck was on my side. I turned in an almost happy frame of mind and walked along the rivulet in the opposite direction to the bridge, came rapidly upon a single plank thrown across from bank to bank, crossed it and pursued my westerly walk.

Everything slept. In the silvery starlight I passed farmhouse, field and spinney. In my present mood, and in the silence, these things held a tranquil beauty which soothed the spirit. I did not, as it happened, journey far. As I rounded some trees I saw a sizeable brick-built building in front of me which I concluded to be a closed-in barn. At this I stopped and decided to investigate the interior, for the principal reason that I wanted a smoke. The door stood slightly ajar. I tried it very gently, but it opened easily and noiselessly enough and I stood for a moment peering round it into the dark recesses of the interior before committing myself. In the dim light I could see strips of white hanging down from the high roof, which, for a moment or two, had me wondering. I stood indecisively in the doorway, unwilling to move toward those puzzling, rectangular white patches. Then, as my eyes became accustomed to the dimmer light within, I recognised them for what they were, laughed at myself for my doubts, walked across to the furthest corner, sat down on a pile of straw and pulled out my pipe.

The place was a barn all right, but it was also a kind of airing room. The white objects were sheets hanging from horizontal beams, and, considering the nature of the fields outside, I could not wonder that the lady of the nearby farmhouse chose to dry her washing indoors. I filled my pipe and lit up. The spurt of light afforded by the match disclosed the fact that my watch showed the hour as a little before two o'clock. Dead silence reigned as I smoked. It would, without question, have surprised not a few that I, notoriously forgetful as to trivia — such as where my pen, pipe or matches were at any particular time — should, in my present predicament, have had the chance to smoke. But so it was. I had, in point of fact, thought this one out rather carefully. There was, in the winter of 1944/45, distinctly less than one chance in two of successfully completing a Bomber Command operational tour. At earlier stages of the war the odds against had been even more unfavourable but the present ones were bad enough. It was not that one sat down and thought long and deeply on the chances of living to see the spring, for that was a certain way to neurosis and what, in the flying trade, was known as 'the twitch'. I had seen perfectly healthy aircrew slowly battered by the strain and danger of operational flying into a state where their faces grew drawn and pale and their hands twitched involuntarily as they wielded their knives and forks in the mess. Those were often the thoughtful, sensitive types. The thing undoubtedly to do was to live for the hour and let the future take care of itself. It had, however, registered that I might very well one day find myself in a miserable, lonely situation in some foreign field, and I had come to the conclusion that, in such an eventuality, the thing I should most desire would be a smoke. My pipe was my inseparable companion. Therefore I carried it on each operation thrust deep into one pocket of my battledress trousers and a full box of matches thrust deep into the other. My tobacco pouch, well filled, I kept ensconced between my battledress blouse and my shirt. I had every hope that they would all remain with me during a baleout and such had been the case. Our squadron motto happened to be Semper Paratus. In this respect, at any rate, I was always prepared.

I sat, then, on some straw in a corner of a Dutch barn enjoying undoubtedly the most satisfying smoke I had ever had; and, as I smoked, I thought, carefully.

Was I really in Holland? It was a question that demanded an answer. I had glibly assumed so from the first and, indeed, had had the temerity to shout as much over the intercom to the crew. But it was hairline stuff based on weak, bleary radar pulses barely visible through a welter of German jamming. Again, there was the effect of the south-west wind. Throughout the ten minutes or so it had taken me to descend, that wind had been blowing me at a steady twenty miles per hour straight back towards Germany, and would have nullified any gain made as the aircraft limped on past the border. Also, it was very possible that the coiled barbed-wire I had seen was the border itself. The truth was that I could be anywhere within two or three miles of the frontier, in either direction.

Memory and a little thought decided me that my route from here on should be south-westwards. That would take me towards the Rhine and Nijmegen; and there, in the narrow neck of land that separates Rhine from Maas, where they both turn westwards toward the distant sea, was the battle and, therefore, the British Army. I had no intention at present of knocking up the nearest farmhouse on spec', for that was obviously dangerous. Nor did I think there was any more chance now of meeting up with another member of the crew than of finding a needle in a haystack. I had to go it alone.

Questions still niggled at my mind. There were no flak positions, so far as I knew, within ten miles of where we were hit, and yet no warning cry of a fighter attack had come from either of the gunners. It was an enigma. All I knew was that four of the crew, including myself, were out, and that I did not rate Fowler's chances very high if he had been many seconds after me in getting through that blazing front hatch.

My pipe had gone out; the light, for some reason, seemed dimmer than before. I felt sleepy and the straw in this corner was comfortable. For two pins I would doss down here for the night and let the morrow take care of itself. A warning bell rang in my mind. It told me neither to be weak-kneed nor gormless. I rose and went out of the barn.

I looked at the sky in search of the Pole Star. It was not there. The cloud, which may well have been our undoing, and which had since come and gone as wantonly as a coquette, had covered the sky. The absence of a star to guide the way and the fact of a now very dark night made life difficult; but by no means impossibly so. Also stuffed in my battledress top I had, in addition to my tobacco pouch, two useful items of equipment: an escape kit and a silk map of western Europe. The escape kit was contained in a perspex box six inches long, four inches broad and an inch deep, made in two parts and sealed by strips of adhesive tape. The underside of the box was concave and fitted neatly either over the breast bone or round the calf of the leg. It was almost incredible what they managed to pack into that small box. It contained about twenty Horlicks tablets for sustenance, four benzedrine tablets to ensure sleeplessness should the need arise, a fishing line complete with hook for angling, a rubber water pouch for storing a small supply of fresh water from a stream, a needle and thread wrapped round a card for sewing and darning, a phrase-card with a list of the most apposite phrases necessary to ensure a snappy conversation in French, Spanish, German or Dutch, and a small compass no bigger than a button with north marked by two phosphorescent dots on the needle to cope with just such an emergency as I now found myself in. The silk map resided in a small, brown, waterproof canvas bag marked clearly and somewhat fatuously in very large block capitals MAPS ONLY. Only one piece of this assorted array was of the least use to me at this point in time. I could not read a map in the dark, neither had I the slightest inclination to stand chewing Horlicks tablets in the wet chill of a February night. But that little button compass was vital. In their wisdom the authorities had evolved a system whereby the kit was packed with the compass, right side up, close against the perspex so that one could read it without opening the box. Or so it was alleged. I had not checked my kit in any way, so I withdrew it now from my battledress hoping that the packer had done his job right, and ready to heap distant curses round his head if he had not. The thing *was* right. Through the perspex of the box I could see the phosphorescent dots marking north quite clearly. I held the box steady for a moment, took my compass reading and went off in what I estimated to be a south-westerly direction.

It was one thing, I discovered, to walk in full starlight keeping the North Star at your right shoulder, and quite another to blunder along in the dark constantly stopping and holding a tiny compass close to your face in order to check your direction. It would have been easier had the night been lighter, for then I could have picked a suitable mark and walked to it. But now, the combination of the moonless period and the cloud cover made the night pitch black and that mode of progression impossible. No night in the open is, however, absolutely black. I had not cat's eyes, nor could I seriously vie with Norman Levick in the matter; yet I had averagely good night vision and, after a while, my eyes grew accustomed to the darkness to a degree and my stumblings less pronounced.

I found that I had developed a marked distrust of woods and copses. The area was well endowed with both and I worked my way round them with caution. They seemed, after my initial experience, to be darker areas containing eyes which pried on my movements. Deviation from my set course or not, I went round and not through them.

The sky to the west cleared gradually. Far, far away — so far that there was not the slightest trace of noise — vivid flashes of incandescent light zig-zagged upwards into the heavens. For a second or so I thought that it was distant lightning, which seemed improbable in the existing weather conditions. Then I grasped the fundamental fact that the light was flickering and pulsating upwards, and the truth was plain. The flashes came from the heavy guns in the Rhine/Maas salient and provided me with the easiest of marks at which to aim. I walked on steadily in their direction.

The land I traversed varied little. It was basically a low-lying, level, spongy pastureland. To say that it was as flat as a board would be an exaggeration. There were almost imperceptible undulations in it which probably explained the varying degrees of wetness of the fields. At times I walked meadows where the going was relatively easy; not infrequently I thrust myself with increasing tiredness through swampy conditions which slowly sapped the strength from my legs. One of the main obstacles to my progress was wire. I found that the majority of fields were divided by strips of barbed-wire slung between wooden uprights two or three feet above the ground. Over these I repeatedly climbed. At first I scaled them but then began to treat them with a contempt born of cautious familiarity. They were a bind.

The countryside had become more desolate, the trees more sparse. The stars came out again, the gun flashes to the south-west continued unabatedly. I saw neither man nor beast as I plodded on; I seemed to be the only thing that moved over that dreary landscape. Farmhouses became fewer, but they did provide a clue to something that had, during this long solitary walk, caused me to rack my brains. Nature had endowed me with a particularly acute sense of hearing, and I could not understand how that soldier at the very start of the game had got within twenty yards of me walking on a path or minor road without my hearing him. The isolated farmhouses provided, indirectly, the answer; and for my purposes it was worth careful noting. Leading to them were invariably farm tracks or, occasionally, very small tree-lined roads. The instructive point was that these minuscule arteries of communication consisted of virtually pure, compressed sand. The sand, like the fields, was wet, and made for muffled walking. I made a mental note.

The gunfire ahead became desultory. The guns, which had for an hour or more blazed away furiously at each other, seemed, like me, to be getting tired. Their vigour waned by the minute, and finally they petered out. That harlot cloud reappeared and I blundered on in the dark over a sward that had become wetter than ever and infuriatingly uneven. I fell heavily over a log which some idiot had left in the middle of a field, and got up wet and cursing the misspent activities of its owner. I seemed for ever to be coming upon strips of wire in the dark and climbing over them; to be crossing and re-crossing sandy farm tracks; to be making my way round small belts of woodland which contained prying eyes. The night became a phantasmagoria of wire, copse, sand and vague imaginings. I went to duck under a strip of barbed-wire slung between two posts some four feet above the ground at the juncture of a farm track and a minor road. The barbs sank deep into my forehead and I could feel the blood gushing down my face. This really was no good. I was walking in my sleep. It was imperative that I pull myself together.

I sat down by a tree and began to shake my head from side to side to wake myself up. The blood was flowing freely down my right cheek and saturating the top of my roll-neck sweater and the collar of my battle dress. I felt the wound gingerly. It was tender and more than a mere graze. That did not bother me overmuch. Of much more consequence was the time I had spent floundering on in a daze. Since the termination of the guiding gun flashes I had, for heaven knew how long, ploughed on without heed to my tiny compass, and therefore without a clue as to my direction. It was more than likely that I had wasted a lot of time and effort waffling round in a circle. I drew out my escape kit, placed it on the ground beside me, struck a match and cupped my hands round the flame to shield it from the wind. Then I replaced the kit in my battledress top.It had been my intention to unfasten the seals which kept the box closed, open the kit and take a benzedrine tablet. But, being trained always to keep a sharp eye on the time, I had automatically glanced at the watch on my wrist and dismissed the idea. The hour was past five o'clock. In two hours from now it would begin to get light, and there would be little future in wandering around the countryside in broad daylight clad in RAF battledress, flying-boots and a roll-neck sweater. I would walk a bit further, hide up somewhere and sleep the day through.

I stood looking slightly downwards from the insignificant crest of a minor undulation on to a row of moving lights. There were a lot of them and they were moving fast. The throb of internal combustion engines came sharply to my ear. For hours I had heard no sound but the whistle of the wind in the bare branches of the winter trees; but now, distant about three fields and right across my track, an army convoy was moving rapidly from left to right across the landscape. It had happened shortly after I recommenced walking, and I was not enamoured of the realisation that there was a major road dead ahead along which a motorised German column was on the move. It was that dark hour which precedes the dawn; I felt very tired, and my spirits were at their absolute nadir. I wanted nothing at all to do with that road, so I swung away to the left and walked on.

Instinct and training began to tell me that it was an error to keep ploughing on to the south. I was, or felt certain that I was, walking in the very south-eastern corner of Gelderland. If that were so another stretch of the German border lay somewhere before me in the dark: and there was no future in crossing that and carrying on towards the northernmost towns of the Ruhr. Therefore, as I passed along the eastern fringes of a wood, which in the scant light possessed a dark look of foreboding, I made up my mind. What I was really doing, I suddenly realised, was funking contact with the main road to the west, along which I had seen the army convoy pass. It must still be to the west beyond this uninviting belt of trees. I turned sharply to the right and entered the wood.

Once inside I found it to be neither so gloomy nor so dense as I had imagined. For one thing, it was, in the main, a birch wood. There was just enough light to pick out the characteristic silver barks of the trees and to see their slender, graceful boughs stretching upwards no great distance toward the heavens. I trod quietly on for five minutes through the trees; and then I stopped dead in my tracks — because I had to. Confronting me was not the road I expected to find but a broad stream. It was full to the very lip of its banks, and to me, a non-swimmer, its waters looked dark and sinister. For the moment I had distinctly had enough. I was dog-tired and clueless. I sat down, propped my back against a tree on the bank, lit up with some difficulty in the still brisk wind, and enjoyed my second pipe of the night in a sullen sort of way.

With dramatic suddenness a series of staccato, guttural noises started up across the river and continued with unceasing violence to disrupt the peace of the night. I, too, started up from my seat by the tree because I could not understand the noise. I listened intently and peered hard across the dark stream, but to no avail. I could just about discern the far bank some twenty yards away and the odd tree that stood upon it; but that was all. Phrenetically, I wondered for a moment whether German voices were as guttural and noisy as they were said to be, and therefore whether I had blundered almost to the edge of an army camp. Then the fact registered that I was the victim of tiredness and an over-vivid imagination. The noise was simply the grunting of pigs. But why, I wondered, should those damned pigs kick up such a continuous din in the middle of the night? The simple truth dawned. It was no longer the middle of the night. Gradually, very gradually, the first faint fingers of a February dawn had begun to steal up the sky. Minute by minute the light was almost imperceptibly increasing. Those pigs, I guessed, were anticipating an early morning feed. They were early risers, and in a short space of time it would be daylight.

The fighter zoomed in from the westward. The beat of its single engine pounded ever louder on the ear as it came towards the wood. He skimmed low over the river to the south, circled round the back of the wood and, with slowing speed, returned a little way in the direction from whence he came. His engine note indicated that he was dawdling; that he was engaged on reconnaissance was obvious. He made two or three slow passes up and down the region where I estimated the road to be, as if examining his chosen territory minutely. Then he swung away and hurtled at the wood full-bore. I had not a clue what to make of this. He was invisible, low and charging straight at me. His engine screamed a wild crescendo as he swooped for the second time over the river; instinctively I took what meagre cover I could behind the slender trunk of a birch tree. I could not fathom what he was up to. Ridiculously, I thought he might be looking for me. In the moment of re-crossing the river he released a fighter flare. All the shadows and glooms dissolved in a moment and became trees, a fast flowing stream and the jut of the top of a farm building beyond the far bank, all sharply etched in a vivid, slightly pinkish light. He zoomed on past me over the roof of the wood, wheeled back over the river again, stooged around for a moment or two, and then roared off confidently to the north, following, I reckoned, the course of the road.

The flare came gently down on its parachute, the breeze causing it to sway and the pink light to fluctuate in intensity. For the moment the immediate area was bathed in that ghostly light and all was silence. The fighter had gone; the pigs, as if bewitched, had ceased their cacophonic serenade to the dawn; I leaned against the tree and wiped little beads of perspiration from my brow. I had unreasonably expected a hail of machine-gun bullets when he swept in for the second time, but none had come. I remained behind my tree for a full minute more in puzzlement. Slowly the flare swung down, plopped gently on to the ground among the trees and went out. Darkness and quiet reigned over the Dutch fields once more.

The reason for the fighter's probing was not in the least clear. On reflection it could as easily have been British as German, for I was no expert on the comparative noises made by Spitfire and Messerschmitt. But whether it was a fighter from 2nd TAF on a dawn reconnaissance, looking for troop movements on the road or flak and field batteries situated in the copses and woods in which the area abounded; or whether it was a German night-fighter trying to find his way home, the import was the same. Day was breaking, and I was in a wood to which a fighter had paid particular attention. It was time I was gone. I turned and strode rapidly northwards along the river's edge, determined either to find a bridge across it or to find a hiding place on its banks.

Fortune favoured me. I had not gone a quarter of a mile when I came upon farm buildings standing on the very lip of the stream. Moving cautiously in the grey, faint light of early dawn, I reconnoitred the farmyard and came upon a barn filled with hay. There was a wooden shutter some three feet high across the open end to contain the hay which rose up at a sharp angle behind it ten feet or so towards the roof of the barn. This was precisely what I had been looking for. Up that pile of hay I intended to go, and there, at the very back of the barn, secreted from all view, I would stretch out and take the sleep I wanted.

I had one foot on top of the retaining shutter and was levering myself up on to the hay with the other when the watch dog heard me. I could not see him, but his furious volley of barking came from a fixed spot round the angle of the adjacent farmhouse, which suggested that he was chained up. The pesky animal had let me cross the yard and pick my spot without a whimper. Only now, when I was within an ace of concealment and comparative comfort, did he choose to rend the stillness of the dawn with his continuous snarling and barking. The dilemma was a pretty one. I had by good fortune found the ideal spot for my purposes; but that racket could not continue for long without rousing the entire neighbourhood. I had to decide whether to remain in the barn or run for it. And if I ran for it, how far would I get in the approaching daylight in my RAF uniform and flying-boots?

I took the line of least resistance, edged further up the pile of hay, wedged myself against the side wall and hoped that, if I remained silent, he might give over. He did not. I heard the sudden rasp of a bolt being withdrawn from its socket and saw a widening slit of light as the farmhouse door across the yard slowly opened. Two men came out and stood in the wan pool of light cast by an internal lamp, shouting rapidly in an undeniably threatening manner. I could not understand a word of it, but the tone was ominous. They made no move towards the barn, probably because they did not know exactly where I was; I, too, made no move, but sat on my perch and observed them silently. The dilemma, however, remained. And this time it had to be resolved. The belligerence of these farming types was understandable. Any farmer anywhere roused by an intruder would threaten. That was natural. Perhaps, in fact, they would prove friendly. Perhaps they might even provide an entrée to the Resistance. It was a chance. I took the plunge, pushed off from my perch, slid rapidly down the pile of hay into the yard and walked across to them shouting, "English, English," above the continued roaring of the dog.

When I reached them I found that I stood face to face with an elderly man of slight build and a taller man half his age. The older man looked very hard at me for a second, and then, without a word, motioned me inside. My lone sojourn in the marshland was over. I went inside; the two men followed and closed the door carefully behind them.

3

First Impressions

The door led, not as I had expected into the farmhouse proper, but into a rectangular, brickbuilt barn which obviously formed an integral part of the building. Half a dozen cows stood in melancholy silence in their stalls, solemnly regarding the proceedings in the dingy light afforded by a single hurricane lamp which hung by the door, as I marched past them with the two men at my heels. There was a further door at the far end of the barn and through this we went. The transition was ultra sharp. On one side of the door were cows, straw, milk churns and all the muck and paraphernalia of a byre; on the other was a corridor complete with hat-stand, mats, a mirror and pictures on the wall. There were no half measures. A flimsy door separated the living quarters of man and beast. It was a first lesson in the sociology of the district. I learned that in the farming districts of Holland, man and beast share the same roof to live and sleep under, but that the roof is large and the quarters sharply separated.

We turned into one of the rooms leading off the corridor, and the scene that presented itself could well have come straight from the brush of Vincent van Gogh. The room was large and high, equipped with old-fashioned, heavy, dark furniture, and lit by the flickering light which issued from a single oil lamp suspended from the ceiling directly over a central table. At this table sat an elderly lady with a white lace bonnet on her head, and a younger woman to whom middle-age was no great distance away. The occupation of the room was completed by a lad of about sixteen, who stood with his hand resting on the back of the chair on which the younger woman sat. They were attired in workaday clothes, and looked as if they were about to make an early start on the day's work when the watchdog had signalled my arrival. There was a distinct air of curiosity mixed with trepidation to be felt as they eyed my mud-bespattered, blue-grey service battledress. A moment of silence ensued, and then the elderly farmer broke into a rapid patter of Dutch as he explained, I presumed, the nature and nationality of the unusual fish he had caught floundering in his barn. The youth detached himself from the chair, came round the table to me and posed a question in tolerable English.

"Who are you?" he asked.

"I am an airman."

"Airman?" he echoed incredulously.

I pointed to the wing on my battledress tunic. "Yes, I am a Flieger. Flieger from the RAF," I retorted, recollecting one of the few German words I knew, and hoping it might register with the Dutch.

The youth was tall, pale and bespectacled. He did not seem particularly convinced. In fact, on a snap judgement, I was prepared to bet that none of them were exactly enthralled either by my presence or by the colour of my uniform, which they seemed, from their repeated stares, to regard with mistrust.

"Your papers, please!" demanded the youth sharply.

It chanced that some pundit in the Air Ministry had forecast in the autumn of 1944 that, with a large part of western Europe in Allied hands, occasions would increasingly arise when shot-down aircrew would need to identify themselves to members of the British or American Armies. Consequently they were equipped with an abbreviated identity-card which contained merely the name, rank, number, and a passport-sized photograph of its owner. This I now produced. The youth glanced carefully at the card and then at me. The pundit may not have thought of this precise situation, but he was a good one. The card helped.

"Ah! Royal Air Force," said the youth, deciphering the words written across the top of the card slowly and deliberately. He looked, I thought, distinctly more pleased with life, and I realised that his English was, in fact, extremely limited. What with my pronouncing the initials RAF as 'Raf' and the interpolation of the German word Flieger, I had no doubt that I had confused him and probably aroused suspicion in his mind. I undid the seals on the escape kit, extracted the phrase-card and passed the box round for inspection. That served no earthly practical purpose, but I felt that it might serve as a token of good will, and I was out to please. The psychology seemed to work; the contents were examined with interest.

"Now," he resumed. "Where is it you are landed and how are you come here?"

"I landed perhaps ten kilometres from here, and I walked across the fields."

"But your aeroplane. Where is that?"

"It crashed somewhere near here. I don't know where."

"Crashed? What is that?"

The phrase-card had nothing to offer on this subject. I was obliged to go through the mime of a falling aircraft, complete with sound effects and ending on the word BANG!

"And were you in it when it has crashed?"

"No, thank God!"

"No? Then how are you come down to the earth?"

"I used a parachute."

He had some difficulty in understanding this, so I asked for pencil and paper, and sketched a man dropping to earth beneath an opened parachute.

"Oh, ja! I understand," he said, and grinned for the first time. "Perhaps you would like that we get for you some food?"

Things were looking up, I thought. I accepted his offer unhesitatingly.

The older lady, who, up to that juncture had said nothing, spoke now, and pointed in consternation to my face.

"Oh yes, excuse me," said the lad. "I had forgotten it that you have a hurt. It must be — how do you say — washed in warm water."

"Hurt? Washed in warm water? What do you mean? I'm not hurt!"
"But your face — look!"
He pointed to the mirror on the wall, and my reflection as I looked into it gave me a minor shock. I had forgotten all about the cut over the right eye I had suffered on that wretched strand of barbed-wire. The right side of my face from forehead to neck was covered in congealed blood, and looked a gory mess. The soaking that the top of my roll-neck sweater and battledress collar had received completed a very sorry looking picture. I tried in vain to protest that the cut had nothing to do with the actual shooting down. But it was no use. Words were inadequate and I could not get the point across. So I gave up and settled for the wounded hero treatment that was just about to commence.
The affair up to now had mainly consisted of a dialogue between the youth and myself. I had had little time to think beyond the next question, but, now that the interrogation proper was at an end, I had time to observe and to reflect that the first round of the battle had, seemingly, gone my way. The two women had departed on an errand of mercy, and the older one now reappeared carrying a basin of warm water and a clean piece of cloth. I sat for the first time to the table; she worked gently away and swabbed the blood from my face. She was a woman of sixty. The white lace bonnet she wore framed a face that was toil-worn and had known its due share of care, but was yet possessed of a calmness that amounted almost to serenity. The lad had naturally relayed my answers to the family in Dutch, but the presence of an RAF type in her house in this remote corner of Gelderland at crack of dawn seemed to perturb her as little as if I were a near neighbour who had called early for a bite of breakfast.
The job done she retired to her chair on the far side of the table and encouraged me by gesture to start on the breakfast the younger woman had brought in. It consisted of a beakerful of warm milk and a large slice of pancake with pieces of bacon embedded in it. Both were delicious! I tucked steadily in and thought out my next move with care. I felt that if I played my cards right I was, by luck rather than judgement, 'in'.
The youth asked where we had been bombing, and I replied, slightly evasively, that it was near Münster. He enquired if I had met any of the crew since I landed, to which I answered frankly in the negative. I did not in the least mind being plied with questions, because I regarded them as a kind of bridge that helped build a rapport between us which would make the posing of the key question I proposed at a suitable moment to put, that much easier. The farmer and his nephew (for such I managed to establish the younger man who had accompanied him out into the yard to be) stood about; the two ladies sat at the table; the youth, who was obviously in large part enjoying the situation, remained standing by my chair as I ate, and continued, haltingly, to ply me with questions on the one hand and to proffer snippets of information on the other. During a pause I posed the question that mattered.
"Are you members of the Underground Movement, and will you help me?" I asked.
There was a period of quiet after my question had been translated, and then a rapid volley of Dutch broke loose as the matter was discussed. I reckoned that much depended upon the final answer. I was, in a way,

being tried by jury, and the verdict would either mean a permanent helping hand, or a smart, 'goodbye, nice to have known you', the moment I finished eating. The psychology of the situation was basically simple, but the outcome vital. I watched the jury closely. That they were helpful there seemed no doubt. Had they, I wondered, links with the people I wanted, and had they guts enough to harbour so dangerous a bird of passage in their midst?

It was the younger woman who bothered me. She seemed scared out of her wits and was talking nineteen to the dozen. The English speaking young man was her son, and they had come recently from their home in Rotterdam to their relatives here in the east in order to eat. Conditions in the large towns in western Holland had been described well enough for me to imagine the sordidness, the squalor, the terror and the empty bellies which had progressively developed under the Nazi jackboot in the Amsterdams, Rotterdams and Haarlems of the fading German Empire. Something of those years of horror was in her spirit now, I felt, as she talked. She bothered me. The old farmer bothered me too. He was a man of comparable age to his wife. Slight of stature, his back was as straight as a ramrod, and his weather-beaten face almost expressionless. But beneath the mask, I detected, I thought, the strain and responsibility he was feeling at harbouring me within his portals; and in my heart of hearts I could not blame him. What became of me was one thing. The fate of all the others here if I were caught in this farm by the Bosch was sealed. Nothing, beyond the bestialities of the concentration camp and a miserable death, awaited them in such an event.

The argument waxed and waned. They were, quite obviously, in a quandary. I watched the farmer's nephew out of the corner of my eye. He was a tall, lean, dark-haired and dark-skinned countryman not a deal older than myself. There was about his face a merry, devil-may-care look that boded well. I reckoned he was young enough and bold enough to take his chance and be on my side. In him and in that serene elderly lady I pinned the bulk of my faith.

During the debate on my future there was a great deal of smoking. The Dutch language, I found, rather to my surprise, tended to be spoken by some at a rate bordering on the speed of light. I began to comprehend how the phrase, 'double Dutch', had found its way into the English language. It was not that the old farmer or his wife said much. He smoked away at an old, gnarled pipe and interposed a word here and a judgement there; she, when she spoke at all, was very gentle of voice. But the younger man and woman went at it hammer and tongs. He was of a quick, impatient disposition, and smoked his way rapidly through a couple of acrid-smelling cigarettes; she, I could sense, was full of womanly qualms, and emoted volubly. There was nothing in the least that I could do, except to let the family settle the matter between them. So, not to be entirely outdone, I fished out my pipe, lit up and let them get on with it. A fug of tobacco smoke built up steadily on the male side of the table.

At length the conversation-piece came to an end, and the youth delivered the verdict with a slow, almost weighty dignity.

"We are not of the Underground," he said, "but we think that we can, perhaps, help. You must now leave our house with the farmer. He takes you to a — I think that the word is shed?" He looked for support, and was delighted when I nodded my approval. "In that shed must you stay until we bring a man."

He was adamant that I should on no account leave the shed for fear of capture, and that, if by any chance the Germans stumbled upon me, I was to say that I had walked into the place of my own accord.

I thanked him carefully, made my adieus to the others and followed the farmer out.

It was eight o'clock of a cold, dank February morning as I followed the farmer to my place of refuge. During my sojourn in the farm a thin, wintry drizzle had set in; the trees dripped, and the skies were leaden. The wind had dropped, and the embryo day had a sullen, forbidding look about it which chilled the spirit as surely as the damp air bit into the marrow of one's bones. The hiding-place was, in fact, a chicken-coop constructed of rough boards and possessed of a single pane of besmirched glass which served as a window. Well screened by trees, it stood, solitary and small, a good hundred yards from the farmhouse. The door was open, and a handful of fowl were wandering in and out pecking at the ground and generally taking life as it came. The farmer indicated the straw-covered floor as a place to sit, and prepared to take his leave. The burning question in my mind was as to where, exactly, I was. I had a map, and probably time to kill, so I might as well use it. Laboriously, with the aid of the phrase-card, I made him understand what I wanted.

"Vier kilometres van Winterswijk," he responded, very exactly, and took his leave, carefully closing the door behind him.

There was a rough table in the corner of the coop. What its real purpose was I knew not, but it was covered with a liberal layer of scruffy straw, and seemed mainly to exist to further the gymnastic antics of a horde of mice which appeared to infest the place. The fowl had all wandered off when the farmer departed, leaving the coop entirely to the mice and me. Along the table, down its legs and over the floor they ran. The place seemed alive with them. So many were there darting and scuttling about, that, despite my tiredness, I chose not to sit down, but remained standing with my elbows propped on the table studying the map which I had extracted from its waterproof cover.

I discovered Winterswijk quite quickly. The town lay in the absolute south-eastern corner of Gelderland, a couple of miles from the German border. It was depicted as a railway junction where four lines met. The Dutch lines converged on it from the north and west, and then went southwards to the Ruhr Valley. A main road linked the town with a place called Groenlo to the north; westwards from the German border a river curled in to a point just above Winterswijk, and then turned north and flowed parallel with the road. On that river I undoubtedly was.

Winterswijk was, without question, the focal point of communications for the area: a sort of staging post between the Dutch hinterland and the German Ruhr. I calculated that it was a fraction under twenty miles from the Rhine. It all meant, though, (so far as I could estimate my landing point) that all I had to show for a solid night's slog was a maximum of five miles, albeit roughly in the right direction.

The study of mice and maps palled. Operationally the week had been busy for within its compass we had attacked the marshalling yards at Siegen, east of Cologne, and done a similar job on Karlsruhe, before embarking on this ill-fated Dortmund-Ems sortie. Tomorrow, as like as not, the attack would be switched back to the oil targets. But, for me there was no operational tomorrow. I had spent the night trudging through a marsh which had sapped my strength, and was stuck now in this miserable coop waiting for something or someone. I was tired.

With tiredness came nagging doubt. Occasionally, as much to relieve the monotony as from any sense of need, I withdrew a Horlicks tablet from the perspex box, unfastened its neat, individual wrapper, and stood like a reflective ruminant chewing the cud. The light that streamed meagrely through the muddied window was of a morbid grey that matched my mood. I had never possessed much patience. When ten o'clock came and went without sight or sound of life I began to wonder.

It was a known fact that the percentage of people in occupied Europe who were actively engaged in Resistance work was low. There was not the slightest question that the vast bulk of the conquered peoples hated their Nazi masters like poison, but RAF escape lectures had made it plain that the finding of a local Underground Movement when one needed one was usually about as easy as finding the proverbial small needle in a large haystack. This was in no way surprising when one considered the fiendish treatment doled out by the Nazis to the miscreants they caught. A lucky man might be pitchforked out of a blazing bomber into darkest Europe and find the local partisans with unerring accuracy. But, the Germans apart, a less fortunate individual could as easily blunder into the hands of that other minority who had sold their birthright for a mess of pro-German potage. Coming down to brass tacks, it was all a matter of luck. And how lucky was I? I seemed, by pure chance, to have stumbled on a family on the fringes of the local Movement. But had I really? Where then, after nearly three hours, was the help they had promised?

I felt in a cleft stick. It was true that the people on this farm had proved hospitable to the extent of feeding me and bathing the cut above my eye. But that was later. Initially they had looked very much askance at my uniform. Indeed, my first impression had been that they loathed the sight of it, and first impressions were usually, in my book, right. Was it all a trap? And was I standing here of my own accord awaiting the arrival of the enemy? I hated the idea of being duped.

The door remained, as the farmer had left it, closed. I had only to open it and walk away to ensure my immediate freedom. The inactivity choked me off; instinct told me to 'scarper' and take my chance in the open. Then reason told me that I was being a devious bloody fool. The elderly lady in the white lace bonnet did not look like a traitress. There was, in the end, no certainty. The logic was inescapable. When that door finally opened it would admit either friend or foe. Through its portals would come either some Dutchman bent upon aiding my escape, or the Gestapo.

When the eleventh hour of this dismal February morning sped on its way, my doubts became major forebodings. I knew that I could not stick this business out much longer. I decided, much against half of my nature, to remain for another hour. I had at least had ample opportunity to study the lie of the land between here and the Rhine. I folded up my map, put it in its cover and thrust it back into my battledress in disgust, watched the wretched mice with a similar feeling and smoked testily away at my pipe. And then, at half past eleven, flak guns to the south opened up. They were close. The nearest, I judged, were no more than a mile away. The roar of aircraft engines and the dull crump, crump, crump of bombs began to mingle with the staccato barking of the guns. Very quickly quite a party was beginning to develop in the neighbourhood. The bedlam outside had whipped itself up rapidly into a feverish crescendo when, silently and without warning, the door opened as if by magic, and into the chicken-coop stepped two Roman Catholic priests.

I was dumbfounded. I had not heard them arrive, and whoever or whatever else I had expected to come through the door, it had not been the clergy. Dead tired and woebegone I might be, but hardly, I thought, ready for the last rites.

The first of the two priests to enter was a spare, dark, intense-looking man in his forties with ascetic features and keen, almost black eyes as sharp as needles which glittered behind a pair of thick, horn-rimmed spectacles. He opened the proceedings with a speed and fluidity which rocked me.

"Good morning. How do you feel now?" he breezed.

"Perfectly well, thank you, except that I'm rather tired," I responded, lamely.

"I should perhaps explain, that I was for six years at Mill Hill in London, and I therefore speak English quite fluently. My colleague also understands English well, but does not claim any great ability in its speech."

Here was corn in Egypt. I could scarcely have been luckier. I had not thought to find a fluent English speaker in this neck of the woods. The answers to a few questions I had to ask ought to be forthcoming.

Physically, his associate could hardly have been more dissimilar. He was as fair-complexioned as the first priest was dark, was much taller, and possessed a girth whose ampleness contrasted sharply with the other's lean and hungry look. His eyes were of a bright blue, and tended, for some reason, to roll in their sockets as he stood and listened attentively. On the surface he looked a picture of ease and contentment. He might have been thirty years old.

"I must also say," resumed the dark priest, "that we are leaders of the Underground Movement in these parts and that we are here to help you."

There was a flicker of a smile in his gimlet eyes for a moment.

"You looked, I thought, surprised to see us. Not so?"

"Surprised and relieved, I can tell you!"

"Surprised I can understand. You would not expect members of the priesthood. But relieved. Why so?"

"Well, I have been standing here for the best part of four hours, and not seen or heard a soul in all that time. I was beginning to wonder whether, when that door opened, I might not find myself face to face with a Nazi Stormtrooper instead of the Dutch Underground. I had made up my mind to walk off if nothing happened by twelve o'clock."

"So you thought this family might betray you?"

"I'm afraid it amounts to that, yes."

"Then you do them a great injustice. They are, as a matter of fact, very honest, hard-working people, and have risked much for you this morning. It is scant thanks you have given them in your thoughts."

I felt a complete heel.

His mood changed suddenly from one of censure to one of considerable warmth.

"Do not feel ashamed, my son, for thinking as you did. I believe I understand your feelings. A good soldier has always an element of caution in his nature. It is, perhaps, proper that it should be so."

There was, undoubtedly, a lot of force in this man. He had about him something of the fanatic, something of the Jesuit, which suggested a deep reserve of power and determination. He never raised his voice, and yet, by intonation, he drove his points home with conviction. He had been quick to chide when I showed suspicion toward people who were my benefactors, and had made me feel ashamed of myself. Equally, once he sensed that I was honestly contrite, he had been quick to show a human side to his nature.

"Where is the air raid taking place?" I queried.

"Oh, that is on Winterswijk. It is quite an important railway junction, and the Tommies are bombing it, for we have just seen their aeroplanes going in to attack. I am always glad to see the Tommies."

Praise indeed! Bully, I thought, for the medium bombers of the 2nd Tactical Air Force.

"Now let us get down to business," the priest resumed. "When you landed, what did you do with your parachute?"

"I threw it and my Mae West life-jacket into a ditch."

"And do you think it probable that a life-jacket would sink?"

He had a sharp, cutting logic and turn of phraseology that was more reminiscent of the lawyer than the priest. It was disconcerting.

"No, I suppose not," I faltered. "But there was a German soldier working in a nearby wood at the time, and it was difficult to do otherwise."

He clearly did not find the excuse very satisfying. Sackcloth and ashes for me again, I thought. This priest had his human side, but I was prepared to bet that he was a firecracker at the Confessional.

"Does the name Copley mean anything to you?" He injected the question suddenly and watched my reaction like a hawk.

"Why, yes. He's our flight engineer. Have you found him too?"

"I did not say that. What we have found is a flying-cap with the name E. H. Copley written inside it. He, too, has left incriminating evidence about the countryside."

Sackcloth for Eric. But still, the 'gen was welcome. It at least meant that the odds were better than ten to one that Cop' was safely down. The clot had evidently jumped with his helmet on, and that was dangerous. The length of flex attached to the ear-piece for the purpose of plugging into the intercom was known to have the distressing habit of wrapping itself round people's necks in a bale-out and strangling them on the descent. However, since the helmet was there and Eric not, the inference was that he had got up and walked away.

The asperity of the priest vanished like snow under a hot sun. He was, suddenly, charm and reassurance itself.

"Well, you are the fourth airman we have visited this morning. We have three more of your crew under our protection. What have you to say to that?"

"Marvellous! What are their names?"

"That I will not say. If you remain with us for any length of time you will learn that we rarely use names. If we do find it necessary, we use false ones."

"You say 'if'. Does that mean that my stay may be short?"

"Possibly. We have means for effecting the escape of airmen back to England, and, for a start, our method shall be this. One of your friends is in hiding two miles from here, and at two o'clock a man will call to guide you to him. All you have to do is to walk with that man."

"Isn't that a bit bloody dangerous in broad daylight?"

I had put my foot in it again, and I knew it immediately. He said nothing, but just regarded me with eyes which held more of a hint of amusement at my embarrassment than they did of reproach.

"I'm sorry, Father, I did not mean to swear. Force of habit I suppose."

"Do not worry about that. I was more amused by your obvious embarrassment than hurt by lack of reverence. You interest me, though."

"Oh? Why?"

"Ten minutes ago you were telling me of your intention to leave this place by midday and walk abroad in your RAF uniform. Now, when I talk of your doing the same thing with a guide, you speak of danger. Where is the logic in that?"

I had to admit that, put in so blunt and succinct a form, I was being irrational.

"You must not be afraid to take risks, young man. Remember that we, also, must take them. But I do not mean that you should walk abroad dressed as you are now. Shortly the farmer will bring you an old coat, some rough trousers and a pair of boots. So equipped you will set forth with your guide in the guise of Dutch farm labourer. Better?"

I agreed that it was, but indicated that I did not need the boots.

The younger priest had said nothing during this conversation. Now, however, he brought the meeting effectively to a close by observing to his colleague, in English, that there was work to do.

"Yes, that is true. We must now bid you goodbye and a safe walk," said the older priest, proffering me his hand.

"Before you go will you answer one question that has puzzled me?"

"Yes if I can."

"One source of doubt in my mind about the people on this farm was the way they looked at my uniform. Unless I'm much mistaken they looked as if they loathed the very sight of it. Why was that?"

Amusement flickered back into his piercing eyes.

"And you cannot think of the reason?"

"Not for the life of me."

"Well, your uniform is blue-grey is it not?"

"Yes — but . . ."

"Well, it is very simple really. The people on this remote farm have never before seen an RAF man. The only thing that they associate with a grey uniform is the Wehrmacht, of whom they have seen far too much. The answer, then, is that they thought at first that you were a German, and suspected a trap."

"Good Lord above!"

With a handshake and an exhortation to be of good cheer the priests were gone as abruptly as they came.

The priest from Mill Hill had left an encouraging mark upon me. His alternating bursts of asperity and affability coupled with a sharp and probing mind gave an inkling of a character that was subtle yet forceful, and not in the least lacking in humour. Above all I liked the liberality of his approach. At no point had he enquired whether I was of the Catholic faith or adjured an immediate conversion and the uttering of a couple of quick Paternosters and three Aves before he was willing to take me under his clerical wing. I might, for all he knew, as equally have been atheist as christian.

The thought pleased me. Sectarianism, with its concept that only if you belonged to faiths A, B or C (depending which lot you were in) could you get a first-class ticket on the boat to Heaven was, to me, humorous. In my opinion we were all basically in the same boat, and I, at the moment, was glad it was not rocking too much. The priests had, after all, brought the welcome gen that three more of the crew were in their hands. I felt that the hands were capable.

After a while the farmer reappeared bearing a bundle of old clothes and some food. The food was tucked away in a small basket, over which the clothes were draped; they consisted of a tatty raincoat that had probably seen its best days before the war commenced, a pair of worn, corduroy breeches which might well first have seen the light in the twenties, and a cloth cap.

I ate the food he brought with relish, and then prepared for the role of itinerant Dutch farm labourer that I was about to play. First I removed the small knife secreted in the top of my right flying-boot, hacked through the deliberately weak stitches round the ankles, discarded the uppers and kept the knife for possible future use. Then I switched trousers, handed my battledress ones and my flying-boot uppers to the farmer for burning or whatever else he proposed to do with them, and donned ancient mackintosh and cloth cap. The old man gazed quizzically at me for a moment, — there was even a suggestion of a smile on his expressionless face — and then stepped forward, seized the lapels of the raincoat, and began with appropriate noises — which might have meant, "there, like that," — to adjust the coat further to cover the top of my battledress. The mac' lacked a top button, and he seemed avid in his intention to obscure from view that which lay beneath. I felt like an actor being prepared for the moment of going on stage. The dressing done, he departed once more and left me waiting for my final visitor.

The light filtered as uncertainly as ever through the window; the day was as uncompromisingly grey and drizzly as at any time during the morning; the mice performed their never ending gymnastics; I stood and smoked my pipe and waited.

The view I had from that small window was restricted by the trees which surrounded the chicken-coop, so that I saw little. Six hours I had spent within these cramped confines, and I was completely brassed-off with waiting. I leaned against a wall and began to doze on my feet. For the second time I was caught completely unawares. The door suddenly burst boisterously open, and in an instant I was wide awake, on my feet and face to face with a big, solid man, whose appearance amazed me equally as much as that of the priests had done two hours earlier. His large, florid face was surmounted by a flat black cap with a peak, and he was attired from neck to foot in an outfit of rough cloth of a bright royal blue. It actually consisted of a blouse which fitted closely at the neck and billowed out, leg o' mutton fashion, at the sleeves, and a pair of baggy trousers drawn in tightly just above the ankle. On his feet he wore a pair of clogs, and in his right hand he carried an old, rusty sickle. He was the epitome of what I imagined the traditional Dutch farming type to look like; he might have stepped straight out of the pages of Alexandre Dumas's *The Black Tulip*.

The apparition was a jovial one. He stood and talked in an easy way to the farmer who had accompanied him in, and turned to me from time to time and grinned like a Cheshire cat. For a while I wondered whether my appearance in this rigout was enough to make the proverbial cat laugh, but decided, eventually, that that was not the import of his mirth. He looked as comfortable as a duck on a tranquil pool, and he exuded confidence. The notion of taking me across a two-mile chunk of German-held territory in daylight appeared not to bother him one jot. The penny finally dropped; the meaning of his behaviour was conveyed without the use of a single word of English. Doubtless a sleepless night and the trepidation I felt at wandering abroad in so thin a disguise were showing. After all, if stopped by the Germans, the game was undoubtedly up, and I did not relish the consequences of being caught in civilian dress. But what this man was trying to show me was the need to drop that line of thinking — to cheer up and look confident. His mime succeeded. I perceived that he was no fool. The sickle in my guide's hand was our raison d'etre: to outward appearance we were to be a couple of farming types moving towards a spot of hedge trimming or ditch cleaning. Providing we displayed no furtiveness the odds were that there would be no problem. He looked cheerful and untroubled. All that was needed to fulfil the rules of the game was that I should do likewise. I grinned back at him to convey that the mime had worked, he nodded blandly, and at a fraction past two o'clock we moved toward the door.

I shook the old farmer's hand and expressed my appreciation as best I could in English; he responded in Dutch, and we parted. The coop had been a place of impressions. My last one was of a small farmer who had mastered his fears and given of his possessions for a cause, and of a very large, traditionally-clad Dutchman whose characteristic was a kind of jovial unflappability. We set off together side by side confidently enough. The more dismal aspects of a smart canter through enemy territory in daylight no longer occupied a leading place in my mind. Mainly I wondered which one of the crew awaited me at journey's end.

4

A View of the Road

We started briskly across the fields, turned after a while into a narrow sandway flanked densely on either side by trees, and pursued a track roughly parallel with the river.

My guide's pace settled down into a long, unhurried stride; the canter slackened into an untroubled saunter. We followed the sandway for a time, went through a gap in the hedge, and started along a grassy track. He took the lead at this point, and I was able for the first time to observe the gait of a man who habitually wears clogs. Because clogs are wooden and do not give with the feet, the wearer must, perforce, push his feet forward in a flat-footed, sliding sort of motion. As my imperturbable friend trod his untroubled way in front of me, his mode of walking caught my attention. He did not lift his feet, rather he slid them forward a mere fraction above the ground, and the result was a peculiar, rolling gait, vaguely reminiscent of a sailor. On the wet sand there had been little perceptible noise, but on this track there was a distinctive swish, swish, swish, as the blades of grass were pushed aside by his clogs.

For the most part we kept along the secluded sandways, and for the first quarter of an hour saw not a soul. The weather had in no way improved. The day remained bleak, the low cloud and drizzle dully persistent; the wind, which had again arisen from its slumbers, had an edge like a knife. It was the sort of afternoon on which one would, from choice, have spent a couple of hours curled up in an easy chair in the mess, close to the fire and sipping the odd whisky.

Eventually we came out from the cloistered narrowness of the very minor way into a fairly broad road, made, inevitably, of sand. At the juncture of way and road was the first observable sign of life since we left the farm. A man was bending down, ostensibly working on clearing out a ditch; but I saw as we approached, that, although his back was turned on us, his eye was active. Quite distinctly he glanced backwards towards us from his stooping position while we were yet a fair way off, and then resumed his work assiduously. My guide stopped for a moment and exchanged an affable word or two in Dutch. Then we were off once more up the middle of the road. Mentally I marked the worker down as look-out man, for the position he occupied was strategically dead right both to command a view of our approach and to give the latest gen on the road we were just beginning to tackle. All very cunning, I concluded. The gen had evidently been favourable, for we pressed on without pause. I began, almost, to enjoy our stroll. It was quieter than I had thought likely.

My whistle was a thing of embarrassment. It hung from the left lapel of my battledress tunic strictly according to regulations. All aircrew were issued with them in order to be able to attract attention in the event of being injured in a parachute jump. There was no doubt that it was preferable, having suffered, say, a broken leg in the drop, to whistle up for Jerry rather than lie and rot where one had fallen. This one was, however, no more than a flaming nuisance. The missing top button of the raincoat meant that it was virtually impossible in the blustery conditions for me to keep my neck area covered. The whistle repeatedly popped out in the most disconcerting manner in spite of my every effort to keep the lapel of the mac' tucked in place. I understood now why the farmer had tried so hard to impress upon me the need to keep the top of my coat across my chest. What a bevy of German soldiery would make, should they come upon us, of a farm labourer with a whistle hanging from his collar, I hardly dared to think.

A line of short, concrete posts placed at roughly ten yard intervals, stood along one side of the road, separating a two yard width of the sandy surface from the rest. They had me puzzled until a cyclist suddenly breezed down upon us along the narrow strip and proved it to be the cycle-track. That he merely flashed close by without giving us so much as a second glance was comforting. We passed a country school standing all alone in the flat countryside with no sign of a village near it. It seemed to be playtime, for the school yard was full of children, and a number of them were cavorting about near the gate. We strolled by very near to the little group, my guide turned his large, rubicund countenance toward them and smiled his urbane smile, and we excited not the slightest attention. It was all extremely encouraging. On he went, sickle in hand, and I walked by his side.

So far, in spite of the twists and turns, my sense of direction told me that we were, generally speaking, following the line of the stream northwards. I felt certain that I was retracing my hard-won, southward steps of the night.

We reached a junction of main sandroads. Up to this point we had not seen a single German soldier, but I gathered from my friend's behaviour that the crux of the whole business was upon us. The noise of spasmodic traffic was closer at hand; we crossed the river; my guide seemed, for a moment, to tense up perceptibly. He scarcely paused in his stride, but looked and listened intently. Satisfied, he resumed again confidently, and there, confronting us as we rounded a bend in the road, was a level-crossing gate. The single-line railway track ran parallel with the edge of a broad arterial road. We paused long enough to scan the road as we passed over the metals. There was not a vehicle in sight. Over railway and road we went at an ambling sort of pace, manoeuvred gently to the left on the far side, and turned into the drive of a substantial, attractive residence that stood in its own grounds perhaps twenty yards back from the thoroughfare. The guide tapped quietly on the front door, a thin, rather studious-looking man with receding hair admitted us immediately, and the walk was over. It had taken just forty minutes.

The two men stood chatting quietly together in the hall. The house was large and well appointed. It was, I thought, a farmhouse, but of more modern vintage than the one in which I had first made contact with the Dutch, and lacking, I judged from the brief outside view I had had, the dual capacity for shelter of both man and beast. I stood for a moment, uncertain as to the next step, for they prattled steadily away in Dutch and paid me no heed. The uncertainty was resolved by the appearance of a lady in early middle age, who arrived on the scene, smiled gaily and motioned me to follow her along the hall. I was ushered into a pleasant living-room and seated in a comfortable chair. Of my crewmate, whoever he was, there was no sign, but, as I passed along the hall, I had noticed two teen-aged girls busy with scissors on the stairs cutting up what was undoubtedly the remains of a parachute. Parachutes were made of nylon, and nylon was a commodity eagerly sought after by the women of war-torn Europe for obvious reasons. These two had their prize and were wasting no time in putting it to use. And, if the prize was there, the donor, presumably, was not far away.

I must, I suppose, have evinced some surprise at not finding my aircrew mate in the room, for the lady stood by the door regarding me with amused eyes.

"A moment," she said, and went away.

The moment stretched to perhaps five minutes. Despite the luxurious comfort of the chair I began to fidget a bit in impatience. From the length of time it was taking him to surface, I wondered, testily, whether these people kept their itinerant aircrew hidden down a mine.

The door opened quietly. Into the room stepped first the lady of the house, and at her heels with a couple of steaming beakers in his hands, Geoff Cheeseman, the spare mid-upper gunner who had deputised for the sick Stan New on that one, particularly fateful, trip.

"Well, well, the navigator," he said. "I wondered who it would be. Nice to see you. Here, have some hot milk I've just brewed up."

We scarcely knew each other. Spilsby was a large operational drome possessed of two squadrons of Lancasters, for No 44 (Rhodesian) Squadron inhabited the place in addition to us. Therefore there were some four hundred aircrew on the station, and I knew Geoff only as a face I had seen a couple of times in the briefing room and as a voice I had heard as often over the intercom.

Cheeseman was a chap of rather stocky build, possibly a year younger than myself. His hair was flaxen, his face a touch on the pale side, and his voice proclaimed that he came from the south country. I reciprocated his sentiment. It was nice to see him.

"You look," I said, "as if you're well installed. How long have you been here?"

"Since about one o'clock this morning. I landed just on the far side of the railway, poked about a bit stowing my kit in a hedge bottom, walked across the road and banged on this door. They took me straight in, and I've been here ever since."

"Lucky man! I passed the night flogging my way through a marshland, the other side of the river, and I've just spent three quarters of an hour retracing my steps"

"River? What river?"

"Haven't a clue, but there's a fair-sized stream running roughly parallel with the road and about half a mile east of it hereabouts. By the way, weren't you afraid of winding up in the wrong hands when you knocked on this door?"

"Took a chance. I remembered your shouting out over the intercom that we were over Holland. We're a long way from home, mate, and I had no yen for mowing about in the dark, so I chanced it."

We were left alone lolling comfortably in the easy chairs, sipping hot milk and talking. Some people, I mused, had all the luck. While I had trudged, this type had ensconced himself within half an hour in a nice comfortable house, simply by being impetuous enough to knock on the first door that had caught his eye.

"Have you had any sleep?" I queried.

"Not a flipping wink. I had a good sprawl in one of these chairs, but I didn't sleep. Since daylight I've been about the house. This place is on a main road as you know, but apart from taking my battledress blouse away nobody seems to give a fig. I've spent a fair old time peeping through curtains."

"Seen much sign of Jerry?"

"No. A big convoy of supply wagons moved up during the night. Since then I've seen one Kraut on foot and another on a bike. The area's not exactly swarming with the bastards."

"I see the people here have got your parachute."

"Yeah. Didn't waste much time about that! I told them where it was, and at first light they went and retrieved it. No messing about with these bods. They take risks and they take 'em cool."

So much was apparent. Nothing about this place suggested anything other than the cool approach: particularly the chopping up of an airman's parachute into serviceable pieces on the stairs.

My big, placid guide ambled into the room together with the owner of the house. The guide gave me a firm shake of the hand, Cheeseman a benign nod, and went his way. Our new mentor quickly showed that he had a little English at his command.

"I think that it is good that you shall have a little sleep. Would you like that you should go to bed?"

The idea met no opposition. It was by now late afternoon, and the mention of sleep after thirty-six hours without it sounded like Utopia.

We were taken upstairs into a spacious bedroom at the front of the house and left to our own devices. A large double bed was made up ready for use, and seemed to my tired eye to beckon me to its voluptuous comfort. The bed was scrupulously clean; the well laundered sheets very tempting. The proximity of the house to the main road argued that a very hasty retreat from this haven of rest might become essential. But I really could not bring myself to climb between those immaculate sheets clad in the stinking old pair of corduroys I wore.

"Come on, Geoff," I said. "Jerry or no Jerry we shall have to strip off. The last thing I want is to be caught without my trousers, but I'm taking this muck-spreading pair off."

"I was going to anyway. You worry too much. There's no problem at all, mate. You'll get used to this place."

The bedroom commanded a perfect view of the road. Before climbing into bed I stationed myself cautiously behind the window curtain and surveyed the scene. It was unreservedly quiet. The single railway line stood inoffensively on the far side, and nothing moved along it. On the road itself, three pedestrians passed by, a dingy old car lurched uncertainly past heading south, and two ancient lorries lumbered with a decayed sort of dignity in the opposite direction. Peace was the order of the day. After five minutes I had seen enough. I prepared to shed some of my tiredness in sleep.

Cheeseman, who had taken up his station prone on the left side of the bed was already nodding off, and I was in the process of clambering into my post on the right, when, without the slightest warning, a minor riot seemed to start up outside and grow louder by the second. In less time than it takes an agitated squirrel to shin up a small tree we were both at the window, secreted behind opposite curtains, and viewing the road anxiously. The damned road was as clean as a whistle; the cause of the ribaldry not in the least apparent. The noise grew in intensity, and slowly all was made plain. Into our view a large, old, open lorry with stanchions and chains round its flat deck slowly chuntered. It was stacked high with beer barrels, and, squatted precariously on top of their load in a variety of histrionic postures, half a dozen members of the Wehrmacht were singing snatches of German songs and shouting the odds as they ferried their precious wares southwards to the troops on the Rhine. They made enough noise for an army, and it did not require an exhaustive effort of the imagination to know that, as provisioning party, they had tested the worth of the brewery before they set off. It all seemed heavily Teutonic and very harmless. Consternation gave way to tolerant amusement. The lorry rumbled away into the distance; the revelry gradually faded; we climbed back into bed, and prepared once more for slumber.

"A bit cool, our taking afternoon naps in a house on the roadside like this, wouldn't you say, Geoff?" I ventured.

"Well, I suppose so. But not to worry. These people aren't that dim. They've got the effort covered."

With those words of comfort I sank down and drifted toward sleep, the bed gradually lulling me into that blissful state between waking and sleeping.

I found my thoughts running on the Dutch folk with whom I had made contact. I had heard that the Dutch were a hard-headed race, and I found it, so far, to be true. They seemed to conduct their Underground business in a brisk way that impressed me, and to possess more than a touch of cool. Guides in occupied Europe, we had been taught, invariably walked or cycled a hundred yards or so ahead of their charges in order to be in the clear if things went wrong. But mine had disdained the principle and walked by my side.

It was reassuring to feel sheltered, but there was, of course, always the chance that an adverse spin of Fortune's wheel might find us forced to go it alone. And here I felt my night on the loose might prove useful. I reckoned it a mistake to try to forge any definite path by ploughing across the open fields in this well-wooded country. The answer clearly lay with the sandroads. They offered plenty of cover and were made for stealthy walking. Judiciously used they offered the real chance of progress to the south-west.

I was lulled to the very brink of slumber when my ear caught a trace of a distant but alarming sound. It was faint but unmistakeable, and portended no good. For a moment or two my sleepy mind tried to dismiss it and reject the obvious, but in seconds the alarm bell rang loud and clear. The rhythmic tramp of marching feet sounded rapidly nearer.

"Hell! Do you hear that?" said Cheeseman, and sat bolt upright in bed at the same moment that I did. We were back at our posts by the window curtains quite as quickly as the time before. Into view from the Winterswijk direction, and on our side of the road, a detachment of German infantry with a portly Unteroffizier at its head stepped. Their march was executed with precision; the Mauser rifles slung upright over the right shoulder looked ominous. On they came until they were virtually level with our gate. I found my heart to be beating rapidly and loudly in my chest, my mouth to be more than a little dry. In a moment it was all over. They looked neither to right nor left but passed straight on about their business.

Geoff breathed a sigh of relief; I burst out laughing.

"What the hell are you laughing at? I don't find it funny. It was quiet round here until you came."

His voice held an aggrieved note that had something to do with being snatched abruptly on two occasions from the very brink of a sleep he needed.

"I'm laughing at you, boy, standing there in your underpants watching the cream of the Wehrmacht at work."

Possibly it was reaction or relief or something, but the picture of two half-clad British aircrew peering furtively behind the curtains of a Dutch bedroom window on to the manoeuvres of the German army struck me as rich.

Installed once more between the sheets, I aired my doubts about the exposed nature of our position a second time.

"There's more Krauts about than you reckon, and I still think it's a bit dicey afternoon napping as near the road as this. There's a Lanc spattered over the countryside a mile or two from here, and at the moment Jerry's missing at least four of its crew. What are we supposed to do if the next batch turn in here looking for us? Become the answer to a maiden's prayer and dive under the bed?"

"Shut up and go to sleep. I've told you they're not that dim. There's a hiding-place cut into the stairs. I know because I've seen it. That's where my parachute is now, and if things get tricky they'll stall Jerry at the door and bung us in there."

His confidence was catching. In the moment before consciousness dimmed entirely I asked a final question.

"I suppose you had a visit from the priests?"

"Yes they came to me after visiting the other two."

"Who are the other two?"

"Sorry, no dice. The priests wouldn't say."

It was no use flogging the imagination to divine who they were. They could be any permutation of two from five, and they could be hiding singly or as a pair. Maybe I would never know until the game was over, whenever that would be. I fell asleep.

When I awoke it was pitch dark. Cheeseman was shaking me and telling me to get up. The bedroom door was ajar, and in the faint light which issued from down below, a young man was standing on the opposite side of the bed. We fumbled about in the dark, donning trousers and footwear, and eventually followed him downstairs. The time, I noticed as we entered the hall, was seven o'clock.

The place seemed deserted. There had been no sign either of the parachute or of the two teen-aged girls on the stairs as we came down; and here, in the farm kitchen, no-one was to be seen. An old clock ticked solemnly away in a corner. A pot simmered gently on the kitchen range, otherwise it was as quiet as the grave. In the centre of the room a table bedecked by a white linen cloth and surrounded by half a dozen chairs stood waiting. The three of us sat to the table, and the type who had awakened us began to talk.

"I am come here to speak with you in English and to tell you what you now must do," he said.

He was a chap of about our own age, this Dutchman. His face had a touch of pallor that suggested a none too frequent contact with the fresh air.

"You do not live here, then?" Cheeseman asked.

"No, I am from the west of Holland. At the moment I live with friends of my father on a farm in the near of here."

"What do you do for a living — I mean, what is your work?" I enquired.

"In Amsterdam I was a student. Here I am a diver."

"A diver?" Cheeseman and I echoed in unison. The mind boggled at what a diver could possibly find to do on the flat plains of eastern Holland.

The student laughed at our amazement. He hastened to explain.

It seemed that in the previous September, when the Allied armies were sweeping everything before them, the Germans had issued a decree that all Dutchmen between the ages of sixteen and sixty must report for work duties, which, in practice, meant digging fortifications behind the Rhine. As a consequence many thousands had disappeared quietly from the scene and gone to ground. This method of dodging compulsory work was known as 'diving'. Gelderland, the student said, was full of 'divers' lying low. Many had migrated from the west. Hereabouts, there was at least some food to be had.

We mentioned the episodes of the beer lorry and the detachment of troops.

"Oh yes," he said. "In Groenlo there is a large brewery, and the Germans steal our beer. Soldiers also march often on that road. That is all right. It is when they do not march but search in the houses that it is not good. So is it about that, that I am come here to tell you. When I was a student I have studied English much, and therefore can I now give our instructions for you."

I began gropingly to perceive quite an organisation in the background. There was evidence of division of labour. When the Underground wanted a guide it found one quickly; when it needed a linguist it soon rustled one up. It seemed not to lack for cards in its hand to play.

"You see," resumed the student, "it is here too near to the main road, and so is it dangerous that you should stay in this house. Two friends of you are together hiding on a farm two kilometres from here, and at eight o'clock a man will come and he will take you to them. I think that you shall then all start on a journey towards the river Rhine."

The news was great. Our hosts reappeared; a plate of thick soup, some bread and butter, and a drink that smacked vaguely of hot tea but had a bitter taste were quickly rustled up; Geoff's battledress top was restored to him and a raincoat of much the same vintage and degree of threadbareness as mine provided, and we settled down to await our guide.

We were not kept long in suspense. There came a knock at the door, a lean individual with an angular, markedly Saxon face and a cap on his head was admitted, we made our farewells, and were off without fuss or effusion.

The night was dark, but by no means pitch black. It was a night in much the same mould as its predecessor. A brisk wind blew fragmented stratus across a moonless sky. The stars popped in and out according to the vagaries of the cloud as we pursued a short series of minor sandways and farm-tracks. On such a night an RAF greatcoat would not have come amiss, for the threadbare coats we wore did little to keep out the biting breeze. I had a slight advantage over Geoff Cheeseman, for at least I possessed a cloth cap to keep my head warm. Naturally, as I trudged, I fell once more to wondering who the illustrious pair were who awaited us on the farm.

Our guide stopped abruptly outside a farmhouse that stood to the left of the way. A man detached himself from the glooms of a position he occupied in a gateway in the hedge opposite, and came across to us. I had not noticed him in the darkness until he was on us, but a terse conversation with our guide ensued, we followed the man through the gate, and came, after a two hundred-yard walk, to where a wooden hut stood all alone under the stars. Outside this we paused, and Cheeseman and I stood talking quietly together. Suddenly, through the closed door, a familiar voice wafted.

"Good God! That sounds like Hanson! But it can't be! He can't be alive! He'd never remember his parachute!" it said.

5

Four Men in a Coop

The voice had a booming quality. Its intonation owed its origin to the hunting county of Leicestershire. It belonged undoubtedly to Eric Copley, the flight engineer. And Copley would not have been Copley without a touch of bucolic humour.

"Yes, impossible though it seems, it's me, Cop'," I answered. "But sod a man whose memory's so bad that he jumps with his flying-helmet on! By the way, who's your mate? Is he asleep?"

"Aye, I think he is," boomed Copley aggrievedly. "Hey! wake up Young you dozey bugger, we've got company."

That was it, then. Ron Young, the bomb aimer, completed the quartet.

The Copley-Young hen-coop was by no means spacious. Copley, who was no midget, sat nearest the door with his back against the wall, his flaxen hair surmounted by the odd wisp of straw. The darker, elongated form of Young was sprawled almost at full length across the straw which lined the floor, his long gangling legs pushed out straight in front of him so that his feet were pressed against the far wall. We were anxious to get inside out of the cold, and it was clear that the guides also wanted it that way, albeit for a different reason.

"Come on, bunk up, Youngey," I said. "Shift your spindly shanks and let's get in and sit down."

"Take my advice and stay on your feet," replied an irritated Young. "There's fleas by the thousand in this place. As a matter of fact I'm going to get up anyway. I'm half bitten to death."

When the door was closed behind us there was neither much light nor much room. Copley had roused himself, and we stood there in the dark, four English aircrew stationed for the fleeting hour in a hen-coop in the remotest corner of Gelderland. Between us we represented England from the far north to the deep south. Young came from Northumberland, Copley and I from the Midlands, and Cheeseman from Kent.

The darkness seemed to have a smothering effect. After the opening burst of minor repartee between Eric and I, a long, moody silence ensued.

Fowler's crew was a happy one, and a bomber crew could be very clannish. Once airborne, its members lived in a noisy, highly dangerous little world bounded by the confines of the aircraft, and, since they flew almost always by night over blacked-out Europe, they rarely saw anything so comforting as an accompanying Lancaster. The danger and the isolation bred a belief in the skills of the people on whom one's life depended, and forged a bond of comradeship that was deep.

It was not that we always agreed. Fowler and I, for instance, had arguments from time to time about the 'book'. He was an excellent pilot with an unshakeable belief in regulation flying, whereas I had a nonconformist streak and was inclined to bend the rules a bit when it suited me.

But this sort of thing was of small consequence. Off duty, we tended to stick very much together and indulge in the pub life. We all had bicycles, and practically all non-flying nights saw anything between four and all seven of us cycling to some village pub in the vicinity of the airfield. We had but two lights between us, one white and one red, and both Australian. Chuck Fowler rode at the head of the convoy and Johnny Eaton at the tail. The rest of us wheeled away in a noisy gaggle much to the annoyance of one particular Lincolnshire village policeman. Mostly we used a pub with a back room complete with piano, where Chuck played and we sang bawdy songs into the night until we were thrown out. It was a great life, if you didn't weaken.

Mood can be a strange and communal thing. No-one spoke his thoughts, but three of us worried like hell about the missing members of that bicycle convoy. Where, at this moment, was the junior member who sat in the rear gun-turret? And where were the two Australians?

"Why," asked Young, suddenly, "are we waiting?"

It was logical that he should ask the question, for he was very much the press-on type. In fact it was surprising that he had kept quiet for as long as he had.

"We're waiting to cross the Rhine," I replied.

"Good show! But how do you know?"

"Because an English speaking Dutch student told us so. That's why we're all here in one block, boy. We're going to have a shot at the Rhine tonight."

"Flipping marvellous," said Copley. "Me with my gammy foot, too. You'll have to carry me. I've twisted my ankle and can hardly walk. Just for good measure I've bitten half way through my tongue as well."

Alas! poor Yorick!

It was an age of nick-names, and in Stan New — the forty year old gunner who had not flown with us last night — we had an ace exponent of the art. He was a Londoner, very quick both of speech and manner, and, unlike the rest of us, had a wife and family and some money of his own. Not unnaturally he had himself acquired the name of 'Papa', but where putting a name to it was concerned, the ancient Greeks had nothing on him.

During his early operational training Ron Young had endeavoured to give his officer's cap the battered look of the true ops cap. In order to help him, three of us had spent half an hour one evening skimming it upside down through the froth on the top of a pub bar, but the distinctive thing was that by fiddling with the wire stiffener he had accentuated the height above the peak, so that, by chance, it resembled the cap of an eminent German general whose picture we had seen in the newspapers. In Papa New parlance Ron immediately became von Kluge — pronounced KLOOGE.

Copley was a chap who chose to hide a quick, widely-read mind under a kind of bucolic exterior. He was, on the one hand, an insatiable reader with a photographic mind which could take him through a book in a night; on the other, he was ever ready with the buffoonery. Because of the half rhyme with Eric, and because his capacity to jest was infinite, he unfailingly became Yorick.

"I can understand your twisting your ankle, Yorick," I said. "But how the hell did you come to bite through your tongue? Tell us the tale!"

"Well," said Yorick, "you're not going to believe this, but I fell slap in the middle of a bed of flipping roses. Ruddy great gnarled efforts they were with thorns as long as your arm. I sailed down just past the roof of a house, landed plumb in the middle of the bed and twisted my foot out of joint in the process. I must have had my tongue between my teeth because, as I hit, I nearly bit the bugger in half. The people of the farm had obviously heard our Lanc come down, because they were all standing in the doorway about ten yards away, gawping at me. They made no move and neither did I, because I was stuck among the thorns. In the end I managed to get myself free and went up and told 'em it was the RAF not Santa Claus who'd dropped in. There was a lass there who spoke a few words of English, and she said that the house was full of divers and so I couldn't stay. Now, I am as you know a very trusting type. But divers in eastern Holland? I ask you. I thought they were just hostile natives pulling my scotch, till I found out later on what it meant. Anyway, they gave me a cup of milk and sent me on my way to find a particular farm, saying I had to be careful because it was after curfew and nobody ought to be about. I nipped cunningly up the sandroads and came eventually to a farmhouse with a great, long hedge in front of it along the side of the road. What should I hear but some other clot pottering about at the far end of the hedge. The crafty Yorick was not to be that easily caught of course, so he slunk back behind the hedgerow. When I did, the other bod did. I distinctly heard him bunk behind the hedge at the far end, so I came out again. But so did he. Then I started walking towards him, and then drew back because I could hear him coming towards me. This went on. To-ing and fro-ing, backing and advancing we were, like a pair of 18th century elegants doing a minuet in flying-boots. Finally we met, and who should the other bloke be but von Kluge here. Then we went together and found the farm we were looking for. We were lucky, because the priests told us later that the very next one belonged to a Dutch Nazi. Anyway, they took us in, von Kluge extracted a ruddy great thorny branch that I'd got stuck in my backside, and we sat down to early morning tea. Well, that's it, almost. They put us in this hen-coop before daybreak and here we've been ever since. Two priests came in the early morning and gave us the spiel, I offered the older one my packet of Woodbines and he took the flaming lot as a gift, the crafty beggar. Must admit, he gave me some Dutch ones in exchange, but they're ropey. That's the heroic story, ain't it, von Kluge?"

"Take that and leave the country!" said von Kluge, as he moved forward in concurring and trod on my foot in the dark. He possessed a clumsy streak, and those were the words he used when other people might have said that they were sorry.

Yorick's tale had broken the solemn spell. The thought of these two clots cavorting about by dead of night along that Dutch hedge set Geoff

Cheeseman and I roaring with laughter. We described our afternoon in a Dutch bedroom; von Kluge gave a picturesquely obscene account of this pest-ridden coop. The usual aircrew ribaldry began to develop. Suddenly the door opened and the Dutchman who had met us at the gate entered.

"There are many German soldiers near, and I think that you should not speak so loud," he said.

We had not for a moment supposed that he could speak English. It was a first-class opportunity to attempt to lift the veil on two questions.

"Do you know of any more airmen who have been seen in this area?" Ron Young phrased the question slowly and carefully.

"Yes, one is caught in the town of Lichtenvoorde some kilometres to the west. It was in the very early morning, and one of our men has seen it. It was near where your aeroplane is fallen."

"Also, then," continued Young, "why do we wait here?"

"You wait because I have sent out a man who will see if it is good that you further should go. If it is good, then shall you this evening start towards the River Rhine. It should then take three nights to walk."

The Dutchman left us again.

"While we wait, let's have a count of heads," said Ron Young. "Anybody know anything about any of the others?"

Geoff demurred. He had had, he said, a hell of a job scrambling round the holes in the underside of the fuselage on his way to the exit door and had seen nobody until I turned up on the following day.

"Johnny Eaton's OK," I said. "He floated down past me within shouting distance."

Holes in the bottom of the fuselage was a slant I had not thought about. It was true, now I reflected, that I myself had felt the shock of the explosion to be towards the tail of the aircraft before my attention had been drawn to the fire on the wing. Come to that, rather crazily, I had never asked the man who ought to know, what had got us. I did so now.

"Night-fighter," said Geoff. "I was watching forward towards the flares when I saw the tracer belting into the port wing. He attacked from the port quarter and I saw him just as he broke away. Junkers 88 I think. But I can't understand why we never heard from your rear gunner. It was his bit of the sky he came from."

I thought hard on my geographical studies of the morning in the mice-ridden chicken-coop. Lichtenvoorde, the Dutchman had said. That was too far to the west for John Eaton, who must have landed near me, to reach by the early hours. On the other hand, it was in the direction in which the aircraft had flown on, and Chuck Fowler had stayed with his aircraft longer than we had. It all began, not too happily, to gell.

"What happened to you, then, von Kluge?" I asked. "You seemed to be dying from the row you kicked up over the intercom last night."

"I don't know about any row. A chunk of metal carved a neat little groove across my cheek. But so what? I wasn't much hurt."

"Well, you seemed like it. You were flat out on the floor and groaning."

Copley agreed with me.

Young thought carefully before replying, and that, in itself, was not typical.

"Stunned I was, but never unconscious. I did *not* groan," he said.

Normally one took von Kluge with a grain of salt. That was the way he played life. To him it was mainly a bit of a joke. But he was serious now, and it boded no good. The combination of broken layer-cloud and fighter-flares had made last night a night-fighters' paradise. It would almost certainly have been Chuck Fowler who had been caught in Lichtenvoorde. That cannon-riddled fuselage and the silence from the rear gun turret made Norman Levick's fate look grimmer.

Time dragged. Outside the hut there was no vestige of noise; inside, there was no desire to create any. We merely stood there in the dark and waited, and thought our own thoughts. The gathering possessed suddenly all the hilarity to be expected from four mutes at a funeral.

"Got a match, Hanson? I think I'll smoke one of my Dutch fags." Yorick's voice held a touch of resignation.

The spurt of light revealed that the hour was nearer eleven o'clock than ten. Cheeseman and I had been in the place for more than two hours. Vaguely and without reason I had the impression that things were not going well.

The Dutchman returned. Previously he had had the tendency to bob in and out, but this time he stayed.

"I suppose," said Cheeseman, at length, "that this Rhine trip really is on?"

"Pardon," said the Dutchman. "I do not understand."

"I mean to say, is it possible that we *can* cross the Rhine?"

"Oh yes it is possible. It has already been done. A walk, a little boat where Germans are not, and over the river. Understand? But I am, as I think it is said, worried, for the man I have sent out. He is not yet come back. I have looked for him, but cannot find. If he is not back in one hour then we go from here, because it is then possible that he is caught by the Germans. And he can tell them things."

This man, I felt, was tough. He did not lack for education: his English was too good for that. But he had a snap and an air of command about him which suggested both leader and autocrat. It was too dark to see him properly, but I felt that his visage was of the grim variety. The news, in any case, was grim. The failure of his spy to return portended little good. If the Germans had him and ran true to form, they would be wasting little time in persuading him to talk.

Time went on with lead in its boots. We seemed marooned in this dark, cramped hut in which no-one spoke and no ripple of noise disturbed the melancholy. It was oppressive.

Then things changed. There came in successive instants a quiet step on the grass outside and a knock on the door. The Dutchman was across and through it in a flash. A subdued but rapid conversation in Dutch ensued at some length. Then he returned and our next move in the game we were playing was quickly made clear.

"I am sorry, but it is not possible that you start yet towards the Rhine. The man outside has gone many kilometres and has found much trouble to come back. Your army attacks at Cleve. Many German soldiers move from the near of here towards the battle. We cannot now also take you in that direction for much distance."

That the area should be 'hot' was not surprising. The battle in the salient between Rhine and Maas was on, and the prize was the Ruhr valley with all its industry. Jerry was bound to react immediately. He was already doing that by moving his reserve divisions along the route we needed to follow. We were, for the moment, stymied.

"It is also not possible," our Dutch friend continued, "that you all four should hide together. Therefore, shall two men come with me, the others shall go off with the man who waits outside when we are gone. I do not wish it that there should be talk when we walk, but only that you should follow me."

The 'you' referred to was Geoff Cheeseman and I. We took our leave of Yorick and von Kluge regretfully, both for the loss of company and because there is a feeling of safety in numbers, however illogical that feeling may be. There were, naturally, protestations of a speedy reunion, and that was always possible. But in our heart of hearts the impression had grown that the interval might not, in fact, be of the shortest.

We traversed a couple of fields with our guide and then dropped quickly on to the secluded, and by now inevitable, sandways. No-one spoke. We settled down into a steady, rhythmic step, and forged, as I saw from persistent glances at the luminous dots on my tiny compass, a steadily south-westward trek. The night was by now inky; the cloud cover absolute. Darkness wrapped us in a mantle as impenetrable as the thickest London fog. We came eventually to a wide sandroad, moved into the narrow cycle-track, and stole along between the line of concrete posts and the flanking hedge in single file like a small party of Sioux penetrating hostile country. We made almost no noise; the environment was equally mute. The only sound that assailed the ear was the soughing of the wind in the trees. The whole thing had an air of unreality. It was ghostlike.

I found it necessary to play small mental games as we went along. The silent, rhythmic walk had assumed a monotony which tended to lull me to sleep, and I could ill afford the luxury, because a lurch to the right meant a sharp collision with a short concrete post that cracked hard into the kneecap, a lurch to the left would have meant a soaking in the ditch that ran at the foot of the trees. Therefore I kept myself awake by memorising the navigational stars in their constellations, the lie of the land between here and Nijmegen, and by speculating on the nature and background of the man who led us. I knew one thing about him, and that was that his name was Karl. At least twice in the conversation that had taken place outside the door of the coop I had heard the other man use it in such a way as to leave little doubt on that score.

South-westwards we continued to head, and the walk was a long one. I brought up the rear of our little group and became increasingly aware of the stealth of the operation. Indian braves or ghosts, the simile was equally applicable. We were slipping through a chunk of lively enemy territory in the most professional of manners. It was quiet.

So monotonous had the walk in the dark become, that when Karl stopped suddenly and spoke, the effect was electrifying.

"There is a railway line that we now come to," he whispered. "Where it crosses with this road is it sometimes by the Moffen guarded. I think that we shall not go there. Let us now go on the fields."

The train came on us with increasing clamour. The clank of its piston rods, the chug and hiss of escaping steam and the rattle of metal as buffer collided with buffer sounded gargantuanly loud in the still night as we waited. We had taken to the open fields and were moving towards the line when the locomotive had first heralded its approach. We stood now in the deep gloom behind a large tree, motionless until it had passed. Through it came, hissing and clanking in the night a hundred yards or so away, the backward glare from the firebox illuminating redly the first few of a line of goods wagons, the remainder of which were too dim in the blackness to be seen as more than dark, moving blurs against a funereal backdrop. Karl offered the opinion that it was a supply train moving Rhinewards by night in order to avoid the ever-strafing day-fighters of 2nd TAF. The point was encouraging.

When it had gone we moved rapidly towards the line. Nothing more substantial than a double wire strip separated the track from the surrounding fields. We paused and listened intently for any trace of a German sentry. There was none. Through the wire, over the metals of the track and out on the far side we went and continued across the fields without pause. We made no attempt to regain the sandroad. The train that had passed was still a faint metallic rumble in the far distance towards Winterswijk when we pulled up outside a farmhouse. Geoff and I waited in the shadow of the building. Karl went inside.

The dull murmur of voices came to us from within as we stood there. The tone suggested more that an argument was taking place than a discussion; but I could have been wrong. The door opened, and a man stumped by through the farm buildings without so much as a glance in our direction. In the momentary flicker of light as he came through the door, I noticed that he carried an elongated object perhaps a foot long in his right hand, but I had not a clue what it was. The patter of talk from within continued for a few minutes. Then Karl appeared in the doorway. He uttered the one word, "Come!" and motioned us to follow him. He led us through the farm buildings in much the same direction that the man who had departed minutes ago had taken, and then out on to an open field. We might have gone perhaps a hundred yards across the meadow when he stopped, bent down, and began to scrape about in the grass as if searching for something. The procedure was incomprehensible to me. I had expected to spend the night tucked neatly away in this isolated farm. What the devil we were now doing standing in the middle of this wet field at midnight while a Dutchman played 'hunt the slipper' in the sward was a conundrum to which I found neither obvious solution nor in which I took much pleasure. I was feeling brassed-off with the whole business, when the answer came, literally, in a flash.

He found what he wanted, heaved upwards, and instantly a slit of light appeared, seemingly from out of the very bowels of the earth; a slit which broadened rapidly to reveal a square, lighted hole in which the head and shoulders of a man with a hurricane-lamp in his hand appeared. It was unexpected and completely grotesque.

"Now!" snapped Karl. "Jump quickly in the hole!"

The man inside stepped back. First Geoff and then I lowered ourselves into the uninviting pit. The hole was four feet deep and rectangular. In the uncertain light of the shaded lamp it resembled, almost precisely, a tomb.

6

The Tomb

Karl followed us in, the trapdoor was rapidly pulled back into place and we were able to take stock of the hole in the lamplight. The cavity was some fifteen feet long, six feet wide, and four feet deep at the end at which we had entered. The floor, however, sloped upwards, so that at the far end the space between floor and ceiling was no greater than three feet. Along the walls on either side ran a series of stout wooden props which supported lateral beams, on top of which the roof, composed of substantial planks of timber butted together, was laid. We had not, in the darkness, been able to see the outside effect, but in imagination I saw the level field over our heads, with the roots of the grass pushing smotheringly down on to that wooden ceiling above us. It felt very much like being in a grave. I was conscious of a cold shiver enter my soul.

The entire floor area was covered by a deep layer of loose hay, which was, for the most part, wet. The place gave me the horrors and I seized upon the sopping nature of the hay as a reason for getting out.

"We cannot sleep here," I said. "That hay is soaking wet."

"It is unlucky that it is so," Karl replied. "Not often is such true. But there was here heavy snow until two days ago and it is come in. It is, however, necessary that you sleep here. In this part is it now most dangerous, and here is it that you must stay because there is not another safe place. It will be all right. My friend has found dry hay for you and put it at that far end."

The man who had passed us while we waited outside the farm had been at work and made us a dry bed. All we had to do was lie in it. Oddly, that required mental effort. It required acceptance and a degree of conscious fortitude.

"There is a pipe there which will bring you air," Karl resumed. "It is not good that you should very loudly speak, for there are many Germans about, and voices which shout can sometimes be heard through the pipe. We shall now go, but in the morning I shall return and bring breakfast."

The two men departed and took the lamp with them. In almost the last flicker of light before the trapdoor closed upon us we discovered the pipe. It was no thicker than a man's index finger, and projected inwards for three or four inches at an angle of forty five degrees through the end wall. It was immediately behind our heads as we prepared to bed down in the hay. And that was comforting. Something, however slender, linked us with the world outside. The time had moved on. It was twenty four hours precisely since the crash.

When the trap door was closed upon us and the light removed we were enveloped in absolute darkness. The night outside had seemed dark, but it was not comparable with this. Utter darkness cannot be adequately described: at best one can only say that it is almost 'feelable' in its denseness. I found our present situation to possess a quality almost of unearthliness. It was, for one thing, most eerily quiet. The darkness and the silence of the tomb engulfed us.

"My God, this is some place, Geoff," I murmured, "talk about a better 'ole!"

"Yeah, not exactly up to that place we were bedded in this afternoon. That seems like the Grand Hotel now," he acknowledged.

It was surprisingly warm in the dug-out. We threw our old raincoats further up the hole because we did not need them for blankets, and prepared for sleep. There was a question I was resolved to ask Karl in the morning. On the way here he had taken us across the fields because of a level-crossing guarded by something that sounded like the 'Muffin'. I wondered vaguely what it meant. It was unexpectedly warm and comfortable here. I went to sleep.

At some time later I awoke feeling terrible. My head ached and my mouth felt like the bottom of a particularly mucky birdcage. My heart, I could feel, was beating over rapidly, my breathing quick and shallow. Cheeseman was already awake, for on hearing me stir, he said, quietly.

"Are you awake, Stan?"

"Yes, but I feel bloody awful."

"So do I. It's the foul air."

The same intense darkness and deadly silence enveloped us as when we had gone to sleep. Geoff Cheeseman, lying in the hay two feet away, was merely a voice in the void. I could not see him.

"Do you know what time it is, Geoff?" I whispered.

"Sorry, mate. No watch. Even if I had one I couldn't see it in this bloody hole." His voice held a touch both of irascibility and something akin to despair.

"Not to worry. My navigation watch is still OK and I've got some matches in my pocket. We'll find out the time at any rate."

I fumbled in my trouser pocket, found the matches and struck one. It sputtered faintly and went out. I repeated the performance a second, a third and a fourth time. The result was the same. What the hell was the matter with the cursed things? Were they damp? I carefully felt the remaining matches and the brimstone of the box. All were as dry as tinder. The terrifying truth flashed across a none too perceptive mind. The air was so devoid of oxygen that a match would not strike. We were breathing a mixture of nitrogen and carbon-dioxide. We were entombed in a virtually hermetically sealed dug-out, the oxygen in the air of which, we had almost completely exhausted.

The effects of oxygen-lack were not unknown to me. In order to impress upon us the vital importance of wearing oxygen-masks at heights in excess of 10,000 feet, the whole crew had at one stage been placed in a decompression chamber and shown what those effects were. The demonstration had not been a pleasant one. The worrying thing about that memory now was the fact that in the initial stages an insidious failing of the mental functions occurs, of which the sufferer is unaware. The violent headache and the feeling I had of muzziness made thought a tremendous effort. In the inky blackness and utter silence, the imagination tended to run riot. The phrenetic state was present. I felt an almost overwhelming compulsion to dash into the black void ahead, find the exit door and get out. I had somehow to master it, and think clearly.

I thought of the air pipe behind our heads. The protruding section came in some eighteen inches above the floor. From its position and angle it had to run obliquely upwards through the earth and be at least three feet long. I groped for it, put my nose to it and sniffed. I thought I could detect air, but only faintly. I sucked the wretched thing, but was aware of nothing but the bitter taste of slightly rusty metal in my mouth. If the pipe were straight and daytime prevailed outside, light should be apparent at the far end. I put my eye to it and looked. There was no light. The pipe might, of course, be bent. Worse, it might be blocked by debris brought down by the recent snows. The test was inconclusive and solved nothing. It depressed me further.

We tried the roof above our heads. The wood was firm and did not yield a fraction to a forceful push. There was a way out. That much was certain. Somewhere in the darkness ahead of us was a trapdoor. If things became too bad, and before they actually became impossible, we must locate that by touch and force an exit. But was it openable from the inside? It was logical that it should be, but fear and a muzzy brain represented alarmingly that it was not. The last thing the Dutch would want would be for us to emerge just as a bevy of Germans was passing. That would spell death to them. Perhaps they had secured it in such a way that we could not get out. In that case we were in truth entombed and dependent for our lives on the offices of a man we scarcely knew, and who, in an area as hot as this, might even now be in German hands.

Conservation of energy was of prime importance. Movement required oxygen, and oxygen was scarce. We resolved simply to lie as near the pipe as possible and wait until we could wait no longer.

We had little desire to talk, and lay, each wrapped in his own thoughts. Forced logic told me that the conditions were not worsening rapidly. They must, in fact, be worsening, because the place was reasonably fresh when we went to sleep and demonstrably foul when we awoke. But the fact that we woke at all indicated that we were not then dangerously short of oxygen. The process of de-oxygenisation was slow. We could probably continue for some time yet. For all that, our plight was not pretty. I detested particularly the persistent, sour, dank smell of the earth which surrounded us. It stank of decay and death.

"Why, in God's name, do you think they've put us in a dump like this?" Cheeseman's voice, breaking the silence, seemed to echo hollowly round the dug-out.

"I can only think that the Dutchman meant exactly what he said. That it's a bad moment to be landed with a couple of RAF types on their hands. If the outside is as I think, then I can't imagine a hiding-place more safe."

"Nor more foul," said Geoff. We relapsed into silence.

I realised, suddenly, that I was falling asleep. That I must not do. My imagination had tended toward over activity for a time, but the mood had passed, and a slow, yielding descent into unconsciousness had followed. I levered myself up into a sitting position and found by touch that Geoff was similarly positioned. We could not sit upright because of the confined space. We sat, crouched sullenly forward in the manner of crows which sit on the branches of a tree doggedly riding out the winter's blast. It was uncomfortable, but it was better than lying down and falling asleep.

"Stan," Geoff whispered — it was a peculiar fact that we did whisper — "I believe it's daylight outside — listen!"

There was a sound, so muffled and indistinct at first that I did not recognise it. So muted was it that it was impossible to place it or to determine its distance. It was the first sound, other than our own breathing and occasional voices, we had heard. Sound argued activity, activity life in the world above us, and animated life probable daylight. It was a small boon but we hung on to it. The sound resolved itself into the throb of a car engine. We were confident of a speedy release from the place of darkness.

Nothing happened. Time, the cripple, limped on. After that one break in the silence there came no more. The thought that Karl had been apprehended forced its way back into my consciousness, but I did not speak of it. It did not bear dwelling on. There was a morbid temptation to do so, but I succeeded, just, in suppressing it. There was, after all, not the slightest evidence that it was so.

Conditions were slowly worsening. But in any case I was probably an easy victim for oxygen-lack. I never had been able to abide a hot stuffy room. I was not normally in the least claustrophobic, but airless conditions were my 'bête noire'. Breathing became more and more difficult, even to the point of pain; dizziness succeeded muzziness; imagination alternately flared and was dead. When it flared I saw in a sort of mist that danced before my eyes a kaleidoscopic medley of faces and places; I saw strange birds that inhabited the remotest mountain fastnesses, and weird fishes that swam in the uttermost depths of the sea; I saw most clearly the silent worms that worked in the smothering mat of grass roots above our heads; I saw a rather authoritative Dutchman named Karl sitting in the glaring lights of the Gestapo interrogation room resisting the bestial techniques practised on him by thugs who demanded to know where we were. It was a phantasmagoria of rapid change and far reaching proportions, and it shaded downwards from the vivid and fantastic, through the dark side of the mind where all was sombreness and despair, to find its base in lame acceptance and mere nothing. It was a delirium of the dark. The Powers of Darkness had my mind and Asphyxia had me by the throat. I craved for light; but I hungered even more desperately for air. It was appalling.

When imagination died — as it had an increasing tendency to do — I was aware only of a deep desire for sleep. There was this state of passive acceptance. It was perhaps years since we had awoken to the Stygian gloom, decades since we had heard sound of human activity. In this mood I was unsanguine of ever getting out of the place of darkness, and I did not much care. Keats and his nightingale that sang in the ageless dark came slipping remorselessly into my mind, and stayed there.

It was a fact that I carried a small attaché case full of books inside my travelling trunk, and that I had a tendency to be found reading something or other just before a raid. A love of literature and poetry was one definite side of my nature, countered, many said, by a fondness for the Bohemian that made me a natural for the marvellously bawdy aircrew life of the pubs. But now, as I felt consciousness wobble, it was not a snatch of lewd song that came to me. Persistently and persuasively the opening, sensuous words of that ode concerned with darkness and despair and the unattainable, sweet voice of the nightingale haunted me.

My heart aches, and a drowsy numbness pains
My sense, as though of hemlock I had drunk,
Or emptied some dull opiate to the drains
One minute past, and Lethe-wards had sunk.

Perhaps it was sheer despair and the shadows numberless that had caused it to rise into my mind. Perhaps it was a defence against the mental tumult that had assailed me; a panacea that offered a solution to all troubles in sleep.

"I can't stick this any longer, Cheeseman," I said, haltingly. "I think I'm going crackers. Let's unbolt that door if we can, and get out while there's time."

"Hang on, mate. You were the one who said they'd put us in here because things were tough. Something's wrong or they would have let us out before now. If we can open the trap and get out we shall probably walk slap into the Krauts. That would be the end of our escapade, but it would be curtains for the Dutch here. Stick it out a bit longer!"

I took his point and admired him for it. Oxygen-lack I knew to be, in part, subjective, and he was probably feeling its effects less than I. Still, he was undoubtedly right.

The 'bit longer' stretched; but not far. There was an abrupt change. The sound of rapid footsteps boomed hollowly right above our heads, there was a scraping sound at the far end of the hole, the tomb opened, and Karl was lowering himself down through the trapdoor, bringing with him a draught of cool,fresh air and the blessed light of day. My first reaction was to look at my watch. I perceived vaguely that it was almost midday.

"You do not look well," Karl said, as we scrambled into the light by the trap.

We told him in no uncertain terms of the unbearable air conditions, but relief mollified our vituperations.

"That is bad. Perhaps it is that the pipe has become stopped. We did not mean it that you should so long stay here, but there were Germans near the farm this whole morning and I could not sooner come. You must now go with me to the farm."

We rose shakily from the hay, and with his help clambered out of the hole.

"Go quickly over there," he said, indicating the farmhouse in the near distance.

When we had gone a few yards I turned and looked back. He had put the trapdoor back into place and was busily trampling on the grass surrounding it. The field looked perfectly normal, the turf as innocent a piece of pasture as was conceivable. We were never to know exactly how the trapdoor opened and shut, or whether we could have forced an exit from the inside. Neither were we ever to discover whether the air-pipe had, in truth, been blocked.

The reviving effect of the air was not immediate, but the feel of it on the face was a joy that would normally have gone unnoticed. Karl caught us up as we trooped uncertainly into the farmstead.

"Stand here by this door and breathe the air for some minutes, I will soon return," he said, as we entered a brick-built cattle-byre. We did as we were told.

7

The Buccaneering Type

Karl reappeared after a few minutes. He had a basket over his arm and was accompanied by a youngish man clad in farm attire. We walked with them to the end of the long, rectangular building. Twenty cows gazed steadily at us from their stalls as we passed them; and they were lucky cows, because in the farthest corner of the byre a huge mound of fodder was piled eight feet high against the walls. Opposite this pile we paused uncomprehendingly. The farmer began to pull away at the fodder, which was matted and hung down curtain-like in tight-packed strands. Cheeseman's face had a bluish tinge to it and was strained from the effects of the incarceration; his mind, like mine, dulled into the dimmest of states. Neither of us grasped in the least what should have been plain. It soon became patently obvious. The curtain of hay parted; the outline of a door and its surrounding brickwork appeared; we stood outside yet another hiding-place.

Karl's face was the picture of amusement. He had stood and watched our bemused looks with glee. "Come into our office," he said, grinning all over his face. Through the fodder and the door we went, and found ourselves inside a solidly-built room some nine feet square and seven feet high. It was a permanent building — not, in fact, unlike a works office — built on to the inside walls of the byre. The sound of the hay being manoeuvred back into place came gently through the door.

The room was barely furnished. Against one wall stood a small, rough table; two old chairs with wicker-work seats provided places to sit; clean straw covered perhaps half the floor space and, on top of the straw, were a couple of blankets. A single electric light bulb suspended by a foot of black flex from the ceiling provided adequate light, and although the means of ventilation was not readily apparent, the air was reasonably fresh. The room was not untenanted. On one of the chairs a man was sitting motionless with his back towards us, gazing, I thought, fixedly at the far wall. When we were inside and the door closed behind us he turned and said something in Dutch to Karl. He was a tall, lean man with a white, cadaverous face. He wore spectacles and possessed an air of concentrated attention which suggested the studious type.

"I promised I should give breakfast, and here is it," said Karl. "It is perhaps a little late; but eat well!"

He laid the contents of the basket he was carrying on the table. A hard-boiled egg each, a few rounds of bread and butter, some lumps of cold meat and a mineral water bottleful of a lukewarm liquid that had a vague taste of coffee and which we each swigged in turn constituted the feast. We, who had not eaten for nigh on eighteen hours, tackled the spread with relish; Karl expressed his approval.

"So!," he observed. "That is good. When earlier I came for you, you did not look well. Now I see that you become quickly better."

It was so. The effects of our sojourn in the dug-out were rapidly wearing off. The fitness needed to stand up to the rigours of the thirty operations which constituted a Bomber Command tour was considerable, and the RAF had seen to it that that basic fitness was there. They toughened you progressively over a considerable period of time, particularly in the earlier stages, where, in the bottlenecks which invariably occurred between one training station and another, there was, inevitably, a commando course or something equally fiendish to be endured. I always thought of it as a form of sadism: but it worked.

It was perfectly true that as one neared the operational stage this sort of nonsense stopped. Life became by, say, army standards, unconventional in the extreme. There were few or no parades, no compulsory PT, and, if you cared to miss your breakfast, you could often continue to lie abed half the morning. Discipline was applied according to individual characteristics in the air, which was one's element. But on the ground there was a deal of drinking, smoking, and a disposition to consort with women of one sort or another.

However, to offset the known proclivity of the aircrew animal for the beer pot, ample sporting facilities were available. Cricket, rugby and soccer were there for the taking, and no self-respecting RAF station lacked its badminton court. In eight months Norman Levick and I had scarcely let a day go by without an hour's badminton. The life tended also to be concerned largely with the open air. The Bomber Command stations were strung out in a long line from Durham to Suffolk, always in the country, and always swept by those bracing airs that stream down the east coast of England. In winter, most people used an epithet other than 'bracing' for those airs. In Lincolnshire it was usually cold enough when the wind blew to do irreparable harm to a brass monkey. But one got used to it. In fact we were fit; very fit, in a hard sort of way. The hours in the airless dug-out had been gruelling. That, however, was in the past. It was to the immediate future that we had to look.

The man who sat by the table announced that he was a school teacher. He said that he spoke English quite well and that he was in hiding. Geoff squatted on the blankets, Karl propped himself casually against a wall, I occupied the remaining chair. The scene seemed set for a gentle afternoon's diving.

The talk centred on bombing and the RAF. We had been busy of late working on the oil targets, but Pölitz, that vitally important refinery which stood on the desolate Pomeranian Plain close to the point where the river Oder empties into the Baltic Sea, meant nothing to them. The huge oil complex of Leuna-Merseburg, near Leipzig, and the refinery at Brüx, in Czechoslovakia, suffered a similar fate. We mentioned the marshalling yards at Siegen and the attack at Ladbergen, but may as well have saved our breath. The incanting of a list of No 5 Bomber Group's strategic targets worked no charm. It did not seem even to register.

"Have you never bombed Berlin?" the teacher interposed. He sounded incredulous that the name had not been mentioned.

It obviously had deep meaning for them, but we were obliged to admit that we had not.

"That is a pity," said Karl. "If I was an RAF man I should most like to fly and drop bombs in the centre of Berlin, and so do much damage to the Moffen."

There was a light in the eyes and a soft edge to the voice which proclaimed that he meant exactly what he said.

I sensed a hatred greater than I was accustomed to. To the majority of aircrew, bombing was a job done in the course of total war without overmuch consideration for the non-technical consequences. I, for example, had always found a state of unreality pervade my mind when I flew on business. Like most others I never operated thinking that the tons of bombs we carried might account for perhaps a hundred German civilians; that arms and legs would be severed from bodies, heads roll and blood spurt down below on account of us. Thirty trips we had to do, and, once started, I had to admit that the thing held a peculiar, rather specialised fascination that made me resent delays. Fear I had known more than once, but no particularly virulent hatred. It was a job of work one did for one's country as clinically as possible. I sensed that these men held a different view.

"Do you then hate the Germans so much?" I queried.

"Oh, yes," snapped the teacher. "There was once a fire raid on Rotterdam in 1940. Many hundreds were killed on that day. We were defenceless then and have since been slaves. Our land is not our own. Many good men have died because they resisted this. You cannot, I think, understand why we hate the Moffen so. But you have not lived in a conquered country. It is not possible that you should understand."

I thought that perhaps, in reality, I did. When so confronted, a deeper stratum of my mind asserted itself against the blasé cynicism I often affected, and represented alarmingly what a hell Europe must have been for the last five years. The continent was in thrall; all the Jews in it in danger of extermination in the gas chambers of Belsen, Buchenwald and their likes. The Germans had set the game afoot, so, he who had sown the wind at Warsaw, Rotterdam, Coventry and London with mere Heinkels, Junkers and Dorniers half a decade ago, must not now grumble if his Reich was being decimated by an Anglo/American whirlwind of infinitely greater striking power. These men were right. I was, however, aware of one thing. They were, though educated, extremely hard cases.

The teacher was a morose man. His extreme pallor may have been caused by illness, suffering, or too little contact with the fresh air. Whatever its cause, it matched the unsanguine tenor of his conversation. He was by nature a critic, and had little encouraging to say. But at last he hit on a bull point in our favour.

"I will say one thing for you Tommy pilots. You are most careful with your bombing in Holland. Our houses are not much damaged by it."

That was good to know. I seemed to remember something similar from the bilingual priest, even to the word Tommy.

I protested that neither Geoff nor I were pilots.

"To us you are all pilots," he said, without the flicker of a smile.

Our education was advancing. To the Dutch, all aircrew were pilots, and all British serving men Tommies. The Tommy Atkins of the first World War had extended his range a bit. I thought I would advance my knowledge yet a step further.

"What is a 'muffin'?" I asked. "You use the word a lot."

Both men spoke a considerable amount of English but neither was bilingual. There was a lengthy discussion in Dutch. The best we could mutually arrive at in the end was that Moffen was the equivalent of the English word Huns as a derogatory reference to Germans. Because of its connotations with Attila and brutality, the Germans had banned its use. Therefore, these men used it: usually with an upward curl of the upper lip.

The talk went on. It obviously pleased Karl, at least, to hear our chitter-chatter about the outside world. We had no qualms about careless talk.

I had noticed the two mens' careful avoidance of names, and so had Geoff Cheeseman. For amusement, and with feigned innocence, he suddenly asked the question.

"By the way, what is your name?" he enquired, addressing Karl.

"I have no name."

"Well, what is your normal work? Your friend says he is a teacher. What are you?"

The answer did not come. Instead came ructions. There was on the instant a terrific crash, followed in quick succession by six or seven more. The walls shook, the ceiling oscillated, the flex from which the single light bulb was suspended seemed to move in all directions at once, and the bulb itself whizzed to and fro in space like a pendulum gone crazy. The sudden mutter of cannon and the answering chatter of light flak coalesced for a moment and then were gone.

"That," pronounced the teacher, "is the Tommies. They attack the railway line half a kilometre from here. It is the main line from Apeldoorn to Winterswijk and then to the German Ruhr." His taciturn attitude did not vary.

Karl, on the other hand, revelled in this sort of thing. He was suddenly on his feet, grinning and winking at us enthusiastically. He, I thought, liked the war brought to his doorstep.

There came a sound of heavy footsteps outside. We both looked at Karl. He had his head cocked on one side listening acutely, but appeared unworried. The rustle of the hay outside indicated that the curtain was being parted. The door opened, and a short, thick-set man with a choleric face entered, puffing like a grampus. He was extremely excited, and began to jabber rapidly in Dutch with accompanying gestures. Karl was all ears; the teacher looked thoughtful.

"What's all this about? What's going on?" Geoff demanded.

"It is all right," Karl answered. "This man is come here with news for me and was crossing the railway when three RAF aeroplanes have made a low attack on it. He has lain himself flat on the ground when the bombs have fallen and has been nearly killed. He has seen that two bombs have hit the railway, and has then come here as fast as he can. This thing I like. I wish that I could be in such an aeroplane."

The teacher interposed in professorial style.

"I cannot understand why your RAF bomb as they do. They attack many times the railway lines here, but it is always across the lines that they fly. They drop perhaps so many as four bombs each, but only one bomb can hit the line, and that is soon mended by the Moffen. If the pilots would fly along the line they could hit it four times."

"It is a matter of technique, if you understand the word," said Geoff, testily.

"I understand. But what technique? It is not efficient."

"Efficient enough to get two direct hits. They came in low, and I distinctly heard German guns. Bugger flying low along main lines studded with flak trains and light flak," I countered.

For the first time on Dutch soil I felt thoroughly annoyed. Two direct hits did not sound bad to me. I saw no reason why he should quibble.

Our visitor, having suffered his contretemps with the RAF and delivered his message, had gone. I began to muse over the difference in outlook of the two men with whom we shared the room.

The teacher seemed a dried-out man. His view was persistently critical and dusty. I began to wonder whether he did too little active work. There are, after all, none so carping as the uninvolved. The armchair, as I had often observed in England, was a wonderful place from which to slate the war effort and those who ran it; a remarkably fine perch on which to sit and hate the Germans. Or was there something more? I found a flicker of suspicion cross my mind regarding this pale man, but dismissed it as being uncharitable. Probably the adverse fortunes of war had embittered him.

Karl, I reckoned, was an entirely different proposition. I realised that the mental picture I had formed of him in the dark last night was false. My picture had led me to expect a grimmer, older man, who was a stickler for the letter of the law. Instead, I found, in full light, a tall, rather slender, fresh-complexioned type in his early twenties who was not at all unhumorous and possessed eyes which were deep-set and reflective in repose, but which held more than a hint of fire when he became animated. The bombing incident told me that he liked action, for when the first bomb had struck he had been up on his feet rejoicing. He was intelligent and an adventurer, I was sure. In England he would have made a good fighter pilot; here, his outlets were limited to what he could do in the Resistance; but that, from the freshness of his complexion, was plenty. He could act, as he had last night, with the assurance and caution of the true professional and seem almost primly severe in the process. Basically, though, he was the buccaneering type.

"I think that I must now tell that in one hour we shall go from here." Karl proffered the information unconcernedly.

"What, move again?" Cheeseman replied. "We're becoming like a pair of wandering Jews."

"It is good that you are not Jews, for if you were Dutch Jews, you would, I think, be already dead. But you must go. It is thought by the farmer and by those who watch, that the Germans are too much interested in this farm. This morning was it so that Germans were too near for too long, and so has it been before. If they suspect, they will come and they will search. In a heavy search they would find this room. So was it that you were put in the hole, for they would never find that. Therefore have I this morning talked with other men and it is decided that you further shall go. In one hour we shall start."

At seven o'clock that evening we were on our way. We had passed through the curtain of hay and left the den in the possession of the farmer and the teacher. What they proposed to do about German suspicions, and when, was no longer our concern: we trod the sandways once more. The night was in absolute contrast to its forerunner. It was cloudless and starlit. Polaris stood out boldly enough above the constellation of the Plough, and we kept it steadily at our right shoulder as we journeyed westwards. In the furthest south-west distance the heavy guns in the Rhine/Maas sector flickered palely, their emissions of light pulsating incandescently upwards into the dark dome of the sky. In the south, and much nearer at hand, the RAF were already busy pranging a target on or near the northern stretches of the Rhine.

The bombers were coming in from the west on a track a few miles to the south of us, and then turning southwards on their run in to the Rhine. The guns at Winterswijk and more heavily those in the fortified German areas to the south, were putting up a curtain of flak; flares and the first of the bombs were going down; there was an abundance of crumping and banging and many-coloured light. Seen from afar the spectacle possessed beauty and as a show of pyrotechnics it left even the largest of firework displays flat. The wind was stilled; the night itself would, in the ordinary course of events, have been a crisp, starlit winter's night of great charm. But the nearness of war had transformed it. It also meant that our progress was not in the least masked by the mantle of darkness beneath which we had slid along like ghosts the previous evening. The main trouble was the searchlights. The area was not exactly bristling with heavy flak guns, because there was nothing of any real military importance other than Winterswijk to defend. But this territory formed part of a great zone that had originally stretched downwards from Denmark to France, in which searchlights and night-fighters operating from beacons co-operated in an attempt to prevent the RAF from reaching the western borders of Germany itself. Those searchlights were very active. Their slender, silver fingers probed the night sky, swung this way and that, crossed and recrossed in a dizzy oscillation as they searched for their prey. They were in the fields all round us, and the ribbon of sand along which we walked was at times as light as day. I felt uncomfortably naked in the changing light.

Karl revelled in it all. Jauntily down the middle of the sandway he strode, whistling softly as he went. For my own part, I felt, after the cautious procedure of the previous night, that the whole gambit was rash. I wondered whether our friend's adventurous instincts and his obvious love of the panoply of war had overborne his caution and would lead us straight into the hands of the enemy. As if mirroring my thoughts, Geoff Cheeseman posed the question.

"What happens if we meet the Germans?" he queried.

"I do not think that we shall meet Germans on this road this night. But if we do I am prepared. Your RAF and the German Scheinwerfer make it not possible that there should be cover for us, and so we go on in the light. I am by the Germans wanted, and if I am caught with you I shall die. It will not be a pretty death. Therefore have I this."

He reached into the pocket of his overcoat and produced a revolver.

"This pistol is full loaded. If we meet one German, then I shoot to kill him. If it is more than one, then I still shoot to kill. Next, if it is possible, I run, and you must run with me. That is what happens if we meet the Moffen."

The exposition was remarkably clear. It held little allure, but at least we knew the exact score. There had again been that soft, icy edge to the voice that proclaimed truth. If we were accosted by his detested Moffen there would be no attempt to bluff our way out, no quarter asked or given. There would be an execution one way or the other. Such was the way of our buccaneer.

We stumped along in silence. The air raid had died as we walked; the searchlights had all gone out together as if operated by a single, many-tentacled octopus, and left us alone with the night. Only the incandescent flickering in the south-west remained to speak of war. We had, I thought, covered between two and three miles when he made his final bow. It was sudden and unexpected..

"I must now leave you," he said, stopping dead in his tracks. "In the right hedge, one hundred metres further, a man waits for you at a gate. Walk to that gate! If he is already not there, you must wait for him."

He loved the surprise element and the quick, dramatic effect. This had come like a bolt from the blue. Remembering his aversion to the use of names, I thought, as a parting gesture, I would catch him out for once.

"And who shall we say brought us, Charles?" I asked, stressing the last word.

I failed to shake him, although he had no reason to suppose that I had guessed his name.

"Tell him that Karl brought you," he replied, gurgling like the proverbial drain. "Now I must go. I wish only that you have a safe journey once more to England, my men of the RAF."

With a handshake he turned and departed along the way we had come. Cheeseman and I watched his tall figure coalesce with the shadows until it disappeared silently into the night. A buccaneer without question, he was. But a shrewd one. He never really missed a trick.

We walked that hundred metres in silence. The ability and the nonchalance of the man who had gone was considerable, but I wondered why he should bring us almost to the meeting point and then turn back. What manner of man should we find by this gate, if indeed he was there?

We were on the gate quite quickly. Five feet or so above the ground a blob of relative white was discernible among the dark shadows. It was the face of a man. He was leaning on the crossbar of a bicycle.

8

The Man in the Hedge

"Good evening, gentlemen," said the man, as we approached. "My name is Leo and I am very pleased to meet you. If you will come with me I will take you to a farm where you can sleep tonight. It is not large, but I think you will find some comfort there."

My mind boggled slightly. Were we peculiarly lucky, or did nearly everyone in Holland speak English? This man was clearly a fluent speaker of the language. His opening remarks possessed a kind of old world charm. He invited us to this farm of his with all the courtesy of a host welcoming his guests to a dinner party.

We proceeded along the sandways in silence. Only the unabating, white flickering of the guns between Rhine and Maas gave evidence that other men were active on the flat plains. In the still, crisp night, the sound of the guns was occasionally audible but very faintly. Otherwise it was deathly quiet.

"We are to tell you that Karl brought us," I said, at length.

"Karl?"

"Yes, that's what he said."

"It has no meaning for me. He is of another group and it is unlikely that I have ever met him. In any case, the name is almost certainly a false one. I ought, perhaps, to say that the Underground here is divided sharply into groups or cells, and beyond the one in which I work I know nothing."

"Remarkable, then, that you knew we were coming."

"There is, of course, always a link to bind the chain."

I thought it better not to pursue the matter. But I remembered the hundred yards of no-man's land through which Geoff and I had walked. Karl and Leo could not possibly betray each other.

We lapsed into silence and moved steadily on. Leo wheeled his bicycle along the centre of the way, Geoff and I walked to either side of him.

"Why a bicycle since you're not riding it?" Geoff asked. "We have been taught that guides in Europe usually walk or ride well ahead of their charges."

"I scorn that. We go together. This bicycle is now a nuisance, and if there is trouble I shall throw it in the ditch. The reason I have it is that I came several kilometres to fetch you and was late starting."

The dense lines of trees which hedged the ways had a claustrophobic effect. I felt eternally to be moving along ribbons of sand that glimmered in the starlight, dividing the black masses of the thickets. I seemed cut off from the outside world. The owls hooted occasionally in the trees as we went, otherwise the silence was disturbing. There were no people in this land we passed through, no vestige of noise, no murmur of traffic. When we spoke, it was automatically in whispers as people do when they look round a church.

"There's not much life round here, Leo, mate," said Geoff. "It can't be much after eight, but the place seems dead."

"The Germans impose a strict curfew after dark, and anyone found moving around is liable to be shot first and questions asked later. They have reason to know that the Underground is active here and they are not inclined to take chances."

"A comforting thought," I observed.

"Do not worry. I use only remote paths, and I do not think we shall meet anyone."

We came to a metalled road. Leo paused for a moment, looked intently to right and left, and then we were across it and into the cover of the tree-lined tracks once more. To pass the time I described our experiences in the dug-out and in the room concealed beneath the hay in the cow-house.

"Ah! That was a real Underground farm. The one that we go to is quite normal, and it has no special hiding-places."

The guns continued their distant, almost silent commentary as a farmstead appeared immediately to the left of the way. The farmhouse was small. Leo paused for a moment by the low fence which formed its boundary. His briefing was short.

"This is the farm. Before we go in I must tell you that no-one here speaks English, except perhaps a Pole who is in hiding in the district and may be here. Even if he is, his English is so bad that you may not understand it. Therefore I will talk with the farmer and determine all that you should know before I go."

He wheeled his bicycle along the side of the house, stood it in a dark spot against the wall and knocked quietly on the door. It was opened immediately, and we filed through the kitchen into the living-room. The time was half past eight.

A table stood in the middle of the room, and seated at it were two small people: a plumpish, blonde woman in her early thirties, and a man who was slightly younger, had a rather unkempt look about him, but rejoiced in a complexion as rosy as an autumn apple. Leo stood by the door, engaged in a long conversation in Dutch with the farmer who had let us in; we took seats at the table, and waited.

"You English?" queried the fresh-faced type at the table. We acknowledged that we were.

"I Pole — was in England — speak English — but make many, many, many mistakes," he sputtered, speaking with the speed of a machine-gun. "My name is Julian Grenade."

Grenade was right. I had not a clue what the Polish spelling was, but phonetically it could not have been more apt. He exuded good humour: but his nature seemed as explosive as a little bomb.

He stood up and shook Cheeseman and myself very enthusiastically by the hand. The farmer halted in his conversation with Leo and also insisted on shaking hands. He was a merry-looking chap who completed the farm's trio of small people. "Tommy," he said, and beamed his approval; his wife returned from a pot she had been tending in the adjacent kitchen, joined in the felicitations and, as if to improve upon her husband's performance by a single word, offered her sentiment. "Tommy, gut!" she said emphatically, and returned to the cooking pot.

The dialogue continued as before in two parts: Leo and the farmer spoke rapid Dutch; the Pole and ourselves endeavoured to make our thoughts known to each other in English. Julian's English was atrocious, fast, and jerky.

"I was soldier — caught by Germans in Belgium — jumped from prisoners' lorry near town Zwolle."

"That's a long way to the north. How did you come here?" I asked.

"Walked — no-one help me till I get here — that was three months before now."

"How did you live?" Cheeseman enquired.

"I live from land — steal carrots and beetroots from fields — carry in pockets — when hungry, eat them. But three months here too long — each day spy I out German soldiers, where they are — soon walk to Rhine and cross it by self — you come?"

"Not flipping likely, not yet anyway," said Cheeseman. "We're for the quiet life for a few days if we can get it. Eh, Stan?"

"Too bloody right, mate," I said, using Chuck's favourite expression.

The Pole did not seem in the least upset by the cool response to his crack-brained scheme. His sputterings in English continued sporadically until Leo and the farmer joined us at the table.

"I have now some time in which to tell you all that you should know here, and also to talk for a while if you wish," Leo began.

"That would be great," I answered. "Your English is exceptionally good."

"It is reasonably good, and I enjoy having the opportunity to exercise it. First, though, I think that you should understand the risk this little farmer is taking for you. The area is now exceptionally dangerous for two reasons. First, there is the growing battle between Rhine and Maas into which the Germans are moving reserves. Second," he grinned suddenly, "there is a certain RAF bomber lying in pieces in a field not far away, and the Germans cannot understand what has happened to its crew. They still search, but find nothing. This farmer has no secret hiding-place, but merely a loft full of hay in which he will put you. You may come down only when he tells you, and you must give him your RAF tunics, because he thinks that a visitor may perhaps see you in them and that could be dangerous. Most dangerous of all, however, is the fact that he has small children, and small children talk without realising the consequences. The farmer is a poor man but a brave one. I must ask you to do whatever he says."

There was an intensity of utterance about Leo that riveted the attention. His hair, like mine, was dark, his mouth firm in a rather oval face, his height and girth a fraction above the average. But it was his brown, rather veiled eyes and this intense manner of speaking that particularly registered. He was, I supposed, about five years older than me, and very sophisticated for a farming region. His sentiment, though, was quite obviously right.

"I have a great respect for such a man as this farmer," I said. "Poor he may be, but there are gentlemen in nice safe niches in England who could do with half his supply of courage."

"And in Holland," Leo rejoined. He looked at me quizzically for a moment, his intensity fading.

"You are, then, no great respecter of persons?" he asked, to draw me out.

"Not really. At least, I've been told to toe the line so often, that I suppose I can't be. The trouble is that I find it impossible to admire a man merely because he's made himself filthy rich or fantastically learned. He may, in either case, still be a bastard. As to being born rich — I really can't imagine that the twinkle in a duke's eye is necessarily any more bright than that in the eye of a peasant."

"You demand something more from men of power?"

"Yes. Power, I believe, brings its own obligations, and I like to see them fairly and generously discharged before I start paying any reverence. Given that, I dare say I'm as respectful as any man breathing."

"You are very left wing!"

"I suppose I am, in a non-political sort of way."

"Like me you are a rebel against what is sham in social convention. You should feel happy among us. It is, of course, the rebels not the conformers who man the Underground."

In a way I was beginning to feel at home. I found a camaraderie among the rebels I was meeting that appealed. Also, it was repeatedly made abundantly clear that Tommies were welcome in Holland: welcome to the point where people took appalling risks for them.

"What, then, do you think of parting with your uniform tunic?" Leo asked.

"I don't like it, but if you say it's necessary I'll do it. What about you, Geoff?"

"Well, with you two setting the world to rights I was beginning to wonder if I'd ever say anything. But, sure. It puts us in bad with the Krauts. In fact we'll probably get shot as spies if they catch us; but, if that's the form, that's the form."

"Good," said Leo.

"Now that you've got off the soapbox for a bit let me ask a question," said Geoff, grinning. After all we still scarcely knew each other, and my philosophising tendencies were not up his street. He preferred the practical. "Tell me," he continued, "your Underground seems very well organised. Who runs the show?"

"That is a question you should not ask. But I will tell you something about our Movement in a general way." Leo moved completely off his intense tack, put his head back and laughed.

"Basically, it is a gang of criminals. There are burglars, thieves, forgers, spies and cut-throats at work in the district, and the Germans know it. The burglars break into premises such as burgomasters' offices and steal official papers; the forgers copy them — and that is particularly dangerous work; the thieves filch whatever they can; the spies survey the land by day and night, and report on troop movements and dispositions; the cut-throats have a tendency to kill a German soldier here and a Dutch Nazi there, whenever the opportunity seems right. Wherever they go and whatever they do, the Germans are watched by a hundred eyes which see and fifty mouths which report — to be general about numbers.

In fact you could say that you were in the midst of a den of observant thieves who have one thing in common. They hate the Moffen."

The first-hand exposition tallied very neatly with what we had been taught in escape lectures. It was a perfect microcosm of the whole.

"I'm surprised about the cut-throats," said Geoff. "Aren't you afraid of reprisals?"

What followed was as subtle a piece of thinking as I had heard for a long time. At the end of it I felt more than ever that the Dutch reputation for hard-headedness was justified, and that we had been treated to a full general exposition of the ways of the Resistance, without ever touching on the specific.

It was apparent that Leo was no believer in head-on attack. He admitted to a particular hatred for Dutch Nazis, whom he regarded as far more dangerous than the average German soldier, because they were fanatical and knew the district. These he referred to as the 'greens' and 'blacks' — according to the shirt they wore — and spoke of a man who had exterminated a few in the region very efficiently. However, his theory was that the work of the Movement should be done in a manner that led to the most harm being done to the enemy without his knowing that he had been hurt. In a flat and highly populated country like Holland he regarded guerrilla warfare with scepticism. Underground work, he argued, should remain underground and undetected. That way there were no reprisals.

"So, in general, you concentrate on a more passive resistance?" I asked.

"Not exactly; but think! Kill a German soldier and what happens? Half the population of a village dies in reprisal. Stop a military convoy by scattering nails on the road and you delay the convoy for half an hour. And then what? Innocent people who live nearby are condemned to the concentration camp. That is absurd. But we know that one RAF or American bomber can inflict more damage than our whole group, provided the Allies have good information and the airmen to fly them. We do our part in gathering and supplying information, and in the return of airmen to England. The last forms some part of my job. I occasionally work on the pilot-line, and I have dealt with a number of airmen."

"And did you get them away?"

"Yes, we smuggled them down to southern Holland. That is the end of our part of the line."

"You went with them yourself?"

"No, we used a courier. He has taken perhaps so many as eighty airmen that way since 1941."

"How?"

"By train. I can tell now how he did it, because he is no longer here."

"Dead?"

"No. When last he went to the south he stayed there, because he knew that the Germans suspected him. He took all those men to Limburg without knowing a word of English. Almost always he started from a small station near here, bought pro-Nazi newspapers for them to pretend to read in the railway carriage, and told them by signs not to speak on the journey, but just to sit reading the papers, with the tickets he had bought in their hands, ready to show immediately. Always he travelled in the same compartment and did any talking that was necessary. But it is clear, I think, that such a journey is not for you, now that the main German defensive line is on the Rhine. The only way with you is to get you over the river somehow, or wait until the British cross it."

"We may have to wait a long time."

"Perhaps, or perhaps not. We shall work on it."

He turned suddenly from English and began to speak in Dutch. With the change in language came a change in mood, for the farmer and his wife found the tale he told uproarious, and laughed till the place shook. This, I thought, was odd. I had mentally classified this man as one who would do his job with the finesse of an artist turned criminal. I failed to see how our chances of getting across the Rhine were improved by his turning comedian and whipping up his audience into noisy stitches.

"I am sorry about that," he said, when the hilarity subsided. "Sometimes I think, though, that it is good to tell a story or two in situations like this."

"You don't find it dangerous? All that noise I mean."

"In no way."

We talked a little further about the bomber offensive, the destruction of the German cities and the high toll taken of their civilian populations. He had no qualms. The song he sang on that subject was very similar to the one the men in the room beneath the hay had sung. More thoughtfully and with reservations it was true. But the song was the same. The years lived in terror of the knock on the door in the night, the arrogance of the conqueror, and the memory of close friends who had been taken away to the concentration camps and never seen again had left no trace of pity in the hearts of the men who resisted. 'Bomber' Harris had no stauncher adherents anywhere. I recalled Eric Copley's scruples about dropping Cookies on marshalling yards.

"What is a Cookie and who is Eric Copley?" asked Leo.

"A Cookie is a large two-ton bomb that bursts on impact and blasts down an acre or two of built-up area. Drop one of those near the edge of the yards and you have a few souls to answer for on judgment day. Copley, one of the crew and probably its most intelligent member, got pretty upset at the idea a week or so ago. But then he's a firecracker on the rights of his fellow men: particularly ordinary men."

The mention of the rights of man seemed to spark Leo off. He reverted to Holland and the Germans. In the process he became eloquently vicious.

"We, the Dutch, have rights. Do not forget that, and do not think from all I have said that our resistance is merely passive. It is only that, for the moment, it must be done in that way. When the time comes we shall rise actively, and the Germans shall know that they have an enemy in their midst."

"When will that be?"

"It will be when the British have crossed the Rhine and are coming this way. When they are one day's march from here, that is the moment to rise, and it will, as you have said, be the ordinary men who will do the work. Certainly not the local pro-German burgomaster. But we will deal with him at the right time."

He had gradually relapsed into his intense mould again; and because of that the bedrock of his thinking became extremely clear. Canny it was, but quite ruthless where the despatch of the Hun from his country was concerned, and completely unforgiving for those of his countrymen who had played the traitor. His brilliant academic English led me to think that he was a teacher of quality, and that was not my line. But that he had a tendency to mix facetiousness with philosophising had at one stage been evident. He was also an admitted rebel. I felt that I should like to know him better. We were, I suspected, basically two of a sort.

Geoff posed a last question. It was a practical one.

"Any last instructions?" he enquired.

"Oh, yes. I had almost forgotten. There is an escape plan. In the loft is a door with two simple bolts. If the Germans come searching, you are to unlock it, jump to the ground, run to a thick copse opposite, and hide there if possible. The farmer will show you how to unlock the door, and, if the worst happens, he will cough twice, loudly. Like this." He demonstrated. "Then you go, fast. Understand?"

We affirmed that we did; he rose to leave.

"You must remain here until I come for you. It will not be long," he concluded.

I, too, asked a last question.

"Wasn't all that laughing a while back a bit risky? It struck me as out of character for a type like you."

"Not in the least. You see, I have a man watching outside. Did you not realise that you were followed here along the sandways?"

"Good lord above! Were we?"

"Yes. You passed the man who now watches as you walked to the gate where we met. He was hiding in the hedge."

"Christ! You're damned efficient."

"Let us just say that I always take precautions," he said, and went out into the night.

9

Under the Hay

An interpreter is rarely fully appreciated when he is present. He is, in some peculiar way, invariably regarded as an automaton who verbally transmits ideas across the gulf that differences of speech cause between the nations. But when he is absent the trouble starts. Such was our case now. The gulf yawned; the language barrier reared its ugly head.

The night was comparatively young; the front door securely bolted; a simple but not unsubstantial meal on the table. There were two Dutch people who knew no English, two Englishmen who knew no Dutch, and a Pole who had a very imperfect knowledge of the one and the merest smattering of the other. The five of us sat round that table in the living-room of a small Dutch farm on a cold Friday evening in early February in the year 1945. The Dutch couple wanted avidly to know something about the two birds of passage who had landed in their midst, and, in particular, to hear about the world in which, until recently, they had lived. Ours was, after all, a free world, in spite of empty bellies and lack of creature comforts. It was a world that five years of the oppressive Hun had almost — but not quite — driven from their memories. They wanted to know of this, and because there was no other way open to them, they used Julian as interpreter.

It would not have been so bad if Julian had not been the excitable type. The Saxon dialect of Eastern Holland tends to be spoken with animation and rapidity, and the Dutch couple, not for a moment appreciating their interpreter's difficulty, put their questions in a quick, lively manner. He failed, I could see, in large measure to understand them, but, being excitable, he tried to jabber an interpretation in execrable English of that which he had imperfectly grasped in Dutch. The deeper he got into trouble, the faster he went. We, for our part, tried desperately to slow him down by speaking in deliberately precise English. But it was no use. Everything about him was quick. When he moved, the action was sudden; when he spoke, he went at it like a supercharged Gatling-gun. Frequently he mopped his brow and lapsed into his native Polish, in which, I suspected, there was a flow of invective sufficient to have made the farmer's wife's hair stand on end, had she understood it. The air was replete with an astonishing mixture of fast flowing Dutch, Polish, and pidgin English, with a counterpart of English so measured as to sound, by comparison, like a funeral dirge. The result was absolute chaos.

Geoff was the first to call quits. "This," he said, "is a complete waste of bloody time," and withdrew into a stony, Olympian silence. I saw no other useful course either, so, after a few more tries at the steady approach, I followed suit. Julian Grenade fretted and fumed on for a while, but it was useless. He never quite lost his buoyant humour, but in the end he gave up. The conversation-piece disintegrated.

The lady of the house, now comprehending fully the frustration, had, in a womanly way, a final drop of oil to pour on the troubled waters. Standing up, she swept her hand round in a comprehensive gesture that included all of us, and uttered twice a term that was understandable in all three languages. "Internationaal!" she said, "Internationaal!" And it was true. There was, of course, no political implication. She simply meant that the five of us ought to remember that, whatever our nationalities, we were deeply involved in a tough game devoted to one end: that we were little tiny cogs in a large anti-Nazi wheel that was beginning to roll very successfully.

The remainder worked like a charm; the waters were smoothed. In the new-found calm, Julian made yet another attempt to embroil us in his projected Rhine crossing.

"You come with me — escape?" he asked.

Cheeseman, his humour restored, shook off his Olympian huff; but only to negate the idea.

"No, definitely not! Too crack-brained!" he answered.

"You then?" said Grenade, addressing me.

"No. I shall stick with the Dutch."

"But I walk here from Zwolle — sixty kilometres — am not caught. Rhine less than thirty kilometres — easy."

In vain we put the case that to wander about in central Holland, far removed from the fighting and with only garrison troops in the towns to worry about, was a vastly different matter from trying without help to work one's way through the fortifications of the enemy's main defensive line and then cross a major river. Our efforts were without point. He was allergic to waiting and was bubbling over with confidence in his solo scheme. He was determined to go. We were equally obdurate in our intention to stay and pin our faith on the Dutch.

Ten o'clock arrived and with it bedtime. The farmer fetched a lantern and guided us up a flight of rickety stairs into the hayloft. The loft was comparatively large in area, but of no great height. The hay was piled in a deep layer over the entire floor and made it necessary to stoop slightly when walking across it near the walls to avoid cracking one's head on the beams of the roof. The flickering rays of the lantern stole across to the far side and disclosed a large door which, primarily intended for the loading and unloading of hay, was now our last line of retreat in emergency. To either side of the door a square window provided a viewing point, should we need it. The farmer took us across the sea of hay, demonstrated that the two bolts which held the door in place were, in fact, simple and requiring no more than a firm pull to unfasten, and then returned us to the wooden staging that stood by the door leading from the stairs. Geoff and I stood and watched; he busied himself in the preparation of our beds. He bent down and began steadily to scoop out two shallow, six foot long hollows side by side in the hay. He worked carefully.

When he had finished, the depressions stood there, eighteen inches deep and three feet apart, waiting for their occupants. He motioned us to get in and lie flat. Cheeseman took the one nearer the window, I the one by the stairs door. When we were lying flat he piled hay all over us until we were almost completely covered. He made a very good job of it. My body, legs, arms and even my forehead were immersed in the stuff; only my face remained exposed. The fact did not escape him, because, attracting our attention, he stood on the staging, pointed first to my face and then to Geoff's, and made a series of circular gestures with his hand. I managed a feeble grin to show that I had grasped his meaning and he departed. I heard his heavy farm boots clumping noisily down the wooden stairs, saw the last flicker of light as the door at the bottom closed after him, and then all was silence.

I particularly did not like my hands and arms being trapped. I felt that the hay enwrapped me like a winding-sheet, and I had a desperately strong impulse to tear the lot away and lie free. But a warning issued by Karl flashed back to my mind. "When the Moffen search, they search often by night, for they think then to catch us asleep," he had said. The meaning of the farmer's mime was plain enough. If the worst happened and we were caught completely unawares, he wanted us to cover our faces and lie still. He had arranged the hay very carefully over us so that the whole area looked level. With our faces covered we might just get away with it. The lurid thought of German bayonets stabbing and probing deeply into the hay as their owners searched, seized my mind for a moment, and I felt a sharp twinge of doubt. But it passed. I left the winding-sheet precisely where it was and determined that, should the need arise, I would cover my face and ride the game out.

The loft was not quite dark, for the starlight filtered gently through the grimy windows and played wanly over the beams and rafters of the roof as they rose upward in a steep pitch to the centre coping. The faint scuffling of the odd mouse was the only thing that disturbed the silence. I could not see my colleague, but I thought I would give him a final hail.

"How do you feel, Cheesey? Are you tucked in nice and comfortable like?" I asked, facetiously.

"Bugger off. I feel like a trussed-up, bloody mummy. Good night!" came the uncompromising reply.

"Check," I said.

I found, after a while, that I was comfortable enough. The hay was warm. Let what would come, come. I drifted effortlessly into slumber.

It was still dark when I awoke. From the regular, somnolent breathing on my right I knew that Geoff still slept undisturbedly. I lay there enjoying the warmth of the hay and rejoicing in the fact that I was about to see the dawn break. It was far from my habit to do any such thing, but something had woken me early this morning. I was not quite sure what.

As I lay there musing, the February dawn slowly came. The faint light of the morning stars, which alleviated the dark and bathed the beams of the roof in the gentlest of glows, gave way progressively to a grey, imperceptibly increasing visitor who steadily turned amorphous shadows and shapes into sharply defined objects. It was not that there were many things to transmute: only the beams and rafters, the walls and the wooden staging, and Cheeseman's face projecting a fraction above the level of the hay. After a while I thrust the encumbering hay to one side, rose and moved quietly over the sleeping, trussed-up form of my partner, and inspected the bolts of the escape door. Satisfied, I turned to one of the windows and gave my attention to the immediate area outside. The ground below the door looked soft and not more than twelve feet distant. The coppice that Leo had mentioned stood directly opposite some fifty yards away. The dawn was cold and grey. The escape route surveyed, I returned to my hollow and pulled my many-stranded blanket back over me.

With the increasing light Geoff awoke. I could hear him turning over and fidgeting as people do when the sleep of the night is almost over.

"Wakey! Wakey! Rise and shine! Come and see the sunbeams dancing on the wall!" I said, quoting the inane reveille beloved of some RAF disciplinary NCOs.

"What's to do?"

"There's nothing to do, boy, except to hang about. In fact, the best thing to do is to lie where you are in your pit. It's a bloody cold morning."

At nine o'clock the clump of the farmer's boots was heard on the stair. He came in, grinned broadly and motioned us to get up. We went across, sat each on one of the broad ledges of the windows and watched him go about his purpose. When he had finished filling in, he smoothed the hay with his hands, trampled around a little with his feet, and finally looked satisfied. "Zo," he said, winked knowingly, and departed.

"I thought he might ask us down to breakfast and a seat by the fire," Cheeseman said, a touch enviously.

I, who remarkably enough had been awake longer, thought he was being over optimistic. The care with which the farmer had immersed us in the hay convinced me that the fear of a German search was a real one. At the very least, the little man who was sticking his neck out to help us had acquisitive German soldiery after eggs and milk, efficient Dutch Nazis, and talkative young children to worry about. He had to be careful. I had the feeling that we should only descend to the comparative warmth and comfort below for short periods. Leo, I reckoned, would soon be moving us on.

There seemed a lack of activity about the farm. There was neither bustle nor stir, and certainly no sound of small children at play. It was unexpectedly and disturbingly quiet.

It was not actually raining, but the sky was a uniform leaden grey, and it was cold. We squatted in the hay in a corner of the loft, talked occasionally, and took the odd chew at the remaining Horlick tablets in our escape kits, as much to relieve the boredom as to sustain ourselves. The dark morning wore on. I decided to review the landscape in a little more detail, so I moved to the nearer window, kneeled in the hay which came almost up to the ledge, and stared out.

On the ground below the door three or four bales of hay had appeared as if by magic. When they had come and who had brought them I knew not, but they had not been there when I had looked out in the half light of dawn. Their significance was plain. They would make our jump so much the easier, should it come to that; they would also provide a valid reason for the fact that the loft door would, of necessity, be wide open after our enforced exit. We were lodging with a man who, as a broad categorisation, could be classed as a homespun farmer. But he did not lack for ingenuity. He was covering his tracks extremely well.

The Gelderland countryside is not, as is the case in the west of Holland, uniformly flat. There is nothing that might remotely be called a hill, but, here and there, there is a roll in the ground to break the monotony. Towards such an undulation I found myself looking. The land immediately outside the window was flat enough, but to the left of the clump of trees it clearly dipped slightly away, because at a distance of somewhat over half a mile, the upper two thirds of the steeple of a large church pointed a long, tapering finger impressively towards the slate-coloured sky. Really large churches may occasionally be found in villages, but the odds are against it. The size of the one I now looked at argued the presence of a town hidden away in that hollow, and meant that we were not, as I had supposed, still out in the backwoods.

It was a matter of some fascination to work out, with the aid of compass and escape map, precisely where we were. There were four towns marked on the map which could conceivably come within the bounds of possibility, but one of them was definitely out. The Copley-Young hen-coop had stood, I knew, quite near to the southern edge of Groenlo, and we had since worked our way some miles southwards and westwards. The latter fact precluded also Winterswijk and Aalten. The southern shank of the compass needle pointed directly towards the church. We were undoubtedly just outside the northern rim of the town of Lichtenvoorde. And that was strange. Karl had said that that was where our Lancaster had crashed. Why should the Dutch Resistance carefully manoeuvre us straight into the region where the search for its crew must presumably be strongest?

"Seen the church, Cheesey?" I asked.

"What church?"

"Shake yourself and come and look through the window. You'll see."

Geoff Cheeseman was normally of a slightly extrovert nature, but not this morning. His mood had been distinctly morose. Nevertheless he came to the window and looked.

"So, there's a church," he said, disinterestedly.

"It's the church of the town of Lichtenvoorde, or I'm a Dutchman."

"That you are not, so it must be Lichtenvoorde. What's special about that?"

"It's flipping strange that they should bring us there. That's all."

"Why?"

"Think hard! That's where Karl said our Lanc finished up. Why should they blather on about German searches, and then bring us straight into the lion's mouth?"

"Yes, pretty preculiar now you come to mention it. Still, there's nothing we can do about it." He was, as ever, practical. That summed it neatly up, without in the least explaining it.

The minor deviation over, we resumed the waiting game. I had no doubt they would feed us when the time was ripe, but became increasingly annoyed by the thought that while we sat up here and shivered, our roll-neck sweaters and battledress tunics were hidden away. I intended to get some more clothing. I began to study my phrase-card.

At noon we were invited below. A youth of about fifteen, clad in an oil skin jacket — for it was now raining — stood at the bottom of the stairs and regarded us quizzically. He remained for no more than a couple of minutes chatting to the farmer's wife who was busy once again at the kitchen range. Then he moved out into the rain, probably, I guessed, as look-out. We sat to the table and consumed a frugal but welcome meal. When it was done I made my point. Indicating the loft, I said, with accompanying shivering motions, "Ik ben koud." "Ja, koud!" said the farmer, nodding appreciatively.

We returned to our vigil in the loft; the hours passed morbidly away. The daylight faded gradually, and with it went the last shreds of our humour. We took a dim view of practically everything. I, for example, gave up the idea that the farmer had understood my meaning about being cold. I sat there and shivered, and decided that he would merely have assumed I was commenting on the wretched weather. Hanging about with nothing to do cloyed the spirit. The art of waiting cheerfully was taking a deal of learning.

Quite suddenly the sound of footsteps on the stairs broke the silence, the door opened and the farmer was standing in the doorway with his lamp, beckoning us below. The time was eight o'clock as we proceeded down the staircase to our evening meal.

We sat as we had done on the previous night in the farm living-room, and made a start on the food provided. Only the Dutch couple were with us. There were no children, and of Julian Grenade there was no sign. The farmer pointed excitedly to a couple of old jackets which hung forlornly over the backs of two chairs. He had twigged my message of the morning and had resurrected them from somewhere. They were so ragged and bedraggled that he might well have plundered them from a couple of local scarecrows, but they would serve. To show our appreciation we tried them on, looked ourselves up and down in the sideboard mirror as if at the tailor's, and muttered the odd bit of German that would be intelligible, such as "Gut, ja?" and so on. It was a small charade, but it pleased him, for he beamed with satisfaction. In point of fact they fitted quite well in a slovenly sort of way, and with our by now generally ill-kempt appearance, I reckoned we should pass for a couple of rough-looking farm labourers should anyone clap eyes on us.

Dinner done, we sat back and made what conversation we could. A little was possible with the phrase-card, but it was an onerous job, and after a while we gave it up. Cheeseman and I conversed in English, the farmer and his wife in Dutch. It was by no means an unhappy little party. I found it very satisfying merely to sit there and smoke my way through two or three pipes of tobacco, for I had not dared to indulge the habit among the tinder-dry hay of the loft. It was an enjoyable relaxation. Nevertheless, we never lost sight of the fact that there could, at any moment, come a thunderous, imperious knocking on that bolted front door, and we were ready at any time to vanish into the loft with the speed of scalded cats.

The knocking never came, however, and at ten o'clock we were ushered once more into our bedchamber beneath the rafters. The procedure was precisely as before. Under the hay we went for the second time. Once the farmer had completed the covering-up process, he departed with his lamp, and we were left to darkness and to sleep.

We slept well that night, for when the farmer roused us it was broad daylight. He had brought a couple of cups of ersatz coffee with him, so we retired to our corner and supped the bitter stuff gratefully while he carried out his ritual with the hay. The pealing of church bells wafted clearly over the fields. It was Sunday morning, and the people of Lichtenvoorde were on their way to church.

I spent hours that morning gazing at the spire of the church, for to me it represented life. I did not suppose that, with most of the men away digging anti-tank ditches or hiding out, the congregation would be a thronging, lively one. But still, in my mind's eye, it was life, and I hungered for it.

Geoff Cheeseman sat, for most of that time, in a corner, lost in his own thoughts. The sky remained grey. By the early afternoon a spit of rain had begun to patter against the grimy windows. We had not been asked down for a midday meal, so we remained, cold, hungry, and decidedly cheesed-off in the gloomy loft. It was a drab, long-winded Sunday.

We enlivened the boredom with an occasional game of hunt the mouse. We could hear the mice working in the hay, and, from time to time, one would pop up, regard us for a moment or two, decide that he did not want our company, and disappear smartly from view. We hunted them with the knives each of us had retained from our flying-boots. We stabbed downwards many times towards the scuffling noises beneath us, but we never made a kill. We did not seriously try. It was something to do. It whiled away the time.

Then, in the middle of the afternoon, came a change for the better. The farmer came up dressed in Sunday best, and motioned us below. Down the stairs we went and entered a living-room which contained members of the family we had not seen before. The farm was a place inhabited by small people, but the two we now met were very small indeed: they were young children. They sat there gazing at us with an expression of wonderment in their eyes. Where they had sprung from was a mystery, for neither of us had heard them about. Whether they had been told that the two ill-kempt gents in scarecrow jackets were of the RAF, I knew not for sure. Somehow, I thought they had, for they regarded us as if we were beings from outer space. But in any case, the fact of our presence was now no secret. The die had in that respect been cast; the cat let quite blatantly out of the bag. I wondered what the change of tactics portended.

We had first a bite to eat, and then sat in sedate fashion in a group round the heating stove. Sunday was being observed perfectly decorously. We talked our different languages, and the time drifted very gently away. The shadows had begun to deepen, the rain to pelt down, as the night drew in. And then, without warning, came the knocking we all feared. One moment all was as tranquil as a Victorian day of rest; the next, all agitation and alarm as the front door was being hammered. Rapidly and urgently it came. It was completely unexpected. I caught the momentary look of alarm in the farmer's eye as he half rose and pointed to the loft. Cheeseman and I were across the room, up the stairs and into the loft like ding-bats. He flew across the hay, and stood with his hand on the upper of the two door bolts; I remained motionless just inside the stairs door and waited to relay the word on the given signal. I listened intently. I heard first the rasp of a bolt as the front door was unlocked, and then the voice of the farmer. What followed was surprising. Instead of guttural German voices and the stamp of inrushing jack-booted feet, came merely the voice of a boy. He had an urgent message to deliver, for he gabbled excitedly away in Dutch and then departed. When he had gone the door was again bolted behind him and, at the farmer's behest, we resumed our places by the stove.

At half past six Leo and a thick-set, rather swarthy man arrived. Both were wet, for the rain had begun to stream down. They sat and warmed themselves by the stove.

"A wet night," said Leo. "We have a long walk to make but we need not start yet. First let me tell you some good news. Cleve has fallen. That was on the BBC."

Good news indeed. It meant that while those distant guns had flickered and Cheeseman and I had whiled away our time in the loft hunting mice, General Horrocks and XXX Corps had broken from their bridge-head south-east of Nijmegen and battered a way into the largest of the bastions that divided them from the Rhine.

"That is excellent news," I replied. "But it is not quite what we were hoping for. We had thought you might tell us that we were starting tonight for the Rhine."

"In a way you will be. We shall go south from here round a small town. The journey will be one of some miles, and at its end you will be less than fifteen miles from the river."

"We go, no doubt, to a farm."

"Yes, and there you must, I think, stay some while. The problem of getting you through the fortifications that now stand behind the Rhine will not be an easy one to solve."

Leo's colleague looked at his watch. It was time to go.

"Before we leave, let me coach you a little," said Leo. "It is Sunday evening, and we may meet people coming from church, or perhaps others who are not. Whoever you meet, say 'Goeden Avond' as gruffly as possible and pass by. Do no more and no less than that. Above all beware of speaking English loudly, for it may betray you."

He had us practise saying good night in Dutch a dozen times before he was satisfied. He was thorough in his teaching.

We had discovered from our phrase-cards that the Dutch for thank you was very comparable with our own expression. "Dank U", we said, and meant it as we pressed the hands of the farmer and his wife. That done, we patted the childrens' heads and went out into the elements.

The night was wild. The cold rain lashed us as we stumbled in the dark between the lines of storm-tossed trees. The gale vented its belligerent force upon us. Rainwater ran down our necks in rivulets. It cascaded off our tattered macs on to our trousers and into the tops of our shoes. The raincoats themselves were in no condition to stand up to weather of this sort, and in five minutes we were sodden. The sandy soil of the road cloyed to our shoes as we trudged, and made them feel a ton in weight. By any standards the going was heavy.

After a quarter of an hour Leo called a halt. He pulled us into the dark shadows of the dripping trees and briefed us.

"This part of the journey is the most difficult. For the next kilometre or more we shall work our way through the town. First, though, we have a major road to cross, and that is the worst point of all, because, three hundred metres to the left, it meets the main street of the town. At the juncture stands the Gemeentehuis or town hall, and, opposite that, a large house which the Germans have commandeered as their Headquarters. Both buildings are of course guarded, and patrols are often on the road. Therefore, we shall cross it in two parties of two with an interval of two minutes between. I must ask that you now be silent until we are clear of the town."

Leo and I moved off and came upon the road within seconds. We stood for a final moment in the shadows and listened intently. Through the murk and the driving rain came the sound of noisy conversation as a group of men moved along the far pavement. I thought the voices were German, and stood stock-still. "Only Dutch people going home from church," Leo whispered. "Come on!"

We were quickly across the road, and immediately into suburbia. The town began abruptly. The transition from country lane to suburban thoroughfare was sharp. It was a tarmaced road complete with pavements that we now trod. Against the loom of the troubled sky I detected the outline of the roofs of detached houses, each lying well back from the road at the end of its substantial front garden. The environment felt strange.

We pressed on for perhaps a couple of hundred yards to where a large tree thrust itself upwards from the very end of an unfenced garden, its bulk adding to the blackness of the night. "Wait for me here, I shall soon return," Leo said, and set off back in the direction from which we had come. I merged myself as best I could with the black trunk of the tree and waited.

Geoff Cheeseman and his guide joined me within a couple of minutes. A trio of thoroughly sodden specimens of humanity grouped themselves behind the tree and spoke no word as the swaying, creaking branches disgorged water upon them. It was, however, noticeable that the gale was beginning to abate.

We stood there for longer than I had expected, and grew wetter by the minute, for a storm-lashed wet tree is as potent a source as a shower-bath when it comes to a soaking. The fury of the elements was undoubtedly decreasing. The howl of the wind in the sandway had largely given place to the spatter and hiss of the rain on the metalled road as the major source of noise. Where the hell, I wondered, was Leo? The question was quickly answered. He reappeared, apologised in his polished way for the delay, and we continued our trudge. He carried now, I noticed with surprise, a square bundle under his arm that he endeavoured as much as possible to shield from the rain.

Round the centre of the town we went. Cheeseman and his guide had now taken the lead as we trooped on. The town itself lay wrapped in darkness; no-one moved except us. Only the houses bore silent witness to our progress — they and the hissing, pitiless rain that had turned the pavements into rivers and the roads into elongated lakes.

We came to the end of the town. The gaps between the houses had increased, and we had exchanged the unfamiliar, hard surface of a concrete pavement for the start of what, by now, had become the normal thing along which one moved: a sandy track. I knew that it was sandy from experience, not because I could see that it was so, for at least an inch of water covered it and made us paddle our way forward as quietly as we could. From the right a second track, equally wet and equally wide, appeared to come in at an angle, turn, and run parallel with the one on which we walked. The two were separated by a yard's width of grass. Geoff — who was immediately ahead of me nearest the grass — decided, for some god-forsaken reason, to move across the verge and take the second track. He veered suddenly to his right and fell instantly, with a resounding splash, up to his middle into the icy waters of a brook. The splash seemed to reverberate round half the silent town. He pitched forward until his nose was within an inch of the water, almost lost his balance completely, and recovered it only by staggering backwards. The initial splash was extended by seconds and enlarged upon as he surged to and fro in the effort to avoid falling flat on his face. Finally he stood upright with the water lapping round the lower part of his chest. He let out neither exclamation nor curse, for the sudden shock had numbed him. For a second or two we were equally mute for the same reason. Then we were galvanised into life. "Hell!" said Leo. "That is bad! Get him out and then run!" We fished him out, took to our heels and sprinted, all four of us, for a quarter of a mile from the scene of the crime.

The town had been left behind and we walked on at a steady pace once more. Cheeseman was, no doubt, the wettest of the bunch. But it made little difference, for we were all thoroughly drenched. He and his guide had resumed the lead.

"Another main road near, I'm afraid, gentlemen," said Leo. "Caution for the moment but, once across, the rest is easy."

There were no problems. The road was deserted. We stole across and moved once more into the cover of the countrified sandways. One acquired gradually the technique of hiking by night through occupied rural Europe. There were times of danger when one kept silent and let the eyes and ears work to maximum efficiency; there were times when the voice had its use to clarify a situation or to forget the rain.

"Why," I asked, "did you bring us to the very place where our aircraft crashed, and hide us for two days where the search was likely to be strongest? That makes no sense to me, Leo."

He seemed surprised, slightly nettled even, that we had been able to pinpoint our position fairly exactly from a view of Lichtenvoorde church. He did not reply directly to my question, but conceded that the remains of our Lanc lay harmlessly in a field a few hundred yards from where we had crossed the first main road in pairs. I reiterated the question.

"The answer is a matter of psychology. Remember that your aeroplane fell within five or six hundred metres of the German headquarters and was surrounded within ten minutes. Only one of your crew was caught, so far as I know. One out of?"

"Seven."

"Any killed do you think?"

"I fear one may have been."

"Do you call one or possibly two men accounted for out of seven very good?"

"Lousy."

"So our local garrison commander would say. A German is invariably a thorough man, and that one is no exception. His razzia or round-up extended for two days, but his soldiers found nothing. The German weakness is arrogance. When an extensive search has been made and nothing found, they conclude, being blinded, that nothing can possibly be there. So, by Friday, I judged that the coast would be clear."

"And yet our little farmer went to great lengths to cover us up."

"Can you blame him? There was always a chance of a return visit. But since neither the Abwehr nor the Gestapo were involved I did not think so. It is all a game of cat and mouse."

There was that subtlety of thought and precision of timing that spoke of the first-class brain. My friend observed closely and thought lucidly. I fancied that the thorough German garrison commander and the pro-German burgomaster would not outsmart him.

We moved through a very desolate spot. Our course had taken us off the sandway and along a deserted farm track. Suddenly, as we came to a gate, I was aware of two men confronting us. "Goeden Avond," said Cheeseman's guide and Leo breezily in unison. The greeting was acknowledged and we passed on. But it was a warning. I had become engrossed in the conversation and failed to notice them until it was too late. They were, as it happened, Dutch. They could as easily have been Krauts.

Later I sought information about Copley and Young, but drew a blank.

"I know nothing of such men," Leo replied. "I have forgotten their names already."

The guide in front held up his hand and said something in Dutch. We stopped abruptly.

"Now we must leave you," said Leo. "But first I have something that may help. These are English books. They will provide interest whilst you are in hiding," he said, proffering very courteously the bundle he had been carrying.

That bundle had intrigued me for some time. Off and on I had wondered, half facetiously, if we were going to blow up a section of railway line en route. It now seemed to me that Leo was prepared sometimes to take a hell of a chance. If those books were discovered in our possession the Hun would have a very limited number of addresses at which to make enquiries. The hauling of that bundle for miles through the pouring rain spoke of the milk of human kindness; also, perhaps, it was a mark of confidence.

"I suppose that we are moving out of your area," I said.

"Yes. It is a hundred metres of no-man's land for you again, then you will find two men waiting in the hedge."

Geoff had a final question to put.

"You do intend to get us back to England quickly I hope? The Pole on that last farm reckoned he could do it alone."

"Julian Grenade is a mad-head. He disappeared on the night that you arrived, and has not been seen since. A cornered animal is very dangerous. The Germans are now like that. Julian will probably contribute to his own death, but that is no reason for you to do so. Do not try alone. Just stay on the farm you go to and read your books. Now, goodbye."

The two men squelched back along their tracks; we dribbled a damp course in the opposite direction. Two figures detached themselves silently from the hedge and fell into step with us.

"Tommy?" asked the one who walked by my side.

"Ja," I answered.

"Kameraad," he rejoined, stopped in his tracks, and began very profusely to shake me by the hand.

Cheeseman's new guide was as extravagant in his protestations of friendship as mine. I realised with a sudden shock how young these two were, and, having a couple of weeks previously attained my twenty-second birthday, I found myself looking slightly askance at the effusiveness of these lads in their teens.

The sandway proceeded in a descending curve to where a farm lay at the bottom of a hollow. As we approached, a watchdog began to bark. Now, as we stood at the door, it growled and snarled furiously, close at hand. We could hear the scrape of its claws as it strove to remove whatever obstacle prevented it from venting its spite upon us.

The door was opened by a very tall, barrel-chested young man with a face tanned the colour of leather by habitual exposure to the air. In the pool of light cast from the open door we could see the dog. He was a savage, black brute who struggled unavailingly to force a way through the stout iron bars of the open pen that enclosed him. At a word from the farmer he relapsed obediently into silence.

A quick, explanatory conversation between the youths and the farmer ensued. The two boys took their leave; but not without a last handshake and a final, almost devout "Kameraad". I warmed to them.

The farmer took a hurricane-lamp from a hook by the door, and motioned us to follow him. We were led round the farm buildings to where, some thirty yards behind the house, a wide, open-ended barn loomed out of the darkness. Against the right-hand wall of the barn and occupying half its width stood a rough wooden shed some seven or eight feet high.

We followed the farmer into the shed, and were instantly aware of the presence of animals. He lit his lamp. By its feeble glare we could see that the place was, in fact, a sheep-fold containing a flock of a dozen or more startled sheep. Uttering the Dutch equivalent of the noises made by an English drover, the farmer thrust his way through the frightened flock, scattering sheep to right and left. Having made a space for himself he knelt down by the inside wall, along which a feeding trough ran at a height of some two feet above the ground. He thrust hard with his hand against the very centre of the wall beneath the trough. A section of the wooden planking swung inwards, and, motioning us to follow, he went through the gap on hands and knees. He spoke no English. When we were inside whatever lay behind the sheep-pen, he indicated that we should remain where we were, and scrambled back out again, taking the lamp with him.

The whole thing was bewildering. The floor we stood on was wooden, and so was the wall through which we had come, there was no doubt of that. The roof had seemed to me, in the shadowy light cast by the lamp, to run up to an apex; but I was not sure, for I had only seen it fleetingly.

"Did you see the side walls?" Cheeseman asked. "They looked as if they were made of straw. Feel 'em!"

I did so, and he was, I thought, about right. But it only made it the more puzzling. Two very cold, wet aircrew stood by the trapdoor with their teeth chattering and the rain-water dribbling off them in rivulets on to the wooden floor. They waited for light to illumine their darkness.

We did not remain mystified for long. Somebody came scrambling through the trapdoor, we moved back to give him access, and he was inside with us. "A moment, boys," he said, as he manoeuvred past us in the blackness and worked his way into the interior.

There was a click in the dark. The place was immediately flooded with light; the truth instantly apparent. Eyes accustomed to two hours of wet sombre night grasped it blinkingly. We were under the hay again. We were inside a hollow, electrically-lit haystack.

10

Behind the Sheep-fold

"So, that is better," said the man. "I am sorry that I was not here when at first you were come. But the farmer's son has told me that you are here, and I am quickly arrived. On the farm is it so, that I am the only one who speaks English. And so I shall — how must I say it? — bring food and talk with you."

"Look after us," said Cheeseman.

"Yes, that is it. I shall look after you. My name is Wim."

We were in luck again. How many people lived on the farm was, for the moment, a mystery. But one of their number spoke English, and he was appointed our keeper. His name, so he said, was Wim — and he pronounced it like the English word 'vim'. Wim might have measured five feet nine in height, and his frame was solid without in any way running to fat. His fair, frizzy hair reminded me somewhat of Karl, and his blue-grey eyes had the same tendency to seem introspective, when, upon a closer scrutiny, they were actually piercingly observant. There, however, the resemblance ended. There was, so far as I could judge, no trace of excitability about him, for his speech and manner were slow and deliberate. He seemed a very calm, exact man, for when he was unsure of something he asked you for the answer. Three times in as many minutes he stopped his flow of English and asked us to rephrase for him, when he could, in point of fact, have pressed adequately, if imperfectly, on. It implied that he intended to get his English right. All in all, he struck me as being a rather quiet, determined type who would look after our interests very well.

"I think," said Wim, "that you are very wet and also cold."

We agreed fervently that we were.

"Yes, the farmer's son has seen that it was so, and I think that I now hear him with something he has brought for you."

There came the sound of a heel tapping against the base of the wooden trapdoor. Wim pulled it open, and the tall form of the man who had scattered the sheep and first let us into our new abode emerged hands first as he struggled to preserve the contents of the two beakers he was carrying. Geoff and I sipped the hot milk gratefully.

"Has this farmer's son a name?" I asked, between sips, regarding the tall chap who stood by, not speaking or, presumably, understanding a word of English.

"No. I have a name, but he is not so lucky. Not all can be so lucky." Wim's retort was quick enough to suggest that he appreciated a touch of humour, however slight its nature.

"Well, do you like your house of hay?" he continued.

"Yes," said Cheeseman. "How thick are the walls?"

"They are perhaps one metre wide. It is so that they let not light in nor out, but air may come in. That is good, because you will find it that the air is so that you will not ever — how shall I say it?"

"Choke," I answered.

"Yes, never shall you choke here, but always can you have light. Also is it possible normal to talk. Unless it is that you very loud talk, it can never be heard from without. What is the word for very loud to talk, please?"

"Shout," Cheeseman replied.

"That is it, do not shout. But now, boys, I think that you should most quickly to bed go. It is not good that our pilots should catch a cold and be ill. We shall now go, but when we are gone this next must you do. There is here a stick, and after us must you fasten the door so." He indicated two sockets on the framework surrounding the door, into which the batten fastened. "In the morning I shall again come, and I shall knock on the door your Churchill's V sign which we hear on the BBC, so." He rapped out methodically the dot dot dot dash of the morse V with his knuckles on the woodwork, and waxed suddenly intense. "Never while here shall you open that door unless you hear such a sign. Many many times come German soldiers here for eggs and milk. We know not when they will come; you in here can never know it. Therefore must you never open the door and go even into the sheep's house, for it is dangerous so to do. If you want that you shall be caught and that we of the farm shall all die, do not as I say, and come out. But I do not believe that RAF men would do it. I trust it to their honour to do as is asked. Goodnight boys. I shall again come in the morning."

It was an old-fashioned appeal that cut to the very core of conscience. We felt honour bound never to open that door without permission. When they were gone we bolted it securely and prepared for bed.

The haystack itself was a fascinating structure. It had been built round an internal wooden frame. Spaced four feet apart, a row of substantial uprights some six feet high formed the bedrock on the two long sides, and these were linked by a series of horizontal slats at eighteen inch intervals from the floor to the base of the angled roof. The inside effect was of a rectangular latticework, against the outside of which the hay was tightly pressed. The roof began six feet above the ground, sloped upward to an apex some three feet higher, and was lined with strong canvas to help take the weight of the hay above it. Wooden planks butted together in the manner of floorboards covered the entire ground area, and, offering a prospect of comfort, the final eight feet or so of the room, at the end opposite the entrance door, was strewn with a deep layer of the inevitable hay, upon which a couple of blankets were laid. Bales of the inevitable piled against the wooden wall of the sheep-fold lined one end of the stack, leaving merely a two foot cubic gap in which the door had room to open and shut. But even that was allowed for, because a loose bale reposed in the middle of the floor near the door, ready, should the desire to do so take root in the mind, to be pushed into place. A wooden staging some four feet high stood behind the sleeping area, while the inner end of the haystack was not actually visible, because of the presence of a large, dark drape, somewhat akin to a heavy tablecloth, which hung downwards from near the roof and obscured whatever lay behind it. This I thought a bit odd. The light consisted of a single, naked bulb thrust horizontally into a socket, screwed, some three feet above the ground, into one of the uprights adjacent to the bed — I noticed in passing that the flex supplying the current came upwards from the ground. It was this end, designed and equipped quite obviously as the zone in which the occupants slept and spent the majority of their time, which contained the one completely unfathomable element in a unique set-up. Along the ground to either side lay a very solid baulk of timber at least ten feet long and a foot square in cross-section. These beams had little to do with the basic construction or solidarity of the haystack, and their purpose was not apparent. I proposed, though, to use the one on my side of the bed as a shelf on which to keep my smoking gear and as a repository for the books Leo had loaned us. All in all the place looked comfortable, was probably reasonably soundproof and certainly spacious. The entire area must have measured twenty feet by eight.

There was but one article of furniture present. An old chair stood on the boarding near the light. On to this we slung our sodden outer garments. Wim was right. There was no point in catching pneumonia. So, it being cold and we being wet, we dived for the warmth of the hay and blankets. We did not bother immediately to put out the light.

"Sod a man who goes paddling in Dutch brooks in mid-winter, Cheesey," I said, slightly peevishly. "What the hell did you think you were at?"

"I thought it was another path. It looked just like the one we were on — covered with rain."

"I suppose it did really. But you might have spared a thought. One second you were walking along the path, the next you'd damn nigh vanished beneath the water."

"Shook me stone cold rigid, I can tell you."

"You can say that again. I was speechless."

We decided that the haystack was not a bad sort of joint. For my part, I would sooner have been sitting in The George or The Shades at Spilsby, with a pint mug in my hand, but things could have been worse. Leo's parting advice and the half dozen books he had given us gave me the sneaking feeling that we were here for a while. But at the moment I did not care. A six mile trudge through heavy weather had completed several days of playing the wandering Jew. We had a fairly comfortable bed, electric light, books, and quiet sheep for neighbours. I felt that I could settle for that for a week. After that my feet would begin to itch.

"Put the light out, Cheesey," I yawned.

"With you all the way, mate."

Cheeseman was the keeper of the lamp. The switch was on his side. He outed the light.

There was a decent feeling of warmth beneath the blankets. We were dog-tired and soon asleep.

The morse V was being rapped insistently on wood. Slowly the persistence and the rhythm of the rapping forced its way through the veil of sleep, and I woke up. It was utterly dark, and for a moment I wondered where on earth I was. Then I was aware that Geoff was already stirring on my right, groping about for the light switch. He found it, the haystack was flooded with light, and a yawning Cheeseman ambled sleepily towards the trapdoor, removed the batten and admitted Wim. Wim looked cheerful.

"Good morning, boys," he said. "I think that you have very well slept. I have knocked your Churchill's V sign on the door until my fingers have hurt. Here is your breakfast."

It was very neatly packed in a basket. There was a hard-boiled egg each already shelled, bread butter and jam in slices which fell just short of the old-fashioned 'doorstep' in thickness, a bottleful of a warm brown liquid, and two cups to drink it from. It was a very pleasant repast, except for the liquid.

"What devil's brew is that?" asked Cheeseman, flinching as he drank the stuff.

"It is tea," said Wim.

"Like hell it is. It's horrible. It's gnat's pee."

"Ah! It is, of course, ersatz tea. Today is a tea day. Tomorrow it will be coffee day, and that is not so bad. You will become used to the both when you in Holland stay."

The meal over, Wim outlined his plan for the morning.

"You are RAF men," he said. "Is it not so?"

We acknowledged the truth of that.

"And RAF men are clean, good-looking men who use razors and combs. Not so?"

He spoke with seeming gravity and absolute poker-face. Only his eyes flickered a fraction to betray the fact that he was, in part, joking. He was the acme of the dead-pan humorist. Joker he had to be from his recent remarks. I reckoned we should have some fun with this chap.

We demurred, naturally, about the good-looking part, but admitted that we usually kept ourselves clean.

"Then closely look in this," he continued, whipping a fair-sized mirror out of a towel that lay in the bottom of the basket.

My gaze disclosed a dirty face with a five days' growth of beard surmounted by a black thatch of ill-kempt hair, within the confines of which wisps of hay were stuck. I looked like a chawbacon. When I really looked at Geoff, his case was very much the same, although, being fair of hair and of skin, the effect was not quite so bad.

"Now," Wim expanded, "here is a towel and soap, and I shall quickly bring water. Also have I a brush and a razor so that you can — what is it in English please when men razor themselves?"

"Shave," I replied.

"Yes, so that you can shave."

The RAF in its wisdom had provided a single-sided safety razor with a short handle to save space in the escape-kit. Wim's razor appeared to be of the cut-throat type, so we declined that piece of equipment.

"That is then good. Now can you come out and stand in the barn. It is quiet of Germans this morning, for many have gone to the battle near Cleve. You can stand and look at your haystack from without for a moment. Then, when I have brought all necessary things, shall you have a wash and a shave."

We trooped out through the empty sheep-fold — for the sheep were dotted over an adjoining field — walked into the surrounding barn, and stood surveying our home from the outside. Wim went into the farmhouse.

I had never been accustomed to find haystacks inside barns before, but the idea seemed sound as a protection against the weather and, assuming that such was a regular Dutch practice, there was nothing in the least to excite attention about this one. It simply nestled there behind a sheep-fold and against one wall of a barn. It looked entirely innocent.

I had noticed as we came out that the masking of the trapdoor was masterly. The horizontal hinges and the necessary cut across the boards were entirely covered by the feeding-trough of the sheep; the two vertical cuts merged beautifully with the cracks where the rough boards joined together. The trapdoor was, inevitably, the weakness. Untenanted, the door would naturally give to a firm push, but when the occupants were in residence I could see no reason why their whereabouts should ever be discovered.

Wim reappeared after a few minutes carrying two large galvanised buckets. The fact that he walked a trifle lop-sidedly suggested that the bucket in his right hand was full of water while the other was empty. We followed him back into the stack.

"So, are we all military men," he said. "I was myself once in the Dutch army, and we shall now make your house proper for RAF men to live in."

"In other words we're going to have the effort shipshape," said Geoff.

"Yes, that is it. We shall make all shipshape."

We assisted in the setting up of our quasi-military establishment.

The bucket containing water was put on the boards on Geoff's side of the haystack near the light for ablution purposes, the empty bucket placed much further away as a latrine, the mirror installed on a hook screwed into the upright above the light, the towel draped over the back of the chair, the cake of soap and shaving brush installed on the horizontal beam beneath the mirror. Everything was very orderly. It was merely a question of letting battle commence.

Being — for a reason I could never quite fathom — adjudged the stubborn type, it had always been my lot at cricket to open the innings. The need for caution required of the opener clashed violently at times with a basic impatience. But I had long accepted the situation and revelled in a slow, dogged sort of game calculated to wear down the fast bowling. History repeated itself here. I was elected first man in, and the other two stood and watched in Machiavellian anticipation as I lathered up and prepared to hack away a considerable growth of beard.

I found it no laughing matter, but they did. However, he who goes in first is, in such a case, soonest finished: even though his face is sore.

"Your turn next, boy," I said to Geoff, and retired from the fray to watch.

The shaving party over, we sat back in the hay, cleaned-up, refreshed in the way that clearing the muck and whiskers off one's face with soap, water and razor does refresh, and comfortable.

Before Wim went I asked him the meaning that lay behind the incongruous wooden beams that ran to either side of the sleeping area. His answer was a fraction more than interesting.

"They are for a good reason. Most possible is it that if the Germans think that men are in this haystack they would fire their guns into it, because they could not know if the men inside had themselves guns. Therefore are these large trees a kind of — how shall I say it?" He fished into his pocket and produced a small, thick book which could only be a dictionary. "Yes, that is it. They are for a protection. When the Germans shoot, then can you lie low on your stomachs by the trees and be protected."

"Gay stuff," said Geoff, when Wim had gone.

"Jolly. But never mind. If Jerry comes in shooting we've always got Wim's horizontal trees to comfort us."

The explanation solved one problem. There was just one other thing about the haystack that intrigued me. What, I wondered, lay behind that dark drape?

We whiled away the rest of the morning pleasantly enough. Curiously, I did not feel any sense of loss at the lack of a view. In fact it seemed to help. It was as if the absence of a sight — or for that matter a sound — of the outside world stifled any desire to be moving in it. Wim had for the second time firmly adjured us to keep the trapdoor locked, and this we did. I found no reason that morning to look upon that bolted door with disfavour, or upon the enclosing haystack as a prison.

Shortly after midday we were revictualled. Some chunks of cold meat, further bread and butter and ersatz tea kept us nicely topped up with food. In the early evening we were fed again, and then taken for a stroll.

"Now, boys," Wim said, as we finished our evening repast. "It is not good that you should all day sit and that your legs should have no work. Put on your shoes and we shall make a little walk."

He took us out on to a long, rectangular field that lay on the far side of the farmhouse. Round the perimeter of that field some three or four times we strolled. The night was clear and devoid of incident. The guns in the salient were stilled; no bombers marauded; the farmhouse slumbered at the bottom of its hollow peacefully beneath the stars; we perambulated gently round our field and noticed, in passing, that a line of high-tension cables ran slap above the centre of it, two of the supporting pylons of which were situated within its confines.

"It seems very quiet tonight, Wim. No Germans about?" Cheeseman queried.

"On the moment all is most quiet." Wim replied.

The walk done, we returned to our haystack and locked ourselves in. The day had been played in very low key, and I, for my part, was in no way sorry. There was a very lazy side to my nature and, just at the moment, that side predominated. There was no point in dragging out the time. We read for a short while, then switched out the light and turned in.

Wim was of the type that brooked no laggardry. So, since we liked him, we saw to it that things were kept shipshape. The beam on Geoff's side had become the ablution bench; the beam on mine the library on which Leo's books reposed. We washed and shaved daily; our meals came with unfailing regularity. I had forsworn smoking because of the obvious danger, but in the circumstances I found the sacrifice a bit much. I asked one morning if I might smoke my pipe in the haystack.

"That is all right if you are always careful," Wim replied. "There is somewhere a tin."

He rummaged behind the curtain at the very end of the stack and produced a sizeable round tin into which spent ash and matches could be dropped. It did not strain one's credulity too far to be certain that men had done this sort of thing here before. What lay behind that dark drape was still a mystery, for since it was clearly intended to be private Geoff and I had decided we ought not to pry. Curiosity, however, still lingered.

"Why sheep?" asked Cheeseman, out of the blue.

Wim, who had remained with us for some time that morning, was puzzled. "Pardon. What of sheep?" he countered.

"Well, I think you're a shrewd lot, whoever you are. Therefore there's a reason why this place lies behind the sheep-pen. What is it?"

The explanation made one thing quite certain. The hiding-place had been built in the previous autumn on the precept that since it was outside the farm it would be a safer place in a German search. Men who knew of its existence could, if surprised in the open, run to it and hide. But the Germans, it seemed, often used dogs, and there lay the cunning of its position. The fugitives could run through the field of sheep and the scent would be lost. Equally, the smell of the sheep would be strong in the fold whether they were inside or not.

"Cunning sods," said Cheeseman in an undertone. "We're not exactly among numskulls are we?"

"Far from it," I replied.

The week drifted away without incident. We took our nightly walk, and returned after the statutory half an hour as regularly as clockwork. The weather was of the mixed variety; the grass of the field, as February grass invariably is, wet. The days alternated between ersatz tea days and ersatz coffee days, as had been forecast. On some evenings the guns beyond the Rhine flashed away, on others they were still. Wim appeared to have no qualms about marching us so regularly round that field. The area, he assured us, had quietened down. At the same time he would brook no question of our emerging from our hiding-place unbidden. The door had to remain locked until the signal to open it was given. Neither was he particularly informative about the occupants of the farm. As the week ended we knew as little about them as when it started. He had divulged that he was the farmer's son-in-law, and we had met the farmer's son on one occasion. That, on the Saturday evening, was the extent of our knowledge. There was no real reason for it, but on that particular evening I felt uneasy. There was, in reality, a world beyond the confines of our haystack. It was a fact that the once almighty Third Reich had begun to totter, but the great natural defensive line of the Germans in the West was unquestionably their legendary river, the Rhine, with its great breadth and quick, treacherous current. However, a sizeable chunk of German territory lay to the west of it, and it was therefore true that the Allies had, in our part of the world, first to crack the vaunted Siegfried Line before they even reached the river. Upon that military world I found my thoughts centring.

The briefing at Spilsby on February 7th had made it plain that the curtain was about to be raised by a mass attack on the northern end of the German West Wall by eight hundred heavy bombers. The Canadian

The original crew formed at No 29 OTU, Bruntingthorpe, in June 1944.
From left to right: Leo (Chuck) Fowler, John Eaton, Norman Levick, Stan Hanson, Ron Young, Stan New.

Left: Eric Copley joined the crew at the next stage of training, and is shown here in his cadet days.

Below: 207 Squadron Lancasters from 'A' Flight snapped on a daylight raid in the spring of 1945 from the pilot's position of another aircraft in the 'gaggle'.

RF144 'EM: H' was the usual mount of F/0 Bob Halewood RAAF and crew, and survived the war: NN724 'EM: X' was a 'B' Flight aircraft borrowed for the night by F/O Fowler and crew, also of 'A' Flight.

The latter was, incidentally, one of 100 Lancaster B.I.s supplied by Austin Motors (Longbridge) and therefore came from the author's home town, *R. W. Allinson, M.A. Garbett / B. Goulding Collection*

Right: The morning after. The reconnaissance photograph taken after the raid shows the parapets of the Dortmund-Ems Canal breached in several places and the canal thoroughly drained. The runnels made by the outrushing water can be clearly seen, and water is standing on the low-lying fields in top right of picture. The Bomber Command assault on the German transport system proceeded well; but for at least one crew it was their last trip.

Weather conditions prevailing are indicated by the dusting of snow covering the area.

Below right: German soldiers examining the wreckage of a British bomber which crashed in a wood near Neede, Gelderland. *via B.W.C. van Albeslo.*

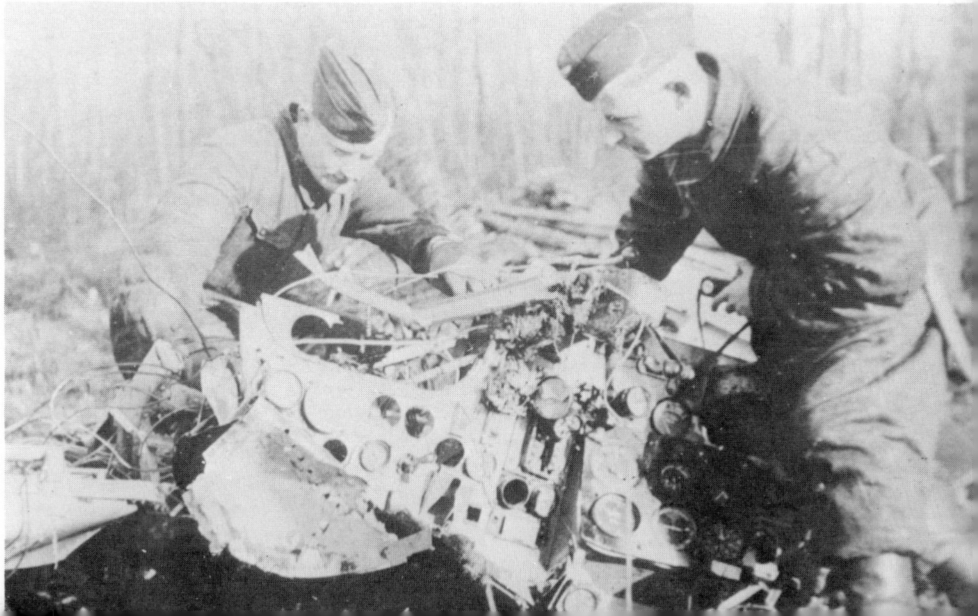

Above: Items from the escape kit, including: the perspex container, waterproof cover for the silk map, phrase-card, map, needle and thread, compass and four benzedrine tablets. Because it was so small, and therefore easily lost, the compass was normally kept in the matchbox.

Left: The farmhouse of the family Halleriet seen from the wooden bridge over the river Slinge. The family gave the author shelter, food, and finally old clothing in which to make his two-mile walk with a guide to meet Geoff Cheeseman.

Right: The Villa Bernarda stands on the side of the main road connecting the towns of Winterswijk and Groenlo. The picture is taken near the point where the broad sandway, along which the author walked with the man in blue, intersects the road immediately beyond the level-crossing.

The bedroom window from which the two aircrew viewed the road can be clearly seen.

Below: The bright weather conditions prevailing as Mr and Mrs Orriens are photographed outside their farmhouse a few years after World War II are at variance with the cold, drab spell in early February 1945 when they hid two aircrew in their hayloft.

The willingness of this couple to shelter such dangerous birds of passage so soon after the crash showed courage of an outstandingly high order; for they had no specially constructed hiding-place, the wrecked Lancaster lay in a field a mere half mile away, and the H.Q. of the German troops garrisoning Lichtenvoorde was roughly equidistant.

Above: Henk Hulshof points to the door of the hayloft from which the two aircrew were to jump in the event of a German search. By chance the set-up is almost precisely the same as in February 1945, for a pile of hay stands beneath the door as bales of it did then.

Something has changed, however, for Mr Orriens, the farmer, has built a new barn which obscures the view from the loft window.

Left: Lichtenvoorde church, the spire of which occupied the author's thoughts one Sunday morning as he looked across from a pretty cold perch in the hayloft.

Right: The hardness of the winters in eastern Holland is demonstrated by the muffled-up figures in the photograph. Taken in April 1949, it shows, from left to right: the author's wife, his son, the author, and Henk Hulshof, formerly known as 'Leo'.

The pilot was caught by the Germans near this signpost.

RUURLO
ZUTPHEN 34
AALTEN
WINTERSWIJK 12

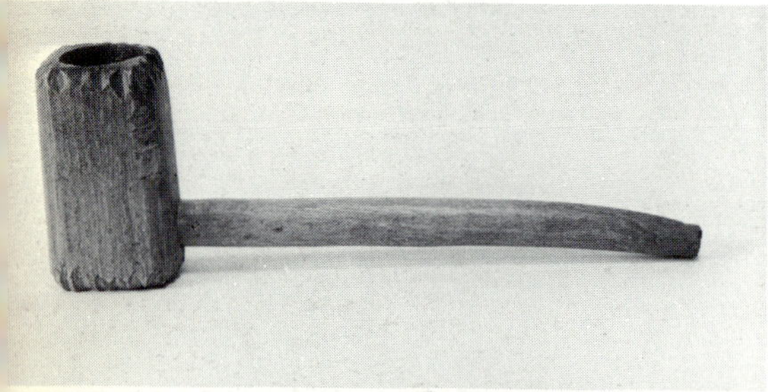

Above: Wim Lensink, in the uniform of the Dutch police, his daughter Hannie, and his wife Sien. Hannie was born on the farm while the two aircrew were hiding in a pile of hay half a mile distant, and is here almost three years old.

Centre left: The pipe made by Wim for the author. The notches mark the passage of the days spent holed-out in the haystack and the pile of hay.

As it turned out, the Dutch sojourn lasted too long to be accommodated by the top and bottom of the bowl, and so the side was in use when the stay ended. The final score was forty-nine.

Bottom Left: The Gemeentehuis (town hall) of Lichtenvoorde. The local German HQ stood almost opposite it in the road taking off to the right. The Lancaster crashed some half a mile up that road, while four nights later Geoff Cheeseman and Stan Hanson crossed it quite near the HQ with their guides 'Leo' and 'Pietje'.

Right: Mr and Mrs te Lindert with their eldest son, Johan, photographed outside the front of the farmhouse. The picture relates to a more carefree time, for it was taken a few years before the events of the book occurred. Nevertheless, these marvellously resilient people never seemed unduly bowed with care, and they still looked very much like this—on Sundays.

Left: The trio stand a few years later with Hanna, Johan's wife, in workaday dress outside the barn which once contained a phoney haystack. The sheep-pen stood against the right-hand wall (where the cart is), and immediately behind, in the recesses of the barn, stood the haystack.

Below: This picture of the farmhouse demonstrates well the situation in the last week of March 1945. On the extreme left, behind the group of trees, are the living-quarters in which the family and others dwelt; on the extreme right, linked to the house by first the cattle-byre (where the arms were hidden) and then the piggery, is the new barn in which the four German cavalry were billetted; at the back of the farm, some thirty yards beyond the gable-end of the byre, stood the haystack in which the RAF resided; out in the cold, within the pen indicated by the white posts, the watchdog prowled.

Nr. 318, Mittwoch, 28. Februar 1945

NACHRICHTEN FÜR DIE TRUPPE

Abwehrkrise am Rhein

4000 Flugzeuge über Halle, Leipzig, Mainz und Augsburg

Die brennende Reichshauptstadt wurde heute nacht wieder mit Bomben belegt.

Gestern bei Tage mussten vier deutsche Grosstädte die Angriffe von mehr als 4000 alliierten Flugzeugen in einer neuen Vernichtungsoffensive gegen das deutsche Nachschubsystem aushalten.

Im Osten wurden Leipzig und Halle von amerikanischen Bomberverbänden angegriffen, im Westen wurde Mainz von englischen Kampfverbänden mit Bomben belegt.

Von Italien aus setzten die Alliierten ihre Bombenoffensive mit einem schweren Tagesangriff auf Augsburg fort.

Bei dem Angriff auf Leipzig wurden gestern grössere Mengen von Waffen und Nachschubmaterial vernichtet als bei irgend einem Luftangriff auf ein einzelnes Ziel.

Dichte Rauchwolken

Die ganze Stadt war heute nacht in dichte Rauchwolken gehüllt, die von den Riesenbränden im Hauptbahnhof aufstiegen, wo Hunderte von Güterwagen ein Raub der Flammen geworden sind. Die Bombenexplosionen schleuderten Lokomotiven und Waggons aus den Gleisen. Die Stellwerke sind zerstört, die Schienenstränge durch unzählige Bombenkrater aufgerissen.

Die Zerstörungen sind so gross, dass Tage vergehen werden, bevor ein Notverkehr wieder in Gang gebracht werden kann, und der Eisenbahnnachschub an die entscheidenden Abschnitte der Ostfront ist jetzt fast völlig lahmgelegt, nachdem die Reichshauptstadt durch den Angriff am Montag als Nachschubzentrum vorläufig ausgeschaltet ist.

Der erste Angriff auf

(Fortsetzung Seite 4)

Zusammenbruch droht von Kalkar bis Trier

GEWALTIGE neue Panzermassen sind an vielen Abschnitten der Westfront tief in die deutschen Stellungen eingebrochen und haben damit die schwerste Abwehrkrise herbeigeführt, die es im Westen seit dem Zusammenbruch in Frankreich gegeben hat.

Von Kalkar im Norden bis nach Trier im Süden ist der Zusammenhalt der deutschen Front in schwerster Gefahr. Eine Abwehrlinie nach der anderen geht fast kampflos verloren.

Alliierte Panzerrudel rasen in allen Richtungen kreuz und quer durch die Landschaft. Schwärme von Schlachtfliegern und Jagdbombern bahnen ihnen den Weg, stossen auf die deutschen Geschützstellungen nieder und zerschneiden die Nachschublinien zur Front.

Und nirgends ist abzusehen, wo den anstürmenden Massen der Angreifer Halt geboten werden kann.

Tausende überrannt

So schnell geht der Vormarsch der Alliierten in vielen Abschnitten, dass Tausende von deutschen Soldaten überrannt werden und den Kampf einstellen, ohne überhaupt einen Schuss abzugeben.

Eingreifreserven werden umzingelt, bevor sie in den Kampf eingreifen können. Nirgends reichen die Kräfte aus, um den Alliierten entscheidenden Widerstand zu leisten.

Nach letzten Meldungen haben die amerikanischen Panzer 23 Kilometer vom Kölner Domplatz auf breiter Front zwischen Königshoven und Zieverich die Erft erreicht.

Kölner Volkssturmmänner in ihren Feldbefestigungen am anderen Ufer liegen unter schwerem Feuer und warten jeden Augenblick darauf, dass die Amerikaner auch dieses letzte Hindernis auf der Strasse nach Köln überschreiten.

Zwei Stossrichtungen

Eine besonders gefährliche Lage ist weiter im Nordwesten entstanden.

Amerikanische Panzer, die in der Montag-Nacht Erkelenz nahmen, rollten unaufhaltsam weiter vor, überrannten Rheindahlen und stiessen von dort aus in zwei Stossrichtungen weiter.

Die eine Spitze wurde zuletzt dicht am Stadtrand von München-Gladbach gemeldet, die andere hat schon Waldniel genommen und rollt weiter in Richtung Venlo.

Die gesamten deutschen Abwehrstellungen an der Maas zwischen Roermond und Venlo sind im Rücken bedroht.

Gleichzeitig kommt aus Wesel die Meldung, dass die Engländer und Kanadier in ihrem neuen Grossangriff

(Fortsetzung Seite 3)

General Crerar, Befehlshaber der 1. kanadischen Armee.

Seine Truppen haben Kalkar erobert.

Auch Köln hat Führer-Befehl, auszuhalten

Die Stadt Köln ist auf Befehl des Führers zum festen Platz erklärt worden. Köln soll, genau wie Berlin, Breslau und Königsberg, bis zur letzten Patrone verteidigt werden.

Zehntausende von Kölnern, die auch nach den Luftangriffen in Köln zurückgeblieben sind, richten sich mit Frauen und Kindern in Kellern und Bombentrümmern auf die Belagerung ein und lassen lieber auch das noch über sich ergehen, als einen Flüchtlingstreck ins Ungewisse anzutreten.

Noch in den letzten Wochen sind viele evakuierte Frauen mit ihren Kindern, die ihre Ausweichquartiere Hals über Kopf für Ostflüchtlinge räumen mussten, nach Köln zurückgekehrt.

Durch Abwesenheit glänzt in dem festen Platz Köln nur die Partei, die auch weiterhin die Gauhauptstadt fernmündlich verwaltet.

Gauleiter Grohé regiert von seinem Schloss Margarethenhof in Much bei Siegburg, und der stellvertretende Gauleiter Pg. Richard Schaller verwaltet sein Amt von Schloss Blumenau bei Engelskirch aus.

Vorstösse auf beiden Seiten in Italien

Deutsche Gegenangriffe und Vorstösse der Amerikaner wechseln am Monte Belvedere und am Monte della Toraccia.

Es gelang den deutschen Truppen, zu verhindern, dass die Amerikaner weiter nach Norden vordrangen.

Im Februar jeden Tag 2 Versenkungen

Wie das OKM mitteilt, wurden im Monat Februar bisher von deutschen U-Booten, neuzeitlichen Kampfmitteln und Torpedofliegern insgesamt 57 Schiffe mit 333 400 BRT versenkt, ferner 27 Zerstörer und Sicherungsfahrzeuge.

Ausserdem gelang die Vernichtung von 2 leichten Kreuzern. Ein weiterer Kreuzer wurde so schwer getroffen, dass mit seinem Verlust gerechnet werden muss.

Damit, so wird amtlich erklärt, beläuft sich der deutsche Erfolg im Februar auf täglich zwei Schiffe mit 11 000 BRT, ein Ergebnis, das zwar noch nicht an die grossen Zeiten des früheren U-Bootkrieges heranreicht, das jedoch nicht unbeachtet bleiben darf, wenn es in der bisher ansteigenden Kurve weitergeht.

Above: The front page of the propaganda newspaper that was dropped on the fields of the farm on March 1st, 1945. Under the headline "Defence Crisis on the Rhine", it speaks of the speed of the two-pronged Allied attack towards the Rhine and the Ruhr Valley, and of the dire defence situation resulting.

The te Lindert farm was approximately fifteen miles north-east of Emmerich (at the extreme northern end of the front), but although the British and Canadians had reached the Rhine in that region it was a further month before the Lichtenvoorde area was freed.

Air news in the paper stated that the burning German capital had again been bombed and that 4000 aircraft had pounded the towns of Halle, Leipzig, Mainz and Augsburg.

Left: The Irish Guards in trouble in Holland. The Sherman tank shown is of the type used by the 2nd Battalion Irish Guards whilst serving with the Guards Armoured Division in north-west Europe in 1944/45.

It was with this battalion, at the beginning of the drive for Bremen and the German North Sea Coast, that the two aircrew made their only landborne military sortie. *via Major P.L. Mercer, Irish Guards.*

Right: Ron Young and Eric Copley show a touch of discipline in their newly acquired army gear on the road back. Their spruced-up appearance and retained flying-boots are at variance with the dress of their two colleagues who travelled the same road a few hours before them and were, at this stage, downright shoddy.

The picture was taken near Goch, Germany, on April 1st, 1945 by an army officer, who sent copies and letters to the parents of each.

Below: The whole family assembled on Good Friday 1949. Trui sits between Mr te Lindert and Wim, while Wim II reclines to Hanna's right.

Left: Want to be a speed cop? Wim Lensink gives the author's son a taste for the game during that same April holiday.

Below: Bits and pieces of the wreck of No. 207 Squadron's X-ray retrieved by the author in April 1949 from the edge of the farm pond into which the aircraft had fallen.

Also shown are four splinters of German flak collected during a night walk in March 1945.

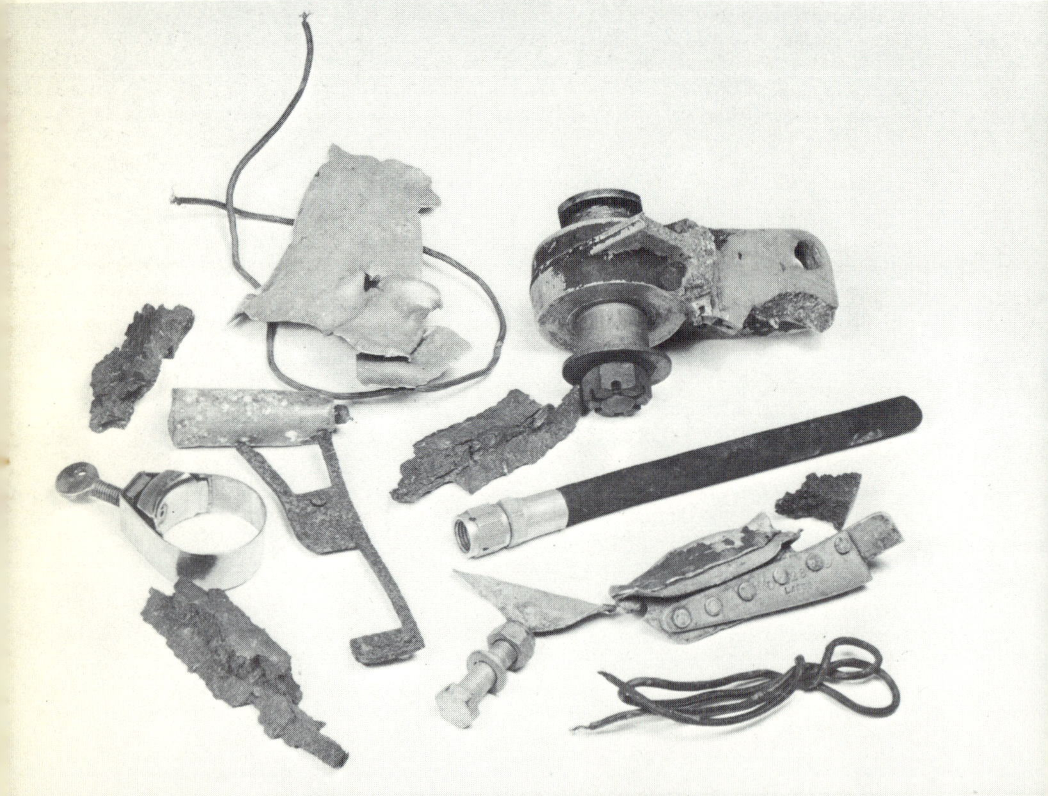

Above: Anglo invasion! In August 1960 three of the crew revisited Holland together with their families. Here, from left to right, Norman Levick, Stan Hanson and Eric Copley are photographed with Henk Hulshof immediately before taking off on a trip to the Münster area for a close look at the Dortmund-Ems Canal.

Lievelde railway station, from which Mr Joep ter Haar (the courier) conveyed the majority of the eighty or more aircrew he helped to escape between 1941 and 1944, stands a very short distance behind the group.

The author sits between Hanna and Johan in the place where he so often sat in February and March 1945—by the fire. It is, however, daylight outside this time, and there is not even the remotest chance of a sudden thunderous German knocking on the door in September 1973.

The plaque of the RAF Escaping Society has hung on the wall for many years, and the photograph of an RAF type and his bride has stood on the sideboard since 1945.

1st Army with the British Armoured Corps in their midst were — from the gun flashes and the sound that had begun to go with them — coming slowly our way. But I had a nasty feeling that Jerry was going to prove stubborn about that neck of land between Rhine and Maas, on the basis that other peoples' back gardens, not his own soil, were the places to knock about in militarily. That being so, we might be cooped up here for some considerable time unless we did something about it. I reckoned we needed a guide to get us moving westward. Cheeseman, I had noticed, never lacked for practical shrewdness. I thought that in the morning I would sound him out.

"Do you remember Julian Grenade?" I asked, as he put on the light.

"Sure, what about him?"

"He had a theory about crossing the Rhine all on his tod. Do you fancy a try?"

"Not on your flipping Nellie. Even if we get to the river by some flaming miracle, how do we get across? If we managed somehow to pinch a boat we'd probably get shot to pieces by some bastard on the other bank, either British or German, whoever happened to be around at that time. Forget that idea, mate. It's suicide."

"Do you prefer to lie here and rot, then? It might be six months before we're freed."

"No. I'm getting fed up already. There's only one thing for it. We'll just have to bind away at Wim to get us a guide."

"Touché."

The Sunday passed. We did not mount our campaign on Wim immediately for there was no desperate hurry. I spent the day somewhat moodily reflecting on the fact that it would be a long time before the countless thousands of miserable wretches who clung on to a living death in the concentration camps would be released. I could not know it, but I was shortly to meet a former inmate of one; though the fact was not immediately made apparent.

We had a diversion that evening. As we turned off the field and prepared to wend our way round the back of the farm to the haystack, Wim stopped us.

"It is Sunday evening," he said. "All people of the farm are this night here. Perhaps would you like to meet them?"

We needed no second bidding.

The room we entered was spacious and high; the dark solid furniture it contained of a sober kind which spoke both of reasonable affluence and strong tradition. The room was brightly lit by electric light, and against one wall was a large heating stove which gave off an adequate warmth. The members of the family, including Wim, numbered eight. Two of them, a man and a woman, looked in their sixties and sat on either side of the stove; the remaining six, equally divided between the male and female sexes, were in their twenties and sat round a large central table.

"This is the father of my wife, and this her mother," Wim said, introducing us to the elderly couple. "Will you not sit by them?"

We took our places in chairs that had been set beside them for the purpose. Geoff sat by the elderly lady, I by the farmer. He was a man somewhat under average height. His frame was lean, but his back was as straight as a poker, and his features possessed the angularity of the true

Saxon, predominated, perhaps, by a proud, eagle-like nose. He nodded affably enough when we entered, but took little apparent further interest. He sat rigidly straight in his chair, puffed carefully, sedately almost, at an old, well-used pipe, and betrayed as much emotion as a Stoic. As a first impression I judged him to be a man of inflexible purpose once his mind was made up.

The farmer's wife had the rosy cheeks of a country woman and as kind a face as one would see in a day's march. She supplied the feminine counterweight to her impassive husband, fussed round us a little, and generally made us feel at home: albeit in unintelligible Dutch.

We were introduced to the younger members of the family. Wim's wife was a tall brunette, the other two girls were blondes. No names were mentioned. The tall chap who had first taken us to the haystack and scattered the sheep in so forthright a manner was the elder brother of a young man of much darker colouring and hair who was the possessor of a well cared for black moustache. Not so tall as his brother, he was, if anything, thicker in build, and decidedly quicker of speech and manner.

"He, also, is named Wim," said our mentor.

"Ah! he is another lucky one with a name," I replied.

"Yeah, Wim II," said Cheeseman, christening him on the spot to avoid confusion.

It was quickly made clear that the two blondes were affianced to the two brothers. They were surprisingly well-dressed, as, indeed, were the whole family. I felt decidedly shabby by comparison. It was, of course, Sunday, and that was an occasion for best clothes and a visit to church for those who could afford to be seen there.

"Have you all been to church?" I asked, by way of conversation.

"The ladies and the farmer have so been. My wife's brothers and I may not so do," Wim replied.

I saw no evidence, as I had done in the two farmhouses I had previously been in, that they were of the Catholic faith. There was neither a statue of the Madonna nor a crucifix to be seen.

"Are you Protestants?" I continued.

"Yes, we are all members of the Dutch Reformed Church."

A small dog nosed his way into the centre of attention in front of the stove.

"Ah! here is Skippy," said Wim. "He will do, what you say, a trick for you before you leave."

It was a quiet and very enjoyable spell we spent in the living-room of that old farmhouse. The family were very interested in their 'pilots' in a steady, Dutch sort of way, and Wim was kept busy in his role of interpreter. It was characteristic that he responded to the occasion, and that his English improved the more he used it.

A civilised hour had passed. Cheeseman and I had finished our nightcap of warm milk, and were on our feet ready to go, feeling in a distinctly better frame of mind than when we had entered.

"A moment," said Wim. "Let us, before we go, first have Skippy's trick."

He knelt down and spoke to the little dog.

"Shake hands with the King of England!" he said.

The dog sat obediently on his haunches, raised his paw, and solemnly shook hands.

"Now shake hands with Hitler!"

The dog remained motionless, and refused to have anything to do with him.

"A clever dog, no?" asked Wim, beaming placidly. "Do you know why he does that?"

We had to acknowledge that we did not.

"Ah! he is a great patriot and friend of the British."

There was a quick translation in Dutch, and the Sunday evening visit broke up on a note of hilarity as the family realised that the little dog's trick had floored us.

During the ensuing night I broke my pipe. I had formed the practice of putting it carefully on the beam by my head at night, but, like a stupid clot, on that one occasion I forgot it, left it in my trouser pocket and rolled on it in my sleep. The break was irreparable; I was annoyed.

"Do not become angry with yourself," Wim opined, when I told him. "I can make for you a pipe.".

"Really?"

"Yes, really. Give to me one day and you shall see."

When he arrived on the following morning he did not immediately knock for admission, but stood outside in the sheep-fold and sang his way lustily in English through the chorus of Popeye the Sailorman. The popular comic cartoon film of the time — the contemporary of Mickey Mouse and Donald Duck — had evidently found a ready market in the Dutch cinema, but we were a fraction puzzled as we sat and listened to the normally quiet Wim's choral effort.

As he brought in our breakfast he was convulsed with laughter, and asked if we had enjoyed the song.

"Yes, very good," I said. "You're wasted here, mate. You should be on the stage."

"Here is what it was about. Here is your new pipe. It is a Popeye pipe."

As one of his main characteristics, Popeye of the cartoon strip smoked a distinctive, tall, square-bowled pipe. Wim, by a piece of very fine carpentry, had produced from a chunk of oak a pipe which almost exactly resembled it. The stem, which fitted like a glove into a circular hole drilled into the base of one side of the bowl, was even shaved into an elliptical shape at its end to provide a mouthpiece. It was, in fact, not inelegant.

I lit up, and it worked perfectly. Perhaps a connoisseur accustomed to best London brier might have demurred a fraction, but I was overjoyed to think I had a smoke at all. To mark his kindness I said that I would keep a tally of the days spent in the haystack by cutting notches in the top of the bowl with my knife. Nine such small nicks I duly cut.

It was at this time that we took to the use of clogs. Our flying-boot bottoms had never really recovered from the soaking received en route to the haystack, and had progressively deteriorated after each nightly walk into a soggy, pulpy state not far removed from absolute mildew. Cheeseman, who reckoned Wim could do virtually anything in a practical way, entered a plea for replacements.

"Fix us up with something, Wim," he said, almost off-handedly. "You're a born fixer."

Wim considered.

"Fix?. I think that means to mend, and I cannot so do. But, if I am a born fixer, something else must I think of."

His answer had been clogs. Mine were several sizes too large for me, but the matter was easily remedied by padding them with hay until a perfect fit was achieved. That done, they were warm, comfortable, and very effective against the wet of the boggy fields.

Our nightly exercise was henceforward carried out in the best Dutch tradition, and we rapidly acquired the swinging gait of the habitual clog-wearer. Up and down and round the same rectangular field we went like prisoners at exercise and, in the process, observed that the battle to the south-west continued to move in our direction. The salvoes from the heavy guns, which had been barely audible during our earlier walks, had, by the end of the second week, become distinct and ominous. Between Rhine and Maas there stands a large forest, and in it at this moment, mayhem on the grand scale was being committed. Gradually the fighting moved eastwards. The Battle of the Reichswald began distantly to thunder.

Our walks began to end, more often than not, in visits to the farmhouse. I suspected that Wim was throwing this in as a kind of sop to allay our ill-concealed discontent. The low key in which we had been playing for a fortnight was beginning to irritate; the inactivity of our existence persistently to pall. We had, during the second week, begun to bind him rigid with the need to get us moving Rhinewards towards freedom; we had failed signally, in any way to shake him or to draw him into rash promises. A deliberate, careful, thinking type was Wim; but, when he chose, absolutely obstinate. The furthest he yielded was to assure us that an attempt would be made to spirit us back to our own lines, and to make a vague reference to the villages of Terborg and Gendringen, which lay to the westward. What he did, subtlely — because he knew we liked it — was to see that our walks ended in the farmhouse.

The old couple, their day's work done, were ever present in their chairs to either side of the heating stove, and we took our regular places beside them. The farmer invariably offered me his pouch for a fill of tobacco, and I always accepted. It rapidly became as natural to me to say, "Dank U," or "Dank U wel," as to say "Thank you." We progressed very amicably. The other members of the family present varied. Wim's wife seemed always to have retired early to bed, and the fiancée of the elder brother lived, we gathered, some distance away and cycled over only at weekends. But the others were usually around — the elder brother, almost as impassive as his father, the younger, darker, more boisterous Wim II, and the blonde girl to whom he was engaged made up our normal party. The tenor of conversation was easy and, for the most part, humorous. But one caught from time to time a glimpse of the stress under which these people lived, and of a feeling of expectancy as they sensed imminent freedom. It also became clear that they regarded the task of getting their 'pilots' back to England with an almost religious zeal.

"My wife's father thinks that perhaps you will not again fly," said Wim, one evening. "How is it with you after such a crash?" When you are again in England, must you more fly?"

It was a good question. Heaven alone knew when this protracted war would end. The resilience of the Germans had repeatedly proved amazing: not least in that sudden, unexpected throw in the preceding December which had carried them devastatingly through the American lines in the Ardennes and on almost to the North Sea. The dangers of the bomber aircrew game had, from the high point in the spring of 1943 when the chances of completing a tour of ops were extremely remote, unquestionably lessened. But the Achilles Heel of Germany was oil. And in defence of this, without which all else must grind to a halt, the Germans had, from the summer of 1944 on, concentrated their guns. The refineries had become fortresses bristling with flak. The Leipzig area, lying deep in the German hinterland, was particularly hot, for there stood upwards of half a dozen large plants, of which Leuna — Merseburg alone was reckoned to be defended by at least 500 heavy guns. The game had become neither funny nor a piece of cake. And yet it was obsessively attractive to some aircrew. Our tour being now a write-off, there was, in truth, a rest period available when we got back. I had no intention of taking it. In any case, what earthly use was there in these people risking their lives for us if we did not resume the fight?

"Yes, Wim," I answered. "You get us back to England and we shall fly again."

"Ah! it is good. The farmer is most pleased that it should be so."

We became involved in the production of tobacco. The Germans commandeered a high proportion of the output of the Dutch tobacco factories and, as a consequence, tobacco, in a land of smokers, had become a scarce commodity. The men on the farm all smoked pipes, and had ensured supplies by growing the plant in the farm garden. The leaves were cured in the house, and cut and rubbed up in the evenings to avoid the prying eye of some itinerant soldier or Dutch Nazi who happened to call. I had, of course, long since run out of my English supply. Therefore I rubbed up with a will. I never lacked for a smoke.

As the month of February drew towards its close and our cloistered, inactive existence entered its third week, Wim the psychologist practised his soporific, diverting medicine yet a fraction more.

"There are some trusted men who know it that you are here," he said, one day. "This night shall you meet them"

When we entered the living-room that evening, two young men stood, almost shyly, on the far side of the large, central table observing us with undisguised interest.

"This," said Wim, by way of introduction, "is Baby, and this is Cowboy. They are young Underground men and wished to see and speak with you."

Using Wim as interpreter they asked a question or two about England and the ways of bombers and their crews, nodded sagely at our replies, stood around a little awkwardly for a while, and then, politely excusing themselves, took their leave. They were a couple of farm lads from this remote corner of Holland to whom contact with two English aircrew — albeit dishevelled, out of work aircrew — was no doubt an event. But they were the stuff of which the Resistance was made, for its membership seemed to know no bounds either of class or of age. The farmer beside me was reasonably well-breeched and nearing seventy; the younger of the two lads poor as a church mouse and no more than seventeen.

What the code name of the next Underground man we met was we were never to know. He was a lean, weather-beaten man in his thirties, and upon his head he wore a tall, well-used felt hat that virtually lacked a brim.

Wim had begun to introduce him. "This is - - -," he had started, when, quick as a flash, Cheeseman interposed with the words, "King Farouk".

Wim looked puzzled. "King Farouk? Why do you say that?" he asked, for once completely taken aback.

"Because of his hat. It's just like a fez. He's King Farouk, king of Egypt."

The joke, when relayed, appealed enormously to the Dutch, who burst into peals of laughter. Even the stern old farmer permitted himself a smile, while the subject of it all, who was obviously somewhat of a comedian by nature, took not the slightest offence, but cavorted about and bowed grandly to right and left to acknowledge his promotion to kingship. Whatever his code name had been he acquired a new one that night.

In the haystack Geoff and I occupied our time as best we could. We had pencil and paper provided, and played noughts and crosses until we were sick of it. Incarceration for twenty-three hours out of twenty-four did not lead to amiability. We argued, sometimes for the sake of arguing, but as quickly made it up. One major source of irritation was the lack of real information about the progress of the British to our west.

At the very fag end of February events began to move. The Canadian 1st Army was, we reckoned, on the Rhine. The big guns became clearly audible even through the thick walls of the haystack; batches of German troops were being billeted on surrounding farms; fighters and fighter-bombers of 2nd TAF flew frequent sorties over our heads. There was a feeling of incipient awakening.

Wim, who had decided for safety's sake to bring our meals twice a day only, arrived on the morning of March 1st with a small newspaper in his hand.

"I have for you news at last, and it is good news," he said. "This morning was this paper found on the fields of the farm."

Dated February 28th, it was in German, headed *Nachrichten für die Truppe* (News for the Troops) and, under a banner headline of "Defence Crisis on the Rhine", it painted a picture that could not have been more gloomy for the German soldier.

Wim had a good working knowledge of German, and with his aid we pieced together the score presented by the broadsheet; though, truth to say, the essence of the matter was easily decipherable in any language. On the front page was a map of the western front from Arnhem to Luxembourg, and, graphically portrayed by the use of arrows, was the picture of a pincer movement designed to capture the Ruhr Valley. In the south the Americans were within fifteen miles of Cologne and moving northwards towards Düsseldorf; in the north — where it mattered to us — the British and Canadians had taken the bastion towns of Goch, Kalkar and Cleve, were already on the Rhine for a twenty mile stretch in the Emmerich area nearest to us and were moving south on

Wesel. The paper said that Berlin was burning and spoke also of mass air attacks by day and night on other German cities.

It was probable, as Wim said, that it was British propaganda dropped by the RAF and aimed at sapping the morale of the German troops who had begun to move into the surrounding farms. There was, however, no reason to doubt the validity of the broadsheet. Our own observations told us that something of the sort was happening.

I sat, late that evening, on the old chair by the light. I had a book in my hand, but I was not reading it. I had read my way through two of Leo's books — a novel concerned with mock spiritualism, which was diverting; and a biography of Asquith, which was instructive — and had now turned to a good old-fashioned tale of the sea. But, at the moment, my thoughts ran not on the book, but on the den of thieves (the words were Leo's) in whose midst we lay. He had had his tongue firmly in his cheek when he used the expression. He knew, as I did, that they were in fact the elite of a nation. We had in our travels met priests, an intellectual of high calibre and radical leanings, a desperado from the professional classes or thereabouts, a teacher who looked always on the black side, and farm people ranging from the reasonably affluent to the very poor. They were all in the same game, and in it voluntarily at pain of death. In a sense they shared this voluntariness with aircrew, because, aircrew being volunteers, nobody, in the end, could make them fly. But at least we were comparatively well paid and enjoyed considerable privileges in food and conditions. These people did not. They deliberately turned their backs on the favours that toadying to the Nazis would bring; they did not even play it safe by stringing along; they chose to risk everything for no tangible reward. I wondered what really drove them to such a pitch, and I found no ready answer. Patriotism, communism, religion, excitement in a dull world, all were possible general answers. And yet I felt that none of these explained fully the case here.

To us this appeared to be a quiet, rather prosperous farm inhabited by a traditionalist, god-fearing family who hid three of their own number within its walls and two RAF types in a brilliantly conceived hiding-place outside. It all argued passive resistance. But the characters in the play did not fit. With the exception of Wim II, who was of a more volatile, hot-tempered nature, the men here were of that slow, steady Saxon kind which does not rouse easily, but once roused thoroughly, pursues its quarry to the bitter end. The elder brother in particular was big enough and tough enough to have picked up two normal sized Wehrmacht infantrymen and broken their backs as easily as he would wring a chicken's neck, if the provocation were right. I could not reconcile them with mere passivity. But then, I had no evidence to the contrary. I was simply day-dreaming.

I had turned from my vague musings and taken up my book. The winds of March were already astir. The haystack had indeed the peculiar property that, while it excluded light, it did admit air. The wind puffed in little eddies through the walls of hay and matched the singing of the wind in the shrouds of the clipper I was reading about. I was deeply immersed in the tale, when, without warning, the light went out.

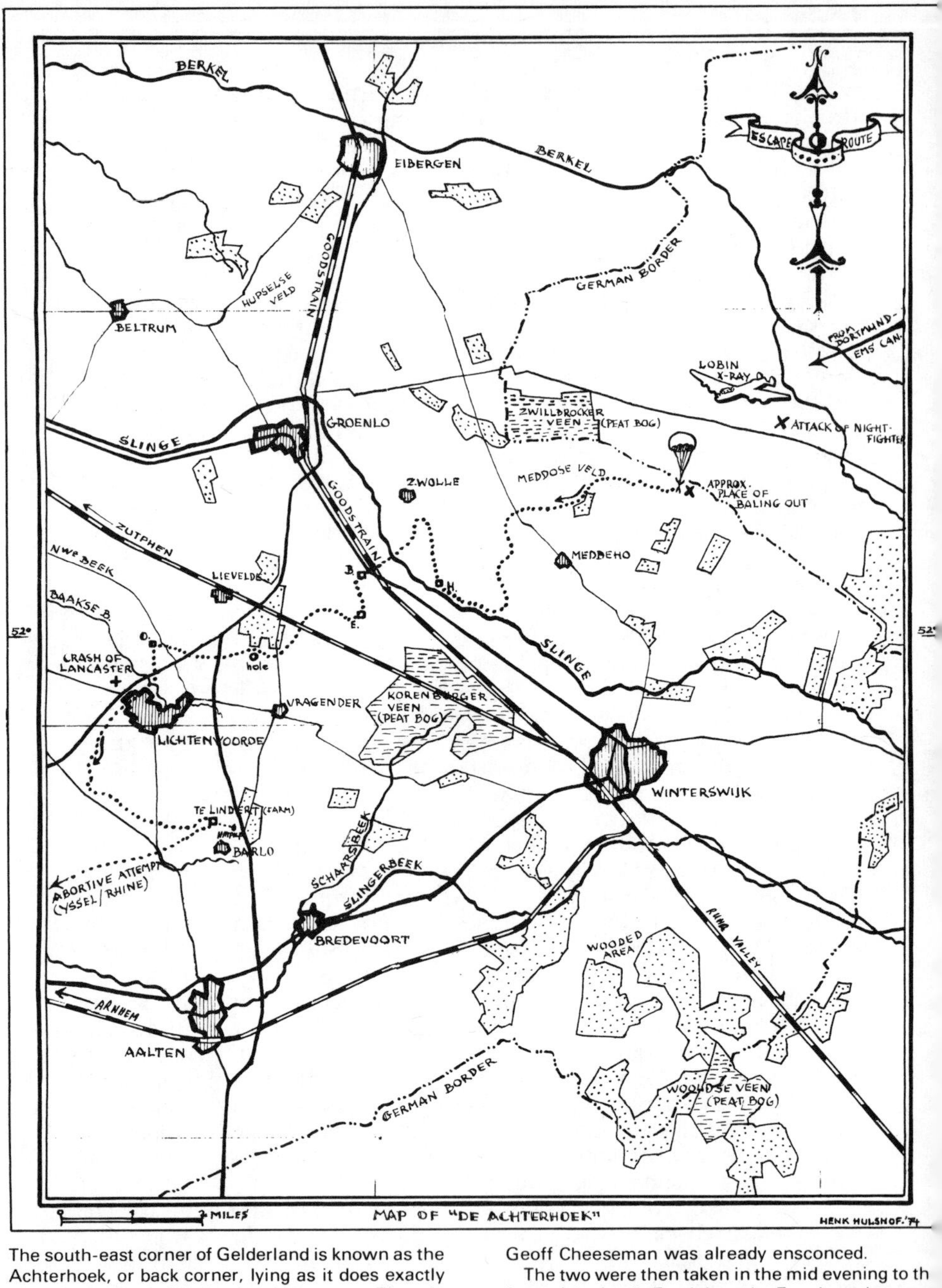

MAP OF "DE ACHTERHOEK"

The south-east corner of Gelderland is known as the Achterhoek, or back corner, lying as it does exactly opposite the Hook of Holland, or front corner. There is, however, nothing backward about its people, and the area is very beautiful in a quiet, copse-bestrewn sort of way.

The map drawn by Mr H. J. A. Hulshof, of Lichtenvoorde, shows the route taken by the author across the Meddoseveld (an unfriendly updraught and a strong westerly wind had carried him well east of the river Slinge) to the point H. This was the farm of the family Halleriet, from where he was led, dressed as a farm labourer, to B – the Villa Bernarda, where Geoff Cheeseman was already ensconced.

The two were then taken in the mid evening to th farm of the family Everink – point E – where they wer reunited for an hour or two with Eric Copley and Ro Young. Cheeseman and Hanson then journeyed we to the grassed-over dug-out in the field near Lieveld while Copley and Young went north to Groenlo.

Point O marks the farm of Mr Orriens who hid t two aircrew in his hayloft, and then came the trudg through the town of Lichtenvoorde to the farm of th te Linderts.

Finally, the abortive attempt to manoeuvre the aircrew to the Rhine is indicated.

11

Darkness Over Gelderland

Morning came. At least, we knew it was morning, because I struck a match and discovered the time to be eight o'clock. The haystack admitted not so much as a flicker of light. Therefore, the darkness was of the same absolute intensity that had ruled in the dug-out three weeks previously. It had not bothered us much before, because we had the ability to flood the place with light at a flick of a switch. Now, that facility denied and no chink of light anywhere visible, the darkness oppressed. We sat in silence, and waited for Wim to rap his V sign on the sheep-fold wall.

Time elapsed and nothing happened. He invariably brought our breakfast by nine o'clock, but that hour passed without sight or sound of him. Sitting there in the dark, the time was slow in passing and solved nothing in its progress.

"Grim, wouldn't you say, Cheesey?" I observed.

"Bloody grim. A question of what to do for the best."

"Continue to sit tight, I suppose. Something's obviously adrift. But we shan't help any by dashing out into the fray."

It was past ten o'clock when the long awaited V sign sounded.

"How is it with you, boys? Dark, no?" Wim said, as he eased his way into the darkened haystack.

"You can say that again," said Cheeseman. "What's wrong?"

"The Germans have locked the place where electricity is made, because there is not fuel more. I do not think that there will again be electric light here. Also is it true that in many near farms are there now German soldiers living, and more soldiers still come. It is, then, not possible that we should make our evening walks again."

Grim was the operative word of the day. But at least we knew the score. Our nightly walks had, in fact, stopped a couple of nights since, and we should make no more. The darkness was not of a temporary nature; it was something with which we had henceforth to live.

In the light of the electric torch he had brought with him, Wim's face was joyless.

"Is it that bad, Wim?" I asked. "You couldn't look more upset if you'd been to a funeral."

At first he would not tell us what else was wrong. Gradually, however, we wheedled part of the story out of him. It, too, was grim.

There had been a fracas between a considerable armed party of Dutch Resistance workers and six German soldiers on a lonely farm near the border. The Dutch leader took no chances. Having rounded up the Germans who had stumbled upon the hide-out, he had them strung up over a beam in a barn and hanged. Precautions taken to dispose of the bodies had not proved adequate. The corpses had been discovered some distance away, still bearing the marks of the hanging round their necks. As a reprisal, upwards of fifty men from the nearest village had been taken away. Wim was certain they would be shot.

The stark brutality of both sides of that particular coin, and the pathetic irony that the Dutch victims had had nothing to do with the case, crashed home like a bomb. This was not war by remote control as we knew it. It was not waged by combatants who never saw each other. There was no element of, on the one hand, pressing a bomb-tit four miles above the surface of the earth and launching tons of bombs upon one knew not whom, nor, on the other, of oneself being blown clinically to pieces by a shell fired by an unknown hand. It was direct, ruthless, murderous stuff in which neither side pulled so much as half a punch. Dressed as we were in assorted scraps of Dutch farm clothing, it was hardly to be supposed that our case would be amusing if we were caught.

"All news is not so bad, boys," Wim said, finally, "I know it now that you shall quickly begin a walk that shall take you to the British across the Rhine."

For the whole of that day and until the evening of its successor we remained in complete darkness, and near complete silence. Nothing disturbed the darkness except three further visits by Wim, who shone a torch while we ate our food; little disturbed the quiet except the jostling of the sheep in the pen and the muted, desultory cracking of the guns on the Rhine. It was a miserable experience unenlivened by any flash of what could even remotely be called wit by the inhabitants of the haystack, for they felt that they had had enough, and succumbed to the gloom in which they lived. In the intense darkness I found no enjoyment even in smoking my pipe. It seemed tasteless, so I gave it up as a bad job.

After forty eight hours in the pitch dark we had a break, for at Wim's behest we paid another visit to the farmhouse. It was lit now by means of an old oil lamp which stood on the table and cast flickering, intriguing shadows across the walls and ceiling as it bathed the scene in indifferent, unsteady light. The mood did not exactly scintillate. The old farmer sat in his usual place by the heating stove and looked weary; Wim, by contrast, seemed incensed, and turned on us, his steely blue-grey eyes blazing.

"Do you know," he said, "that all this day must my wife's father give his eggs and milk and butter to the Germans? They have all day come and demanded it, and he must always give. He would rather burn his food than so do, but he must not, because of his family. Also his sons and I may not help him. It is always he who must deal with the Moffen."

The sudden vehemence took us aback. It was in contradistinction to the normal atmosphere that pervaded the house, and was the first occasion on which we had seen Wim let his hair down, or seen the two brothers sit there scowling. We blinked in the unaccustomed light and were glad that we were not the objects of their wrath; for I would not, at that precise moment, have given more than a brass farthing for the chances of any stray German who had happened that way.

"You should not seem surprised that I speak so strong," Wim resumed. "The farmer was for near a whole year in a concentration camp, where he was beaten and kicked and starved. He was there because he is a kind man and hid Jews on his farm. But he came back. This man" — he pointed to the photograph of a man which stood on top of a dresser, and which, I had previously thought, bore a marked resemblance to Wim II — "was his brother. The Germans have caught him listening to the BBC on his radio and have put him in Dachau. He is not heard from in two years, and we feel that he is dead. We do not know it, but we feel it. That is to us a murder. Since that time has the farmer said that, if the Moffen will so do to him and his brother, he will do worse for them as he can."

Wim broke off his tirade in English, turned to the elderly Dutchman and translated what he had said. The old man sat, as ever, as erect as a ramrod, only his eyes betraying the tiredness he felt. He listened intently to what had been said. At the end he nodded his head, lifted his pipe from his mouth for a moment and said, quietly, "Ja! Verdomde Moffen!" Having damned his enemy, he continued smoking as imperturbably as before.

The motivating force I had recently been looking for was suddenly apparent; the stimulus that drove a family to risk everything for no concrete gain, crystal clear. The farmer was a man of the old school. He seemed to me to embody much that was already passing in England, and probably passing to our detriment. He was a father-figure of the best possible sort. His sons dwarfed him in stature, but his, I suspected, was the dominating will, and, in such a man, that was no bad thing. That he had hidden Jews on his farm to save them from the gas chamber argued compassion; that he had been caught, subjected to a year's corrective treatment in a concentration camp, had come back to his farm, and was doing the same thing all over again for a couple of stray aircrew he did not know from Adam, argued both a continuing compassion and a resolution that was indomitable. I felt that I was in the presence of a very remarkable man. He was a living example of the fact that the spirit of some people is not to be broken. He gave a pointer to the reason why the Underground Movements of Europe grew stronger as the war progressed. The breaking of Resistance rings, and the brutal, lingering deaths inflicted by the Nazis on their members had had the converse effect from that intended. It was ironic that the Germans should have worked so hard for a negative result. But it was human nature. It explained why the Nazis were almost bound to lose the war from the start.

I knew that the farmer was a humane and religious man. The deprivations and punishments he had himself suffered, he might therefore have forgiven; but the murder of his brother for so slight an offence he would not. The motivating force was not simple in character. It was, I judged, a blend of religious belief, humanity, and the older, more basic desire for requital.

It had been the kind of day here when the straw had not broken the camel's back, but had resulted in an explosion of feeling. That explosion permitted a glimpse of the intensity of the emotion that moved this family. Every time a German soldier came to this door and made demands he unwittingly rubbed salt into an unhealed wound. How it would all come out I did not know. But I was sure of one thing. I had smelt the smouldering wrath. This was no place of mere passive resistance.

I thought, as I prepared to bed down in the haystack that night, that this farm would change character in the not too distant future. I had an indistinct vision of a great awakening. Perhaps it was the effects of reading Leo's novel on spiritualism, or perhaps it was the dark, or perhaps — my grandfather having been an Irishman — it was a rush of Celtic blood to the head. Whatever it was I had a presentiment in that direction. But we should not be here to see it, for we were shortly to be on the move. Wim had committed himself to that. And I knew him well enough to understand that the promise would not be empty.

The guide in front of us stopped, knocked surreptitiously on the door of the farmhouse we had just reached, and was admitted. Cheeseman and I merged into the shadows near the door and waited. The time was eight o'clock on the evening following Wim's outburst, and we had been walking for almost an hour.

Our departure from the farm had been sudden. There had been no preliminaries and no tender farewells. Wim had arrived in the early evening with food and the simplest of briefings. The man who was coming knew no English, and wished that we should not speak as we walked, but follow quietly behind him on a journey towards the elusive Rhine.

When things did move here they moved fast. By the light of Wim's torch we had gathered together our scanty belongings and hastily swallowed the food he had brought. There had been no time even to visit the farmhouse.

And so, with my escape kit and map, a well-filled tobacco pouch, matches, and a pipe made of oak strewn about the pockets of my scarecrow jacket and ancient raincoat, I had said a heartfelt goodbye to Wim and set off with my colleague in the wake of our guide.

The man who led was a tall, lean character who went about his business in a cautious, deliberate way. His pace had never been hurried, but had possessed the rhythmic, unflagging movement of the countryman, and, as a consequence, we had made good progress. The route had not been mentioned, but its westward direction made me remember Wim's vague reference to the village of Terborg, en route to Nijmegen. That, I guessed, was where we were headed. On no part of our journey had we walked the sandways, but had moved silently along the fields, using the lines of trees which flanked the minor roads as cover. We had heard little during the walk other than the swish of our own clogs over the grass.

It was while we waited that the air raid started. The darkness and silence of the night were shattered with dramatic suddenness. Flak guns to the westward thundered a staccato fortissimo, heralding the approach. The thundering drew nearer. Searchlights in the surrounding fields ceased their dreaming and shot their brilliant beams upwards. In no time at all a dark, cold, unexceptional March night was transformed. The leading bombers winged their way towards us, turned almost precisely over our heads, and flew on southwards towards the Ruhr.

There was a confusion of cracking sound and blinding light; over and above it all rode the familiar noise of massed Rolls-Royce Merlin engines. It was idle to pretend that, in one way, the sound was not welcome: it had me thinking in a nostalgic sort of way of Lancasters and home. But, for our purposes, an air raid at this precise moment was, without question, a menace.

"Trust the flaming RAF to decide on a pranging job just at this instant," I muttered to Cheeseman. "If it's a big show, the chances are we're buggered."

Our guide reappeared and motioned us to follow him. He gazed testily at the warlike sky to the west for a moment, and then set off once more. We trooped behind him heading steadily into the teeth of the fleet of bombers. We knew that by now every second or third farmhouse had German troops billeted on it. Therefore, we had to be careful, and he had to make no mistake. He was a confident, cool man who proceeded in a proficient manner, but, like any professional, he needed luck, and that seemed to have deserted him. The show *was* a big one. The bomber stream came on and on. The amount of light was an abomination.

We trudged on, slinking furtively from cover to cover. The guns at Winterswijk were whanging their shells into the sky, and the parabola was such that splinters of exploded flak descended in spasmodic shoals and cracked and spattered into the bare branches of the trees alongside which we walked. Without a steel helmet it was dicey. When the shoals of splinters fell we flattened ourselves against the trunks of the trees, and stayed put; when they ceased we pressed on. Our progress was intermittent.

The experience was not entirely new to us. Almost a month ago we had walked in similar circumstances with Karl on our way to meet Leo. Much that was now happening was reminiscent of that. The moonless, stratus-flecked night tallied, the probing searchlights danced the same dizzy criss-crossing reel, the areas and density of flak were comparable. But there were differences. The guide who led us was no buccaneer who went whistling down the middle of the road. He eschewed even the most minor of sandways, so that we crept stealthily across the fields; the bombers were not passing across some vague line to the south of us but roaring on over our heads; the raid, on that night in February, was relatively minor and near at hand; this one was a flat-out Bomber Command effort involving hundreds of Lancasters and Halifaxes in a saturating, battering job on the western Ruhr. As we progressed, the first flares began to light the sky to the southward, and the faint, dull crump of continuous bombing came to our ears in the intervals when the flak guns paused for breath. Some place was being hammered. We took a quiet guess at Oberhausen on the north-western edge of the Ruhr. It could, however, as easily have been Wesel, slightly nearer at hand on the Rhine.

A second farmhouse loomed. Our guide entered. We waited outside. I wondered almost listlessly what our fate was to be this time. The bomber stream caught my fancy. As the flak burst in red and yellow daggers above our heads I could hear, in imagination, the babble that was going on over several hundred intercoms. The stream would be perhaps a hundred miles long and, technically at least, no more than ten miles wide. The pathfinders were on their way home; the tail-enders still miles from the target. There would be a relaxing and a pouring of coffee among some of the lads homeward bound, a chorus of bomb aiming patter culminating in the magic words 'Bombs gone!' among the early waves of bombers, a flurry of 'Target sighted' at the back. I was very envious. As we waited, the sky in the south began to take on a crimson hue.

When our guide reappeared he looked *un*cheerful. He shook his head from side to side in a negative gesture, and then motioned us on. I did not wholly comprehend his meaning. I assumed only that there was no room for us at that particular place.

The last of the bombers had passed above us; the surging engine note of laden Lancasters was becoming increasingly remote; the sky to the south was blood-red, the searchlights going out; relative quiet was beginning to descend. After a while I became aware in half-baked fashion that something did not fit. After three days in pitch darkness the lurid light had hurt my eyes, and the long walk had tired legs unaccustomed to exercise, but despite this I realised with a start that the distant red glow was no longer on our left as we went.

"Look at those sodding fires!" I whispered to Geoff. "They're behind us now. We've swung away to the north."

"I know. I noticed it a few minutes ago. Going round in a flipping circle, that's what we're doing, mate. Still, wherever we're going I suppose we'll get there sooner or later. The sooner the flaming better. My legs are tired."

We journeyed on in silence. Increasing cloud cover made the night darker, and only the outlines of the rows of trees alongside which we moved were clearly visible. Our guide never faltered. He found his field tracks and negotiated the strips of wire which occasionally barred our way with an unfailing technique. Cheeseman's prognostication was right. We had long since turned from our northerly tack to an easterly one. There came the barking of a dog in the night; we dipped gently down into a hollow that seemed familiar; the vague outline of the building we were approaching looked like home. The circle was complete. We were back on the farm.

A quiet knock by our friend on the door, a question from within and the requisite answer in Dutch, the rasp of a withdrawn bolt, and we stood inside the darkened farmhouse. Wim bellowed a command to the snarling dog, and all was silence.

"What is this boys?" Wim asked, as he closed and bolted the door. "I did not think to again see you so soon."

He looked tired, rather as if he had been roused from sleep by the barking dog. We stood in the hall, and no sound other than the ticking of a clock came from the adjacent living-room. It was late and the family had gone to bed.

A conversation between the two Dutchmen ended by Wim's turning to us with a wry laugh.

"He says that your RAF should not make air raids when he is guiding pilots. It becomes too difficult for him. It was his hope to take you a long distance this night, but he found it not possible. At both houses in which he went was there a report of many German soldiers now living in the near farms. In such a bright light as then was, he thought it most dangerous further to go. So are you once again here."

"Sorry, Wim," said Geoff. "It is more trouble for you."

"No, it is not so. It is our duty that we should help English pilots, and so shall we do. But come, how is it with you? You do not look happy."

I suppose that, had we possessed the Latin temperament, the disappointment and frustration we felt might have been expressed in chestbeating and gesticulation, but, as it was, we contented ourselves with a few well chosen British oaths wrapped up in the RAF slang of the day. It was doubtful if Wim understood a word of it.

The tall Dutchman who had led us stood motionless and erect throughout this conversation in English, and looked, I thought, a fraction crestfallen. His abandonment of the operation at the particular point where he had, smacked of good sense to me.

"At least express our thanks to the guide, Wim," I said. "It was a brave effort and very well done."

Wim translated, and there was a moment's talk in Dutch.

"He is happy that you should thank him, for he feels that he has failed. He says that perhaps on a better night shall he try again."

The guide departed. We wound our way round the farm building, across the yard, and scattered the sheep to right and left in the fold. We were back absolutely to square one. In the haystack Wim poured what oil he could on troubled waters.

"Come," he said, "it is really not so bad. You are not by the Germans caught, and it might so have been. A long walk have you had, and it was good work for your legs. I shall see you in the morning."

The part about the legs he could say again. Mine ached like hell after a long period of disuse. As regards the half promise that we should try again, I did not believe it. The region was rapidly filling up with German troops. Our escape attempt had failed ingloriously. I was convinced there would be no second one. Look at it whichever way one would, there was no vestige of light. We lived in the dark in a haystack, an unspecified distance to the west of the road that linked the towns of Aalten and Lichtenvoorde. There was no point in bilking the issue. Gelderland was a dark place. In darkness we were, and in darkness we should stay until XXX Corps came bouncing up that road; and that was that.

Cheeseman said not a word, and neither did I. I went sullenly and obstinately to sleep.

12

The Long Night

On the wooden staging behind our heads a miserable, paltry light flickered and fluctuated, casting wan, ever moving shadows over the walls and ceiling of the haystack. Wim, in an effort to improve our lot by a fraction, had, an hour before, brought a fair-sized dollop of mutton fat in a square tin, inserted a length of wick and lit it. We had, therefore, breakfasted in the light, and Cheeseman was now sitting astride the old chair, peering into the mirror and endeavouring to shave. In the pitch black conditions of the last few days such a feat had not been attemptable. The growth he was painstakingly hacking off was, therefore, considerable, and since it soon would be my turn, I winced at the thought. The RAF had indeed seen to it that a razor was among the items packed in aircrew escape kits. But in that razor was only one blade, and that, after almost a month of cold-water shaving, had become blunt, its single edge visibly serrated. Shaving was a painful business.

Wim had never relented in his efforts to keep us up to scratch. His approach was often not unlike that of a sergeant-major; at other times he virtually mothered us. Life in a black void was not easy. It would have been the simplest thing imaginable either to have gone stark staring bonkers behind that bolted door or, alternatively, to have degenerated into sloth. Wim would have neither. There was not enough light to read by, so he made us shave. At least that was one positive action to take in twenty-four hours. We had become very attached to Wim with his stock of dead-pan humour, his assiduous attempts to improve his knowledge of English by asking questions and using his dictionary, his utter reliability and quiet ways. We even forgave him his insistence on our shaving. But it was useless to pretend that we were not cheesed-off. We were, in fact, bound completely rigid.

Almost in the instant that I finished my barbering job the rudimentary light gave a last jerky flutter, sputtered, and went out. The time as it did so was 10.00hrs. It would be some nine hours before Wim came again with food. Nine hours of idleness in which conversation would gradually fade, and thought alone remain active. The haystack seemed a dark prison; the desire to unbolt that wretched door, and escape, almost overwhelming.

When Wim eventually came with our evening meal we unburdened ourselves upon him with a vigour born of near despair. He listened to our tale of woe carefully, and then proceeded in his quiet, methodical way to shoot us down in flames.

"You think that it is bad for you here, no? But had you rather be in a concentration camp? It is not likely that you now could walk for a kilometre from here alone without that the Germans should catch you. You are not in your uniforms. The Germans would know that you were with the Underground because you wear Dutch clothes. They would say that you were spies, take you to such a camp and torture you to make you tell. That is not good for you, and nor is it for us. Under torture can no man say that he will not talk. It is not much that you can tell of this farm. But possible is it that it would be enough."

In the light reflecting from the torch he held, I detected that he was peculiarly in earnest. I expected a tirade, but it did not come.

"When you think that it is bad for you, think also that it is bad for us," he continued. "Especially is this so for my wife and I."

"Oh? Why particularly for you two, then, Wim?" Cheeseman asked, relieved to break in on the quiet wigging we were getting.

"Because she is soon to have a baby. But perhaps you had already seen that it should be so?"

We had, in fact, only met her twice, and had not noticed. We therefore demurred.

"Well, so is it, and it shall be soon. It is our first baby, and I should like that she should be in a hospital and have all proper treatment. But it cannot so be. She, too, must not be seen on the farm, for that would make a suspicion that I also was here. It is for us very difficult."

As a piece of psychology it was superb. He had, in the first instance, done no more than formulate clearly the truth for us, should we give way to temptation and break out, and, in the second, let us into a secret. But the effect was far-reaching. Self-pity was no part of the RAF code. Our keeper had problems enough to plague him without our adding to them. After he had gone we resolved to face the cheerless issue fairly and cease vapouring. Even though we had no alternative but to live sightlessly, there was still a need to render a true account.

I had one priceless talent to use in a situation like the one we faced. Obviously the ideal solution was to be unaware of as much of it as possible. I could, when I chose, be very lazy, and as a consequence I had a highly developed power of sleep. I began to put that talent to work.

By a peculiar quirk, I, who was so spendthrift of time, was also a great observer of it. When I felt myself falling asleep, I struck a match and looked at my watch; when I awoke I did the same. I found that, despite the increasing cold, I was beginning to sleep at least fourteen hours a day. Lying and waiting came the more easily.

When Wim arrived one morning with our breakfast he did so to an accompaniment of rifle shots. For perhaps the preceding quarter of an hour an intermittent fusillade of small arms fire had been cracking and reverberating round the district, and we were, to put it mildly, curious. I had a feeling that the wooden beam that ran comfortingly along the ground to my left might prove useful.

"What the hell's going on?" demanded Cheeseman, when Wim was safely inside.

Wim looked more amused than anxious.

"It is only the Germans," he answered. "Last week were they short of fuel. So have they locked the power station and there is no light. Today is it that they have not food enough. Therefore shoot they rabbits."

It was on this same cold morning in early March that Wim decided we should bath. He finished setting the wick in a new blob of mutton fat, lit up, and extinguished his torch.

"You have now been here almost one month," he said. "My wife's mother has said it that your clothes shall be washed. Also is it good that you should yourselves wash."

Winters in eastern Holland are hard, and this one was no exception. The damp air of February had given place to the biting winds of March. The breeze scurried through the barn and scythed its bitter way into the haystack. We had never taken our shirts or trousers off since entering our lair, and I was distinctly loathe to do so now. They had become a sort of second skin that warded off the cold. The idea of stripping off starkers and taking a stone-cold, stand-up bath did not appeal to me. We were, though, undeniably grimy, and our underclothes could probably have stood up of their own accord. Wim, in his quiet way, was determined to alter that.

"You shall have all new clothes while your ones are washed," he said. "Do you wear underclothes beneath your trousers?"

"Yes."

"What do you call such underclothes, please?"

"Pants."

"How long are these pants that you wear? Are they so long as this?" he asked, pointing to his leg just above the ankle.

"Good God no," I answered, indicating my upper thigh.

"Ah! that is difficult. We have not such short pants here. All our pants are long."

I was in an obstreperous mood, for the thought of a cold bath remained uninviting. I was also a fraction allergic to anything in the nature of woollen underwear. It made me itch, and I refused even to wear the heavy stuff they issued in the services, but wore instead my own singlet and shorts. I certainly had no intention of taking to long pants, not even for Wim.

"I shan't wear those," I said.

"But you must. It is here cold, and you must not become ill."

"Sorry, Wim, no dice. No short pants, no bath."

I had hoped to floor him and remain in my muck, but, like that intrepid fellow the Bosun of the unrepeatable service rhyme, Wim was not to be outdone.

"OK, I shall fix it," he said. "You shall have your short pants. Now I go to bring fresh water and a large towel."

He trooped off with a bucket of mucky ablution water, shortly to return with the bucket filled with clean water in one hand, and a pile of fresh clothes and a large towel under the other arm. Then he left us to it.

There was no real option. We each had a quick stand-up bath, donned our new clothes and dived back under the blankets.

Later, in the natural course of things, I had occasion to use the latrine bucket. I was aware that something was wrong.

"Hell!, Cheesey," I said. "These bloody pants haven't got a fly."

"They must have, you clot. You've probably got 'em on back to front."

But I had not. Those pants were entirely lacking in a vent of any kind. They were not intended for the male sex. Whose they were, I never had the temerity to ask. But Wim had done it again. Short pants I had demanded, and short pants I had got.

The long night ground slowly on. In a life that was completely black and equally empty I found that the small things mattered greatly. One looked forward to the tap on the door that meant food, and relished the food as if it were divine. On some days we had an hour's indifferent light via the wick in mutton fat technique; on others none at all. When we had light I smoked away at my oaken pipe, otherwise I was a non-smoker. I kept the tally of days by notching the bowl of my pipe most religiously. The score was mounting up.

It was, I found, completely impossible for the mind to be still. Even if one allowed that up to two thirds of each day was spent in the oblivion of sleep, there were still eight or nine waking hours to cope with. I was never aware of having dreamt when I slept. But I dreamt by day plenty. In imagination I saw lush green cricket fields on sunny days, and would have rejoiced to face the most demon of bowlers on the dustiest of wickets with a chunk of hard, red leather whistling past my ears. Mountains, too, had always drawn me irresistibly, and I saw their inviting tops etched against clear blue skies.

Sometimes, however, we had tangible evidence that cheered us up. For two years the Third Reich had been subjected to air attack on a twenty-four hour a day basis. We lay on a route that was frequently used, for we were no more than thirty miles from the northernmost towns of the Ruhr. Thus, once or twice, faintly we heard the American Flying Fortresses by day and the RAF Lancasters by night as they hammered the Fatherland round the clock. It did a bit for our morale.

Life in the dark haystack was, however, not entirely without humour. Wim lobbed in one day bent on one of his jokes. But, with his dead-pan approach, the fact was not immediately apparent.

"You know, boys, my English is very bad," he said.

We naturally assured him that it was improving by leaps and bounds; which, indeed, it was.

"No, such is not true," he maintained. "Often do I get my words in a mix. Is it, for example, proper to say the cock has laid an egg or the cock has legged an egg?"

His pace had quickened suddenly as he asked that one, and, ever ready to help, I fell for it.

"Oh, the cock has laid an egg," I replied.

"And is that really true?" he asked, innocently, while Cheeseman tittered.

"Yes."

"I have heard that your England is a wonderful country. But do cocks there really lay eggs?"

I felt like a village idiot, of course, but I gave him best. It was humour for humour's sake, and that was a precious commodity in a lack-lustre world.

There was also a strand of minor comedy subsisting between the little dog, Skippy, and myself. Although our evening walks round the field had finished, our visits to the farmhouse had not. On some evenings, when we were lucky, we went there for an hour or so. King Farouk, who seemed to like our company and relayed Dutch jokes to us through Wim, was often in the gathering, Cowboy and Baby less frequently.

Whoever was there, the form was always the same. We sat in the light of the old lamp, and made what fun we could. The pièce de résistance was the closing ceremony with the little dog.

"Shake hands with the King of England!" Wim would say, as he knelt down. The dog would comply.

"Shake hands with Hitler!" would come next. The dog would decline.

I had never been able to fathom the simplest trick done by sleight of hand. This one had me floored. Cheeseman had long since rumbled it, but had been told to say nothing. My continued failure to spot the method was an unfailing source of amusement with which to round the visit off, and it therefore served a purpose. When, at Geoff's disgusted suggestion I watched Wim's hands and finally perceived that he offered his right hand for the King and his left for Hitler, a great cheer went up. But the intelligent dog and the dumb airman had achieved something. They had between them persistently raised a laugh. And the quality of humour was of ultimate importance. If we clung on to it we should stay on an even keel; if we lost it I dreaded the consequences.

March had staggered painstakingly into double figures when a visitor arrived on the farm.

"Come with me, boys," Wim said, as he came unexpectedly into the haystack.

Out of the gloom, through the empty sheep-fold and into the blinding light of a glorious March day behind him we went. The air of the farmyard was cold, the sun glittered in majestic splendour as we blinked our way round the farm buildings. It was almost exactly a month since we had seen the light of day. We paused outside a brick-built barn, the door of which was slightly ajar.

"A man waits for you in there," said Wim. "Go in!"

In the middle of the barn stood a couple of upturned boxes, to which we gravitated because, apart from those, the place seemed to be empty. Light streamed in from an upper window, filling most of the building with a glare that hurt our eyes. We stood nonplussed by the boxes with eyes watering. It seemed strange; almost ominous.

"Sit down!" said a voice. "I have to ask you a question."

In the dark area behind the door a man was standing. Our unadjusted vision did not enable us at first to recognise him, nor did he seem in a hurry to disclose himself. We sat on the boxes in full light while he remained for a short while in the shadows. The circumstances smacked I thought of cloak and dagger, and portended little good.

The man moved towards us. We recognised our guide of a month ago.

"Good God! It's Leo," said Geoff. "You had me worried, mate. I thought you were going to interrogate us as a couple of prospective Nazi spies."

"Oh no, we know exactly who you are. You must excuse me. I am so used to the shadows that it is second nature for me to stay in them."

He turned to his business in a brisk, almost professorial manner.

"You must know that I am a member of the Underground, and that it is my duty to further its interests in any way I can," he began.

Sitting on our upturned boxes while he stood above us, the barn became, suddenly, the lecture room. The delivery and formality of the opening gambit was in the classic style of lecturing. He did not, at that moment, seem a bit like the chap who had walked miles through the rain with us clutching his parcel of English books.

"The British have informed us," he proceeded, "that they intend to make an arms-drop here in the immediate future. We have waited a long time for it, and now, finally, it is coming. There is, however, one problem, and you can, I think, help solve it."

"And the nature of the problem?" I asked.

"It is that of recognising an aircraft by its engine note. Everything is arranged. The dropping zone is fixed and, upon receipt of a given signal, the time is known to the minute. However, it involves the use of lights, and in this area we have now to be very careful. We do not want to switch on our lights when a German aeroplane is passing because we have confused it with a British bomber. You would, doubtless, recognise the sound of one of your own aeroplanes and prevent us from making a mistake. Will you come with us?"

The solving of his problem posed a second one. It was no part of our duty to get mixed up in active partisan activities. The RAF firmly discouraged any such thing, and carefully underlined the penalties for being caught on such a job. There was the added fact in this case that the area literally crawled with Krauts and lacked the mountains and moorland that might have made such a drop a relatively easy matter. It sounded dicey to me. Geoff felt the same. We said so.

Leo thought for a moment, conflicting emotions flickering across his face. Then he shrugged, relaxed visibly and dropped the formality.

"You know by now our maxim that the fewer people who are aware of the details of a project the better chance it has of success. But we need you, so I must not be too exact about that. As you say — what the hell?"

He proceeded to tell us the scheme in detail in an effort to persuade. After the European news on the BBC, there had for some years followed a number of code-phrases which had meaning only for those who knew their implications. When the phrase 'Spring is coming' was announced, an arms-drop would be made in a clearing in a nearby large wood at a fixed time on the following night. Lights had to be laid in the clearing in the form of a triangle, and, at the moment the aircraft carrying the arms answered the beaming out of the letter B in morse by a man with a torch, those lights had to be switched on. Clearly, the last thing the Dutch wanted to do was to give away a carefully chosen position by signalling to the Luftwaffe.

"But those sodding lights," said Cheeseman. "Won't they be seen?"

"No. The wood is dense, the lights shaded so that they will only show upwards, and then, we hope, only for a short time while the bomber makes its run in."

I was dubious as to what would happen if the Germans discovered the affair and moved in.

"All approaches to the wood will be guarded by men with Sten guns and rifles. It should be adequate. All you have to do is to stay by me and give the word for the signaller to make contact. The sound made by a Stirling bomber is probably not difficult for you to recognise. Will you come?"

There had been no undue pressure, and certainly no reminders of what the Resistance had done for us. One seemed, in all conscience, not to have much option. The recognition by sound of a low-flying, laden Stirling would be a piece of cake.

I wondered for a moment, why, if the wood was to be so well guarded, our presence was needed, for obviously the show had been done before. But the mental search was not a long one. Never — not even in May 1940 when the enemy had swept victoriously across Holland — had there been anything approaching the concentration of German troops which now lay ensconced on the flat plains awaiting the Allied attack, and never had such an abundance of aircraft scurried across the skies. Efficient recognition of that Stirling was vital; otherwise there would be a mess. As Leo had said — to hell with the strict line of duty! We were bound to have a go.

Before he left, Leo asked if we needed any more books.

"No thank you," Geoff replied. "We live in the dark like bloody out-of-work moles."

As we crossed the yard I noticed Geoff Cheeseman's face. In the bright light the tell-tale marks of close confinement stood out. The pallor beneath the stubble was almost fish white. I concluded, as I realised that the same must apply to me, that Leo had observed us pretty closely while he stood in the shadows and we in the sunlight. He could not afford a couple of deadbeats on his arms-dropping sortie. We had, it seemed, qualified for the next test — provided it came quickly.

We bolted the door, settled down, and waited in the gloomy haystack once more. This time, in more senses than one, for spring to come.

I reflected ruefully on the accuracy of the navigation required to put an aircraft so near to a clearing in an obscure Dutch wood by dead of night that the flickering of an ordinary torch was recognisable. Aircraft and air navigation had evolved by early 1945 to a point where less than two hundred Lancasters could drop more than twice the weight of bombs with pin point accuracy on a precise section of the Dortmund-Ems Canal in ten minutes than could the five hundred German bombers which dribbled during the course of ten hours over Coventry on a never to be forgotten night in November 1940. The essence of the developed RAF method was concentration: which implied that each individual navigator had to perform an accurate, demanding job based on mathematical principles and radar. If he failed, his aircraft would be a lone sitting duck, open to the full ravages of the first-class German night fighter and flak defences. The job offered a superlative challenge, and personally I loved it. But that was of no consequence now, for our Lancaster was just a heap of junk spattered over a Dutch field, and two of its crew lived in the cloistered seclusion of an artificial haystack. It was, as Geoff had said, a sort of mole game, played in the dark, and I hated it increasingly.

The days following the promise that spring was coming were exceptional only in their uniform lack of anything remotely remarkable. Daily the morse V, or the rhythm of the opening notes of Beethoven's fifth symphony, or the victory sign — whichever way one cared to think of it — was rapped on the door, and we were fed. The darkness was tactile; it seemed to smother us. It was every whit as deep as that of the grave, without, however, possessing quite its silence. Noise, particularly sharp noise of great volume, came in muffled form through the walls of hay, and punctuated our narrow existence. The whine of fighter engines, the crack of Mauser rifles as their owners hunted rabbits, the snarl of flak batteries and, with increasing frequency, the distant mutter of the big guns on the Rhine, gave evidence of immediate and rapidly evolving war.

We listened in particular to those distant guns, for we knew that if the Rhine was to be crossed, it could only be done by building a bridge across it under the cover of a lengthy, saturating barrage. Those damned guns always failed us. They would natter for ten minutes together like old crones at a funeral, and then fade. They duped us by raising our hopes, and as soon dashing them.

We had developed a tendency not to want our food, and this perturbed Wim. He chivvied us to eat, but to little avail. He himself went down with a heavy cold at this stage, and his place was taken by Wim II. Wim had taught him the word 'boys'. For three or four days he would bustle in with his torch, set our food on the staging and encourage us by signs to eat. "Zo, boys," he would say, and take his leave. Largely, the food he brought remained untouched.

And yet, despite the growing lethargy there came a time when I could abide voluntary captivity no longer. One day the desire to see got the better of me. I wanted to stand where the winds blew free. This I could not. But I could do the next best thing.

I slipped through the trapdoor and stood for a couple of minutes in the fold to allow my eyes to become accustomed to the light. Then I pressed my nose against the rough boards and looked through one of the cracks.

It was like a glimpse of paradise. All I saw was a long green field that ended two hundred yards away in a copse. Over its surface were dotted fifteen or so sheep who grazed serenely. As I watched, a boy of perhaps fourteen with a long stick in his hand appeared and walked over to the furthest flung of the flock.

It was late afternoon and the sun was setting. The scene was very ordinary, and yet, to me, sylvan. The boy began to round up the sheep and head them in the direction of the fold. It was time to go. While he was yet afar off I crawled once more through the trapdoor and bolted it behind me.

"No prizes for that," said Geoff. "Curiosity will be the death of you one of these days. What did you see?"

"I saw a long green field, fifteen sheep, and a boy shepherd who'll be bringing them into the pen any minute. Heaven must look something like that."

We had both been choristers in our younger days, so we sang, quietly, to keep our spirits up. Not a few RAF ballads were rendered sotto voce in the haystack.

At this time two apparently unconnected tunes ran obsessively round my brain, and I whistled and sang them until Cheeseman, not unreasonably, told me to dry up. The old hymn, "For all the saints who from their labours rest" was an odd tune to be possessed by, since, though undoubtedly from our labours resting, saints we certainly were not. The popular song, "These Foolish Things", was obviously more applicable, for it seemed hardly possible to be more foolish than to live like a zombie in a dark haystack.

The winds of March continued excruciatingly to blow, the cold remained intense, the darkness abysmal. Geoff had become progressively more and more taciturn, while I, I fancied, was going slightly dippy. How long, I wondered, could one bear incarceration in conditions resembling those pertaining in a deep bank vault? Surely nothing worse could follow if we took the chance and broke away? And then I remembered what might happen to the Dutch.

We sat on Sunday evening, March 18th, once more in the farm. It was the evening when things changed and the long night ended. But, at that moment, we did not see the change coming.

"One thing intrigues me, Wim," I said, by way of conversation. "You seem so damned casual about our visits here. We're a long way from the haystack. What happens if the Moffen suddenly descend?"

"What happened when first you came here and when you were returned from a walk towards the Rhine?"

"Can't remember anything in particular."

"Not a noise? A dog barking, perhaps?"

"Yes, he barked like hell, now you come to mention it."

"That is our protection. If any man moves within two hundred metres of this farm he shall bark. Then we shall move, fast. If it happens, then shall you see how fast."

"You have other bolt-holes, then?"

"Oh, yes. We have such. We call them hiding-places, but into them we can, at alarm, bolt."

They seemed, as usual, to have it all sewn up. Nevertheless, I listened intently. The wind outside seemed stilled for once; no sound other than its gently soughing came to my ears. The watchdog slept.

Wim looked as if he had something important to say, but did not know how to begin. At last he dropped the bombshell.

"It is strange that you should on this night be of hiding thinking. Today has the farmer had an order that he must take ten German soldiers on his farm. It is, then, not possible that you longer should stay. It cannot be that you and they are here together. Therefore, boys, we can no longer hide you. You must go."

The thing ought not to have been unexpected, for most of the farms round about now had their quota of the enemy billeted upon them. But we had never faced the realities of the situation. Ostrich-like we had buried our heads firmly in the sand and voluntarily become progressively more dependent upon the good offices of a Dutchman. Now he was kicking us out. It hurt like a blow between the eyes. It felt as if we were being turned away from the inn.

13

Guns on the Rhine

For moments a baffled, pregnant silence prevailed. Cheeseman's voice, breaking it, sounded incredulous, disgusted almost.

"Go, Wim?" he asked, "Go where?"

The question was basically weak. But it might as well have been ascribed to me, for the words were forming in my mind even as Geoff spoke them.

A worried frown creased Wim's ample forehead. He seemed annoyed with himself.

"Excuse me, boys," he said. "I see that I have once again spoken my thoughts to you badly. I do not mean that you should absolute go from us, for we now think of you as of the family. Therefore can you be with us until the British come. I mean only that you shall go to another hiding-place. It is almost one kilometre from here."

He departed from the room, and returned a minute or so later with a loaded provision basket.

"It is not possible that I should come to you before tomorrow in the evening. Therefore, here is food for one day. We go now to your haystack where you can get all necessary things that you want. Then go we to your new hiding-place."

We bade the family a reasonably cheerful goodbye, and went. The farmer's wife looked genuinely upset, and I suspected that she foresaw all sorts of dangers besetting us. But, for myself, I found a flicker of interest rise in me. The move betokened change. And nothing, I thought, could possibly be worse than the dismal life of the haystack.

By the light of Wim's torch we retrieved our escape kits, maps and odd bits of impedimenta. Then we set off.

Scudding cloud driven by a brisk night wind rolled imperiously across a sky rejoicing in a full moon; the feel of the fresh wind on the face was a benison. Our way was illuminated by the moon and darkened by the cloud alternately as we walked. It was, in point of fact, a strange procession which stole quietly through the Wehrmacht's reserve area that night. Against all classical military precedence the provision train was at the front, for Wim, the Dutchman, carried the food, and he led the way. And what a terribly pukkah type would have made of a couple of operational aircrew dressed in jackets befitting scarecrows and wearing clogs, God in his heaven alone knew. Nevertheless, we moved in single file along small field paths which skirted the lines of trees, achieved near silence, and arrived after ten minutes or so at a point where our path was intersected by a deeply rutted farm-track. Wim drew us close. We stood in the shadow of the trees and he pointed out our new abode. Twenty yards away, a long, low rectangular mound stood on the far side of the farm-track, indifferently bathed in the light of the cloud-encumbered moon.

"That is your hiding-place," he whispered. "It is a store of hay. In there must you go, and there stay until I come to you tomorrow in the evening. The walls are very thin. So must you always very quiet talk, and, if you must make a cough or a sneeze, first put your arm over your face in such a way." He mimed the smothering of those explosive human noises by putting his nose and mouth in the crook of his arm. "Also must you most careful be that, when you go to sleep, you never make this noise." He simulated a snore.

"Heaven forbid that we should," I said. "But that is called a snore."

"OK. Be careful, then, that you do not snore, for Germans and Dutchmen walk along this farm-road. Let us now go to the hiding-place."

We approached the hay store quietly, our clogs making the merest swish over the intervening grass. The moon stood suddenly clear, and what had been an indistinct mound was sharply delineated. It was a precise rectangle, fully thirty feet in length, but not more than six wide. It stood about a yard back from the farm-track and was, at most, four feet high. On the outside it was thatched with straw against the weather.

Wim bent down and began to pull away some straw at the base of the nearside narrow wall. A dark, rectangular aperture a foot or so high and twice as broad took shape.

"That is where you must get in," he whispered.

"What? Through that? I'll get flipping stuck," said Cheeseman.

I led the way in.

It was not a hiding-place for fat men. You needed, like Cassius, a lean and hungry look to negotiate that gap. I went down flat on my stomach and inched my way laboriously through the mixture of straw and dirt surrounding the hole, through the gap and into the pitch dark of the interior. I groped my way forward. The floor felt hard, lumpy, and slightly damp. My feet were barely clear of the entrance when my hands encountered an unyielding obstacle which felt like a wall in front of me.

"Keep going, mate!" said Cheeseman, who was manoeuvring in behind me. He was by no means flabby, but he had a fraction more meat on his bones than I, and was finding the slithering process harder.

"I can't move any further, you clot. There's a wall or something in front. I'll veer right. You go left!"

We installed ourselves, sitting upright with our backs to the wall.

"OK boys?" came a query from outside.

We acknowledged that we were, more or less.

"Then stay there and be always quiet! I shall come again tomorrow."

Wim passed the provisions basket inside, scraped the loose straw back round the hole and left.

"Turned out nice again," I ventured, half facetiously.

"Bloody marvellous," came the non-commital reply.

Sleep did not come easily to me. I had become conditioned to too much silence. Here the night wind sang in the trees, the hoot of a stalking owl seemed disproportionately loud, the noises of the darkened countryside irritated. After a while I could tell from his regular breathing that my companion had dropped off. He did not, thank God, snore. I had never known him do that.

I awoke in the morning to light and the sound of animated, rapidly approaching German voices. There was no question of sitting bolt upright in alarm, I was already doing that. Instead I glanced at Geoff who sat beside me, wide awake with his finger to his lips in a gesture of silence. The voices came straight towards us. This, I thought, is it. My heart beat a rapid fandango in my chest. The voices came on until their owners were level with us and not more than a couple of yards away. Then they receded gradually into the distance.

"Christ almighty!" I whispered, in relief. "I thought we'd been rumbled that time."

"Not to worry. Just a couple of Jerries passing by. As a matter of fact another pair went along ten minutes ago."

There came in rapid succession the footsteps of an individual plodding by, the sound of a small group of men speaking Dutch, and, finally, a further pair of Germans of a less vociferous order than their predecessors. We remained quite still and eminently silent.

"Getting like Piccadilly Circus round here, boy," observed Geoff. "I get the impression that the Germans operate in pairs. There always seems to be two voices. They're off to breakfast, like as not."

Well, breakfast was a thought. The light that filtered in had a grey quality that I associated with early dawn. But it was deceptive, for, on looking at my watch, I found the time to be well past eight o'clock. Things had quietened down outside. For some reason I had recovered my appetite.

Outside, almost perfect silence reigned as we munched through half our food and drank an equal quantity of the bottles of ersatz coffee provided.

The amount of light did not vary. It retained its greyish hue and gave the impression of perpetual twilight. Still, it was light, and it offered the chance of assessing the score. The wall we sat against was, of course, a wall of hay. Naîvely we had supposed that the whole of the long pile of hay was a hollow structure, but it was apparent that such was not the case. The obstruction that had barred our way in the night was, in fact, the end of a genuine haypile more than twenty feet long. We occupied a phoney construction some seven or eight feet in length attached to the end of it. The hay which covered the floor had clearly been down for a long period. It had from time to time been soaked, and then dried again. As a consequence it was hard, unpliable and dirty, and it lay in a bumpy, unyielding mass a few inches deep over the ground. The hide-out was, in one respect, a small scale replica of our late abode. The vertical wooden posts and horizontal bracings of the frame, against which the compressed hay and straw thatch were pressed, were clearly visible on the inside. There, however, the resemblance ended. The haystack was, though grim, a comfortable place. Conditions here were extremely cramped, and the cold was even more intense, because there were no thick walls to minimise it. Geoff Cheeseman's face wore a distinctly ruminative look as he ate.

"One thing," he observed, at length. "Did you notice anything remarkable about the footfalls of those Dutch and Jerries who passed?"

"Footfalls?" Conundrums at this hour, Cheesey?" I asked, with a minute attempt at drollery.

"Sod your conundrums! I'm being serious! Think for once!"

It almost never worked. My attempts at undermining the serious situation by some form of flippancy seemed to annoy at least seven people out of ten. The world was, I supposed, full of serious folk. Geoff was by no means always in this category, but he was this morning. So, since he was far more practical than I and had likely hit on something, I thought for once.

There had, on reflection, been some sort of difference between the Dutch group that had passed and the Germans, but I could not place it. I asked him to tell me.

"Well, we're on a rutted farm-track here, aren't we?"

"A sandy one, yes."

"That sand is sandy soil, and it's bone hard because of the cold spell. The Germans, being in pairs, mostly walk along the ruts, the Dutch often along the middle, where there's grass. The German jackboot goes clump, the Dutch clog slithers along in a kind of swish. You can hear anybody coming some distance away, whether they're talking or not. We've got an early warning system."

He was undoubtedly right; his observation brilliantly acute. We had no idea at all who these German troops were who went by. For all we knew they might be the fanatical SS. And in that case, we stood a very fair chance of being shot first and questions asked later, if we made a mistake. It would be nice to know who was passing.

We settled on a plan of campaign that recognised silence at the appropriate time as the only real weapon in our armoury. If we used our ears effectively, the approach of anyone was audible from a fair distance. We therefore resolved that, on the sound of a footfall, we would stop whatever we were doing and remain stock-still until the danger passed. We had to be particularly unlucky to fail on account of coughs and sneezes. Neither of us had colds, and the odd outburst could be smothered reasonably easily. Snoring, if we were both asleep, was a different matter. But each of us maintained that the other did not commit that cardinal sin.

I found myself intrigued by the way the mind worked. In the haystack, where it was abysmally dark but relatively safe, we had degenerated into torpor. Here, where there was light of a sort and danger one measly yard away, Geoff had just evolved a system that could save the day.

I wondered, though, whether we could really get away with it for long. And then I recalled the precept that the surest way to hide something was to put it in a very obvious place. This hide-out certainly qualified for that. Jerry had all the advantages bar one. It would have surprised him to know that the pile of hay he passed so closely by was occupied. We had to keep it that way. Danger was a whetstone. We might just succeed.

"It's a morning of questions and answers, Cheesey," I said, breaking a long, reflective silence. "Let me ask you one. Where do you think the light comes from?"

"I don't know. Through the thin walls, I suppose."

"True. But if you look closer there's a patch on either side where the light is brighter. I'll lay you a quid that those are peepholes. Everything's quiet. You take the one on the track side, I'll take the other. Let's see what gives outside."

The hole through which I peered was cunningly contrived. The compressed hay had been pulled away over a roughly circular area as large as a big man's palm. Strands of the outer thatching of straw had been woven across it to conceal the gap, but woven in such a way as to afford the observer from inside a limited view. The panorama to the rear of the haypile was hardly one that merited the immediate despatch of an enthusiastic telegram home to mother. Behind us, at a distance of a few yards, stood a small copse of trees, their grey, bare branches basking in the glow of a wintry sun. On the far side of the copse, rising above an undertow of thicket, I could detect the jut of a gable end. That was all. But the presence of a farmhouse less than forty yards distant was interesting.

We scrambled across the hay and investigated the opposite peepholes. The Dutch had been more cautious with the one on the side flanking the track. The strands of straw had been woven more densely across the gap, and the view was, in consequence, more limited. Nevertheless, it was possible to see out indistinctly, and both peepholes demonstrated the extreme thinness of the walls. They did not appear to be more than three inches thick.

The morning had quietly given way to early afternoon. After the flurry of activity that had enlivened our breakfast nothing much had happened in the immediate vicinity. The distant big guns on the Rhine had had a desultory bang at each other, the odd fighter had scooted across our section of the Dutch sky. Otherwise things had been quiet. We were aware of the fact that a sizeable road lay two or three hundred yards distant, beyond the nearby farmhouse. The sound of vehicles, large and small, had come to us at intervals, and implied military activity. It could only be the road which linked Aalten with Lichtenvoorde, and the knowledge of its whereabouts was important. If we had for any reason to make a break for it, it was imperative to avoid that road.

Time hung. I took the opportunity to notch up the procession of the days on my oaken pipe. The score stood at thirty-seven. A half century seemed a distinct prospect.

The hands of my ever reliable navigation watch showed the hour to be one o'clock as we took a further swig of the ersatz coffee.

"Jerries!" whispered Cheeseman, insistently.

I heard the footfall at the moment he spoke, and there was no doubt of it. It was the clump of the jackboot, not the swish of the clog that touched the ear. Three further sound impressions registered almost simultaneously: a voice spoke animatedly but relatively softly in German; the speaker cleared his throat nervously; there was a sound of music. The voice grew louder as the soldier approached us. His rapid and persistent monologue was punctuated by a couple of quick, short coughs. The music resolved itself into the unmistakable sound of a harmonica. The two Germans came on until they were within touching distance. The logical side of my brain told me that the harmonica was being played softly, and that the loquacious German was a quiet speaker. Yet, at the nearest point, both seemed unbearably loud. We held our breaths. The beating of my heart sounded to me like the clanging of a knell. In a moment the danger had passed. Musician and compulsive talker receded along the farm-track.

"Strewth!" muttered Cheeseman, surprise oozing. "We've heard it all now. A Kraut with a mouth organ. What the hell next?"

"What indeed? Did you mark his mate, the talker with the cough?"

"I did. Come to think of it I heard him go up this morning, coughing away just the same. Chest case I think. The mouth organ bird's new though, I didn't hear him."

I thought the cougher was more likely a nerve case, and that perhaps the harmonica player only gave lunchtime concerts.

In point of fact, he did not. That evening, as the daylight faded with the setting sun, he played us a serenade. His taste in music, like mine, was catholic. He began in the heights with a snatch of Schubert, descended through clouds tinted with the sentimentality of a couple of the old, somewhat heavy, unmistakably German love songs, to land with a flourish among the hit songs of the thirties. And he was no mean player. His notes were clean and true, his rhythm firm. He was a musician who performed beautifully on the harmonica as the sun went down. He interested me but, look as I might through the peephole, I could not see him. He may have stood round the angle of the farm building, or have been obscured by the thicket which grew among the trees of the copse. I failed to see him, but I did hear the babble of German voices as he played. Eventually he stopped, and silence descended.

"You know what that means," I whispered. "He's billeted on that farm, and some of his mates are too. One mistake and we've had our flaming chips."

Night had fallen, and we sat in the darkness waiting for Wim. I had ceased smoking in the daytime, because of the obvious danger that upward drifting smoke from an apparently innocent haypile would catch the passer-by's eye. Now, I was very loathe to strike a match in case the glow should be visible through the peepholes. The idea of German infantry chasing a will-o'-the-wisp might seem amusing, but that delusion would soon be shattered if they found it. The perch we clung to was a precarious one.

Soft footsteps approached our lair. Someone began very gently to pull the loose straw away from the entrance hole.

"It is Wim," came a welcome, almost inaudible whisper. "Is all well with you, boys?"

We had never really doubted that he would make it, he was that kind of chap. But the actuality of his presence gave us new heart. We said that we were all right.

"Then come quietly out and bring your basket."

We wriggled our way out of the narrow exit, through the muck and loose straw, and emerged into the air. The acknowledgment that all was well with us was an overstatement. Our rumps were sore from sitting and our legs were cramped from lack of use. We stretched them gratefully and breathed deeply as we stood in a tight little group round the haypile.

A small conversation-piece took place in whispers. We enquired, as we did daily, whether the expected child was yet born. The answer was still negative, but all seemed well on the farm.

We were given no more than ten minutes in which to unwind

physically, and then it was back to the hovel for us. In the instant before we began our scramble back I started to put to Wim something which had twinged at our consciences all day. The risk he ran as he sloped along the hedgerows with our provision basket was far from small. The Germans now seemed to be everywhere, and if he were caught it would be disastrous for him. I said we thought that, particularly as he was shortly to become a father, we imposed too much. He did not let me finish. He grabbed my arm almost angrily.

"You must not say that," he retorted, speaking with a fervour I had only once before known in him. "Soon shall we be free, and it is most to you British that we owe it. For years the sound of your RAF flying in the night was the only thing that gave us hope. Always was the noise of their engines music in my ears. Later came the Americans by day, and that also helped. But not always did your aeroplanes fly back. Many RAF men are buried in graves in Lichtenvoorde and other near towns. They were men who did their duty. So also now must I do mine for you. Go back, boys, and hide quietly. Tomorrow shall I come again."

Figuratively I doffed my cap. Bravery coupled with humanity always humbled me.

In the early afternoon of the following day Geoff Cheeseman lay flat on his back inside the hollow haypile, sound asleep and snoring. The snore was not particularly loud, but it was regular and appreciable.

That he should have been asleep at that hour was not surprising. The night had been bitterly cold, and this, together with the uncomfortable nature of a place where we could never stretch out, had ensured a bad night's sleep for both of us. At the warmest point of a reasonably fair day we had both fallen asleep where we sat, side by side with our backs against the one firm wall.

Along the farm-track a detachment of German infantry approached at a brisk pace, talking loudly as they came. The noise of guttural, boisterous voices outside dinned on my sleeping brain. I was awake in a flash and immediately aware of danger. Cheeseman had slipped forward from his sitting position, and lay flat on his back with his knees drawn up in front of him. I hit him a sharp crack in the ribs with my right elbow and brought my left hand close to his mouth in order to stifle any cry he might make. He came to immediately, shook his head and remained stock-still. He made no sound.

The infantry came up until they were right on us. The loudness of their talk seemed to fill our den with clamour. The tension seemed to last hours of psychological time. Had they heard the snore or not? They were level with us, the babble of voices crucifyingly loud. They seemed to be shouting. In a couple of seconds the whole issue would be decided. Those seconds were interminable. There was no pause. The soldiers continued on their way until their voices were lost on the still air. We breathed again.

So much, I thought, for the dictum that, 'the knowledge that he is to be hanged on the morrow wonderfully concentrates a man's mind.' The truth of it was indisputable. Everything about us had sharpened up to the point where our reactions to danger were immediate; lack of effective vision was amply compensated for by acute hearing which gave the Cheeseman early warning system a chance to work. The only thing that amazed me about the dictum was that it applied equally well to the subconscious. For how else could I, a very sound sleeper, have heard those Germans? So far, so good, I thought.

When Wim arrived in the evening he brought good news.

"What's pleasing you so much, then?" Geoff queried, as we stood outside.

"It is that we now have a daughter," he answered, with obvious pride. "She was this morning born in the farm."

"Congratulations, Wim. Good show!" we echoed in unison.

"And what will her name be?" asked Geoff.

"Her name shall be Hannie."

Naturally, and perhaps rather formally, we offered good wishes for the present and future. Wim seemed delighted and perhaps rather touched in reply.

"Yes, all is now very well, and I thank you both for such hopes. I shall tell them to my wife. Thank you."

In imagination I played that little scene over again as we sat in the dark, and I found it not to lack either for the humanities or for humour. If Wim had brought us his news in England we should have taken him off pronto to the mess or the nearest pub for a celebratory drink. Here we had conducted a polite, slightly stilted conversation in whispers, with German troops within easy shouting distance and we ourselves ready to bolt into or behind the haypile at the least sign of trouble. The proud father had received congratulations from a pair of decrepit-looking ragamuffins. Still, despite the difficulties, the proprieties had been observed. And that mattered.

Time slid by slowly and helped us not one jot. Our circumstances remained grubby, cramped and almighty cold. The roof of the eight foot by six box in which we lived constrained us, so that our movements resembled those of an infant learning to crawl. There had been an interlude in which two German soldiers had had the cheek to stand and hold a conversation outside our hovel, but the serio-comedy that would have ensued had either decided to take a rest on it had not happened. Sporadically small-arms fire had volleyed around as the soldiery presumably hunted rabbits. That did not particularly bother us. It did, however, act as a reminder that the gentry who passed so close carried rifles.

We had, in fact, just entered the season of spring. But that was all that could be said about it, for of its vernal qualities there was no sign, and as to the arms-drop dependent upon the code-phrase "spring is coming," that seemed a dead duck. I began to wonder whether spring would ever really come.

Late in the evening came trouble. Wim had been and gone, and we were sitting in our usual spot in a state between waking and sleeping. Outside all was still; inside it was pitch dark. I was jerked rudely wide awake by the realisation that someone was standing immediately outside the entrance hole. Whoever it was had approached softly, for I caught the sound of his footsteps only in the instant before he stopped. A moment's pause. And then I heard the loose straw being pulled away from the hole itself.

Geoff Cheeseman put his mouth to my ear and whispered quickly and almost inaudibly.

"Lie doggo, mate! Whoever this bird is he's on his own. Let him get part of the way in, and then strike a match. He'll be startled by the light, and if he's a Jerry we'll chop him and run for it."

It flashed across my mind that the known presence of one enemy did not necessarily imply the absence of others. A firing squad of the night prowler's companions might well be in waiting. Still, there was no other answer. Either we had to hack him hard with the side of the hand across the jugular vein or be taken here like rats in a trap. That method of despatching an enemy was a silent one, but the situation yelled for discreet violence. When he was half way through the narrow entrance he would be at maximum disadvantage. I pulled my feet quietly under myself to gain purchase, surreptitiously removed my box of matches from my coat pocket, extracted one, and waited, ready to strike.

The intruder had removed the loose straw, and was on his way in. The small noises he made as he slithered along crackled upon the ear. The rustle of the straw as his chest and stomach passed over it, and the sound of his breathing gave the picture of his approach. When his head had first come through the hole it was no more than eight feet from where we sat. Yet we could not see him in the pitch darkness. The sounds of stealthy movement stopped suddenly and completely. I crouched, match in hand. But I wanted him further inside. Little, unfathomable, fidgetting noises came from our unseen foe. He was not exactly where I wanted him, but I could wait no longer. I had to make a move.

In the very act of striking I was forestalled. There came a quick, sharp scratch and spurt of light in the darkness ahead. My eyes were dazzled by the sudden glare. The advantage was his, and we were hoist by our own petard. I cursed myself for a slow-witted fool.

The dazzle of the match was only a momentary disadvantage. The scene resolved itself rapidly. It was sheer comedy. Instead of the gun barrel down which I expected to find myself looking, my gaze riveted on the pale, astonished face of a Dutchman who lay propped up on his left elbow. He was a very tall, thin man who was positioned on his stomach half in and half out of our lair. In his right hand he held the lighted match; on his head he wore a cap; written on his face was a mixture of disbelief and alarm. He looked like a huge, undernourished fish emerging from the water. As the match went out he put his finger to his lips, and retreated through the hole without saying a word. He even replaced the straw.

"Apart from being bloody slow with the match, mate, what do you make of that?" Cheeseman whispered. "Do you think he was a decoy sent in by the Krauts? If so we'd better hoof it."

"Sorry about the match. But no, I don't think he was trying the place for size on Jerry's behalf. He looked too scared for that. I reckon he was an Underground type diving for cover who probably heard our breathing as he scrambled in."

The luck, I thought, continued to go very much our way. With reference to his snoring act, I told Geoff to get his adenoids sorted out, and went off to sleep.

There was not the slightest practical reason for it, and curiosity I knew was said to have killed the cat, but I determined next day that I would have a look at these Germans who passed us by.

The peephole on the road side afforded a very limited view indeed. Therefore, to satisfy my whim, I took up position on hands and knees opposite it, and waited. I started to work a little on the thickly woven straw over the hole to try and improve the view, but gave that up as being too dangerous.

Time passed; I remained obstinately in the praying position. Eventually, the two Germans with whom by sound we were most familiar came striding along the farm-track. The harmonica player and his loquacious friend approached and were gone. There was a snatch of music and a nervous cough or two mixed with rapid speech, and that was that. But in the instant when they were abreast of the peephole I caught a close-up, fleeting glimpse of a field-grey greatcoat and the butt of a Mauser rifle slung upright over the shoulder. The nearer of the two (whoever that was) was too close to give me anything other than an enlarged view of a limited area of a uniformed body. I felt almost as if he had brushed me as he went past.

"Satisfied?" queried an amused Cheeseman.

"Not really. Still, I got a close look at the butt end of a Mauser. Interesting bit of equipment in its way."

"Yes, so long as you don't get on the business end," came the ever practical reply.

That Thursday evening we had yet another concert from the Wehrmacht. The soldier stood, as he had done a few nights previously, somewhere in the farmyard and played loud and long in the fading light. He finished, predictably, on "Lili Marlene", the song that, because it was so good, had spread from the Germans to take its place among the hit-tunes of the Allies. In this he was accompanied by a small chorus of German voices, and he played it through again as an encore. I could almost have joined in myself.

When the music stopped and both night and silence descended, it seemed to me like the curtain going down on the last act of a play. The play might have been entitled, "The Old German Paradox". How was it possible that a nation so rich in music, a nation that included Beethoven, Bach and Schumann among its sons, could, at the same time, have caused so much misery by launching the world into two total wars in the space of twenty years, and even worse, be responsible for the bestialities and degradations of the concentration camps? I found no answer to that question, other than the over-simple and unsatisfactory one of national schizophrenia. That a representative of that nation should, unwittingly, have serenaded a couple of enemy aircrew crouched like beasts in a lair, held a sort of cynical satisfaction. Perhaps, quite soon, the darker side of that paradox would be finished for ever, the play actually at an end, and we ourselves able once more to walk freely abroad in the full light of day.

Certainly the psychology of the situation was fascinating. I wondered, abstractly, whether a man who loved music so much that he must needs play his harmonica surreptitiously as he walked along, would shoot me as a spy if he found me. Was he, perhaps, a part of that paradox that made him fanatic as well as musician?

Circumstances had made Geoff and I as hard as nails. For my part, I knew that, given half a chance, I would have had no hesitation about killing the musician if he had been last night's intruder. That would have been done in defence of a kind of freedom. However badly we lived, the determination to evade capture had taken on an almost fanatical force of its own.We simply had to get back now.That was what it was all about.

Wim was not in the least amused when, later that evening, we told him of last night's interloper.

"Did you know the man?" he queried.

"I saw him for no more than five seconds, but I have never seen him before," I answered. "He is a very tall, thin man, if that helps."

"I do not know who that was. Therefore I do not like it."

Friday March 23rd was remarkable initially for its quietness. It was too quiet, and therefore depressing. There was no air activity and no firing across the Rhine. I cut the fortieth notch in the bowl of my oaken pipe, and reflected ruefully on our days in the wilderness. The wilderness had little to do with sand, but was closely linked with hay. For all those days I had seen nothing but the inside of walls made of hay, and, when I could not see them, I was acutely aware that they were there.

"I think I'm developing hay-fever, Cheesey," I said.

"Oh my god no! You start sneezing now mate, and we're finished."

"I don't mean physically you clot, I mean mentally. There are times when the presence of the stuff we grovel in drives me up the wall. If anybody mentions the word hay to me when we get back I'll ram some down his flaming throat. This silence doesn't exactly help much does it?"

"No. I know what you mean. I begin to think the attack over the lousy Rhine never will come. I get despondent."

We talked morose stuff. Our bodies and legs were stiff and sore, our minds tired out by the necessity of remaining constantly on the qui vive. How long we could keep up this apology for living I did not know. But I was certain that it could be counted in days rather than weeks. Our melancholy humour did not in the least improve as the midday passed and the afternoon began to slip uneventfully and noiselessly away.

Then, towards evening, everything changed. We were jerked abruptly wide awake. The silence was shattered in the twinkling of an eye by a colossal barrage which seemed to open up instantaneously along the whole length of the Rhine front. The nearest attacking British batteries were fifteen miles or so away; the nearest German guns, vehemently belching a reply, perhaps a couple of miles less. But such was the unceasing force of their combined thunder that the earth itself seemed to be in motion. It seemed continuously to rock and pulsate under our feet. We had been disappointed so many times by artillery duels which had petered out that neither of us said a word. We merely sat and listened. The violence of the exchanges continued unabatedly. After a quarter of an hour I hazarded a hopeful guess.

"I think," I said, slowly, "that this is probably it. Rip van Winkel awakes."

"Maybe. In an hour's time we shall know for sure. If it's still hammer and tongs by then, this must be it."

In fact the guns were still crashing belligerently away when Wim arrived three hours later. He removed the straw from the hole as quietly as ever, identified himself softly, and we slithered once more out into the night. To the south and south-west the sky oscillated in countless flickers of yellow light which seemed to play a jagged, zig-zagging game with the cloud base. The noise, beautifully cacophonic, was continous and intense. Wim had recently said that the roar of aircraft engines had been as music to his ears. So was this din to mine. There was no doubt now in any of our minds that this was the saturation barrage we were waiting for. Under its cover it was possible that the sappers were already beginning to throw a Bailey Bridge across the Rhine. Cheeseman and I, in spite of our developed caution, were excited, and so was Wim. He chose, in his steady way, not to show it, but I could sense the animation in him. He had, after all, the most to gain. He had known, as we had not, what five years under an oppressor's heel were like. And he had a daughter just a few days old who would never know what oppression meant if that crossing succeeded. I chose that moment, with what I admitted to myself to be low cunning, to enter a plea.

"How many more days must we remain here, Wim?" I asked. "We have become very stiff in our legs because we cannot stretch out or move about. I do not think that we could now walk properly."

"I know not for sure how long it must be. But I see it that you are, as you say, very stiff. Also I cannot find who it was that came in to you in the night, and I do not like that. Perhaps I can so arrange that you shall soon move from here."

He looked at the sky to the southward and laughed, quietly but contentedly.

"The guns are most heavy near Emmerich," he said. "Perhaps your army shall cross there, and that is the most near point to us. It is all very good. Very, very good. Now, boys, once more to your bed."

We returned, and sat for hours, talking and listening to the never ending ferocity of the guns. My ear did not become sullied by familiarity, nor my pleasure in the aesthetic tainted. It was, in truth, a din. But to me it seemed a sound more sweet than any melody I had ever heard. I fell asleep lulled by the noisy charm of artillery. I was vaguely aware at one point in the night of the duller crump of exploding bombs, but I slept well, and when I awoke it was daylight.

As usual Geoff was astir before me.

"The RAF were in in the night," he said. "Quite a party. But I don't suppose you heard it. You'd sleep through a bloody earthquake."

The continuous heavy barrage had ceased, but intermittent gunfire and air activity to the south spoke of action. In our immediate vicinity, however, things were very quiet. Traffic moved down the road a couple of hundred yards to our left, and the swish of clogs told of the passing of Dutchmen. But of the clump of the jackboot there was no evidence. The day wore steadily away. We scoffed our modest rations and drank the ersatz coffee. For the first time in six days we enjoyed a sense almost of well-being.

"I believe those merchants from the farm have gone. I haven't heard a Jerry all day," said Cheeseman.

"Yes, poor sods. Kraut version of the moonlight flit."

I wondered idly how the musician and our other erstwhile neighbours would acquit themselves in the battle that was upon us, but the real question lay with the entire Wehrmacht. Was it, as the twitterings of the Allied propaganda machines suggested, near its beam-ends or not? The

Germans had proved remarkably resilient in the past. What price now a long drawn out battle on the banks of the big river? I hoped not. Better to dream of a quick crossing, and of British armour rolling hell-for-leather over this flat plain in a bee-line for Hamburg, Bremen, and the German North Sea Coast.

Evening came.

"Come out, boys, and see the fires!" Wim called, rather less softly than usual as he removed the straw.

The sky to the south was the colour of a blood orange. Predominantly red, it yet held tinges of yellow as the towns along the northernmost strip of the Rhineland burned. Where we stood, the night was dark and filled with the noise of war. Down the nearby road a column of German troops came marching towards the battle. They sang as they went, and through the trees separating us from the nearby farmhouse the strains of "Deutschland über alles" wafted as a noisy counterpoint to the tramp of marching feet.

Geoff Cheeseman noticed the absence of Wim's basket.

"No food for us?" he queried.

"There is not need. The German soldiers did not come to our farm, and we now think that they shall not come. Therefore can you this evening return once more to your haystack."

A roaring shadow flitted between us and the stars as he spoke. In the instant of passing, the shadow emitted light. A fighter flare hung low over the farmhouse, its pinkish white glare illuminating the whole scene suddenly. The nocturnal, prowling aircraft banked a fraction to bring its track more parallel with the road, and then, from low altitude, spewed cannon shells into the night. The German choral effort stopped as abruptly as the light from a snuffed candle. Everything in that moment seemed a combination of harsh stuttering noise and the colour red. In my mind's eye I saw that road strewn with shattered, bleeding bodies. I stood, with my two hands gripping the top of the haypile and my mouth slightly open. Cheeseman, I noticed, was similarly affected. We gaped like two village idiots at the fair. We had lived too long like moles. We were not attuned to this.

Wim's voice cut sharply into our bemused minds.

"Yes, it is all very good and very interesting. But it is not our business. Come! Both follow me and let us quickly go!"

The whole incident had occupied no more than a few seconds. The fighter flare still swung on its parachute a few feet above the earth, and in its light I saw that Wim's eyes were glinting, glaring almost. He had revelled in that moment, and I was glad. It was a British aircraft that had roared over our heads and administered the tonic. Perhaps, when all was said and done, nothing could have been more appropriate.

We cut across the angle between the haypile and the path which led to our farmhouse. In the shadow of the trees which flanked our way we forged a gradual path homewards. It would be untrue to say that we walked. Cheeseman and I, because our legs were so stiff, lurched like a couple of drunks homeward bound in the small hours.

"That aircraft was a Mosquito," whispered Geoff. "A good old marauding Mozzy. I just caught her shape for a moment against the sky. It's the first feeling of home I've had in a hell of a time."

I knew exactly what he meant.

We came across the yard once again, disturbed the sheep in their fold, and waited for a moment while Wim pushed open the trapdoor. We had anticipated darkness, but instead a shaft of subdued light greeted us. As we scrambled inside, the source of light was apparent. On the staging at the far end of the haystack stood a hurricane lamp radiating its welcoming beams. On the floor lay fresh hay on which to lie, fresh water filled the ablution bucket, and the latrine bucket was empty. The dark drape hung down as ever, providing the backdrop. We were back in the billet.

"Well, thank God for that!" said Cheeseman. "We're home and dry."

14

Revelations

Wim caught Geoff's idiom perfectly, and regarded us quizzically.

"Yes, you are, as you say, once again home, boys. Sometimes I have thought that you did not like it here. What now do you think?"

We looked at the clean hay, the blankets, and the hurricane lamp shedding its friendly rays. It seemed luxurious.

"Marvellous to be back, Wim," I replied. "If we can't have the Grand Hotel we'll settle for this."

He was obviously pleased at our reaction, but the mask of the sergeant-major was immediately donned.

"I shall now go and bring food from the farm," he said. "But you are still RAF men are you not?"

"Of course."

"Look in that mirror and you shall see men with much hair and dirt on their faces. Water and soap are there, boys. I think that you should wash and shave yourselves."

He was right. We were, in fact, filthy. The haypile we had occupied for six days had undoubtedly been used as a bolt-hole for years. The hay which covered the floor was dirt encrusted, and we had gradually transferred the grime to our faces and hands until both were as black as the proverbial grate. A chance to swill the offending muck off appealed to me; the prospect of chopping off at least ten days' stubble did not.

"Have you got scissors in the farm, Wim?" I asked.

"Oh yes."

"Then bring a pair back with you and I'll have a shot at trimming my beard."

We cleaned ourselves up and ate the food Wim brought. He regarded us approvingly.

"So, that is better. I must now go back to my wife. She is on the moment not too well, you understand."

The night was still young. In fact, when we had finished our barbering, it was still a little short of nine o'clock. Our spirits were high, for things seemed at last to be going our way, and the shaving job passed relatively easily.

"I can never quite place old Wim," said Geoff, in the last moments before sleep descended. "He's quite the disciplinarian, really. He makes us shave, he insists on the drill with the entrance door, and if he says he'll come at eight o'clock, he means exactly that. I wonder what he does in civvy street?"

"Haven't a clue. You know the rule. Ask no questions and you can't spill the beans. Perhaps he'll tell us when he comes in the morning. In the meantime, let's have the light out. I'm tired."

Though morning duly came, the dependable Wim did not. It was pitch dark when I awoke, and I was vaguely aware that someone was fumbling about behind my head.

"What the hell are you doing, Cheeseman?" I snapped. "Go back to sleep! It's the middle of the night."

"I doubt that. I've been awake for ages. This is the haystack we're in. Remember? You don't get any light here until you make it. I was searching for your matches."

The penny dropped. It could, of course, be any time of day here. I retrieved the matches. It was, in point of fact, ten o'clock.

"A pretty kettle of fish," I said. "Where the devil's Wim?"

"I don't know, and I don't like it."

"He might have come, and failed to wake us."

"Not a chance. I've been awake for hours."

The probable truth lay there. Geoff, I had noticed, did not enjoy my halcyon capacity to spirit myself away from harsh reality in the gentle bosom of sleep. When I slept it was a minor death; he tended, almost always, to sleep lightly. It was most unlikely that Wim, if he had knocked early, had failed to waken him.

The morning ground slowly away, and with it went our new found high spirits. By mid afternoon we were hungry and well aware that something was wrong. We had, it was true, a roof over our heads, but we had no other means of survival. Worse still was the fact that we had not the slightest notion of what was happening outside. There was no noise to give us a clue. The thirty yards that separated us from the farmhouse seemed to have saved us, but that strength was of no avail without the lifeline of food and drink which Wim provided. We were in a vacuum from which we dared not move until night fell. We put out the oil lamp, in case we needed its light later, and continued to wait in the dark.

It was a nasty, niggling situation, full of doubt and the unknown, and it played a very jagged tune on the nerves. By early evening Geoff had become convinced that the family had been taken by the Germans.

At seven o'clock Cheeseman had had enough. He lit the lamp and began to assemble his gear. I made no move.

"Well? Are you coming?" he demanded. "Or are you going to stay here like a half-baked drip? I'm hungry and thirsty, and I'm not going to starve in here like a rat in a trap. The Dutch have been caught. Come on!"

"No. I shan't move yet."

"But why the hell not?"

"Well, you're so bloody sure the Dutch have been caught, aren't you? Let's suppose you're wrong. What then?"

"It's obvious to me that they must have been caught. But go on. Let's say I'm wrong. Answer your own question!"

"In that case, if you move out you're more stupid than I thought even you were. It would be suicide, not only for you, but for all the family here, including a six day old child."

"How do you make that out?"

"Do you remember why we were farmed out last week in the hay-pile?"

"Because of ten stupid Jerry infantry who never came. What's that got to do with it?"

"This much. They might, for all you flaming well know, have arrived last night after we came back. If so, you'll run straight into their arms and sink the bloody lot of us. Try the logic of that for size!"

An uneasy truce subsisted between us. A lot of mental heat had flown; tempers cooled only slowly. Each of us held that his own theory was the right one. Still, the chips were down. I was the immovable object, and the irresistible force gave me best, for the moment. Until ten o'clock, to be more precise.

We outed the lamp again. Then lost all patience with darkness and relit the wretched thing. The compromise we had arrived at was an uncertain one. It was more a kind of armed neutrality than perfect peace. I was increasingly aware of a dryness in my throat. I felt dehydrated and more than a touch feverish. The hands of my watch seemed to fascinate me, for I checked the time again and again. It was not that the hands moved slowly. They galloped; time flew. As ten o'clock approached and nothing happened, I had reluctantly to admit that Geoff was right. Therefore, the longer we remained here the greater risk we ran. Nevertheless, I refused to budge.

"Ten o'clock yet?" asked Cheeseman.

"Just gone."

"Time to go, then."

"It might be time for you to go. You do just that if you want. I shan't move till I'm ready."

"That'll be next Christmas by the look of things, and you'll be a heap of bones before that. You know the score. If the Germans have got them, then the Gestapo will be busy. How long it will be before somebody talks is anybody's flaming guess. Then there'll be no chance for us. You said you'd go at ten o'clock. What's the matter? Still funking the issue?"

Sarcasm had no effect. Every scrap of logic was now on his side, and I had made a sort of half promise to leave at ten o'clock. But I possessed, for some reason, an overwhelming feeling that I must remain where I was. And against all sense and reason I was going to do just that.

"No, Cheeseman, I'm not turning yellow," I replied. "The risks are obvious. But I have a hunch that to stay here is right, and I'm backing that. I will not budge from this haystack before midnight, and I'll not be in it after one o'clock. If you like to stay, that's up to you."

Cheeseman thought for a moment.

"Your argument is ropey. You're being obstinate and stupid. In fact, as far as obstinate sods go, you take the biscuit. God knows why I should stay, but I will."

A better relationship developed. The die had been cast. It seemed clear that we had to slip quietly out of the haystack and keep well away from the farmhouse. Whatever had happened there, we could in no way help, only incriminate. By morning light we had to find cover and food, and then hide up for the day. As midnight approached I prepared to carry out my part of the bargain. I began to gather my bits and pieces together in readiness for the start. My head swam dizzily. I finished assembling my gear, sank back into the hay wearily, and waited for the time to come for moving off.

Almost on the stroke of midnight the sheep stirred in the pen. At first it was just the jostling of animals when they are disturbed. Seconds later the stealthy sound of a hand feeling its way along the wooden wall came to my keyed-up ears.

"Somebody's moving in that pen, and it's not Wim," I whispered.

"I know. All we can do now is sit tight. If it's Jerry we've had it. There's no chance of chop and run from this place. We just give in."

The fumblings outside continued. I cursed myself for being an idiot. In the last analysis, when all else failed to provide a satisfactory answer, I always backed instinct. That had told me with absolute certainty to stay hidden and make no move. But I was wrong; instinct had deceived. Whoever was out there was still searching for the entrance door. Therefore, it definitely was not Wim. He knew how to find it to the square inch. My obstinacy had sunk not only myself, but Geoff as well.

The scuffling stopped. Suddenly the V sign was rapped very gently on the door.

"That means nothing," whispered Cheeseman. "The Krauts might have found that out in the interrogation."

"Nevertheless, it's the moment of truth. Whoever it is I'm letting them in."

I moved rapidly down the haystack, unbolted the door hastily, and shot back to my place in the hay. I sat bolt upright — as did Geoff — and watched that door defiantly. It opened tantalisingly slowly. We watched it compulsively like a couple of hedgehogs caught in the magnetising glare of a car's headlights on a road at night. The haystack was long; the amount of light shed by the hurricane lamp very little. We looked into an area that was shrouded in shadow. Among the glooms an indistinct figure scrambled on hands and knees through the aperture and slowly rose to its feet. We could not believe our eyes. Coming towards us down the length of the shadowy haystack was a woman. She tripped across the intervening space and stood with serious face above us before I recognised her. She was young, she wore a smart overcoat and she had a basket in her right hand. It was Wim II's girl friend who stood looking down at us. I goggled in sheer surprise; she put her finger to her lips.

"Psst, Duitsers!" she said softly, and proffered her basket of food.

"Thank you very much. Very welcome," said Cheeseman, mechanically.

I realised that I was gaping at her with as much grace as a clodhopper.

"Sorry to stare," I said. "It's just the surprise."

She understood not a word. She smiled and continued to hold out her basket. We took it.

Another figure came scrambling through the gap, and in seconds her fiancé stood by her side. Wim II was the merry, boisterous type as a rule, but tonight he looked grim. He repeated his girl friend's warning, except that he used the word 'Moffen', sourly.

Within minutes they were gone, and we had secured the door behind them. It seemed so unreal that it might never have happened, but for the presence of the food basket.

"Well, well. How about that?" I asked, shaking off the numbing effects of reaction with an effort. "Spread the cloth, Cheesey. Let's begin the midnight feast!"

The visit explained much, but not all. That we had German soldiers on the farm for company was clear, and, that being so, it was not surprising that succour should have been delayed until midnight. But why the girl and Wim II? Where was Wim?

The food and drink worked a minor miracle. The tensions ebbed; relations became cordial. Geoff admitted to the same light-headed feeling that I had suffered. It was, he said, not surprising since we had eaten not more than two or three lumps of cold meat in thirty-six hours. He asked me where my hunch to stay here came from.

"My Irish grandfather, I shouldn't wonder. Celts are a bit fey."

Our course of action was transparently clear: it meant further inaction. We had now to be particularly quiet. Our rations would last for twenty-four hours.

The night passed, and so, inevitably, did the ensuing day. Nothing of consequence happened, other than an increase in the noise of battle Rhinewards. And that was a help. Sound was always preferable to utter silence. The problem of the missing Wim worried us, but there was nothing we could do about it. It simply remained a problem. By the late evening we were becoming edgy again: at least as much on his account as on our own.

The witching hour seemed, in Holland, to be invariably significant. At or around that hour things happened again in much the same basic fashion as on the previous night. The sheep jostled once more in the pen, the signal sounded rhythmically and softly on the door, in moments Wim was scrambling his way inside. We breathed a sigh of relief.

"Very nice to see you, Wim. Are you all right?" Geoff asked, concernedly.

"Yes, I am well. But all is very difficult on the moment."

He looked tired to the point of exhaustion, but nevertheless, one of us was bound to ask the question.

"What the hell's wrong, Wim? How many German soldiers?" I queried.

"Four horse soldiers."

"Four what?"

"Horse soldiers. They and their horses are in the new barn asleep at this moment. Have you not heard them when first they came?"

"No. Not so much as a bloody sound."

We seemed to be enjoying the luck of the devil. On the night we returned Wim had scarcely re-entered the farm's back door when four German cavalry drew rein at the front, demanding a billet and food for their horses. There had been no chance at all to let us know what was happening. The family had just trusted to luck that we should remain lying doggo. As to my hunch to do so, Wim's laconic opinion was that the feeling was a lucky one to have had. We concurred.

"Why the girl and Wim II last night, then?" Geoff asked.

"I was with my wife. All was not well with her at that time. Therefore it was decided that Trui and Wim should come to you with the food."

"Trui?"

"Ah! I should not have said that. It is a mistake I have made. Please forget the name."

"We'll do our best."

He went, leaving us rations for a further twenty-four hours, some oil for the lamp and, as always, the admonition to be careful. The Germans, he said, had been very quiet since they came, spent the day wandering about the farm and the night in sleep. They had not taken their horses out since they arrived. I wondered about those Germans. They seemed too docile to be true.

"Another twist in the saga, Geoff," I said, as I dropped off to sleep. "The Four Horsemen of the Apocalypse are here. We're due for some revelations. We've had one already."

The four cavalry remained on the farm for a total of four days. In the early evening of Wednesday of that fateful week they left. They and their steeds had occupied the new barn seemingly as quietly as we had occupied the haystack. We heard nothing of them from start to finish — not even when they galloped away. Their coming and their going was a mystery. It seemed almighty strange.

Around tea-time of that day Wim made his presence known upon the entrance door. We admitted him with some surprise, for we had at that time no clue about the change in the status quo. He was in benign, expansive mood, and began at once to talk with a levity and freedom I had never known in him before. To everything there is a season. It was the time for a modest letting down of hair.

"Boys," said Wim, " I have most good news. The Germans are now gone and your British army is come away from the Rhine. They fight now in Isselburg and near Bocholt. Also is it true that they move towards the Dutch frontier at Dinxperlo and south from Aalten, where I was born and have for long lived."

Inquisitiveness, after a long suppression, rose.

"Aalten is a town," said Geoff. "Aren't you a farming type, then?"

"Oh no, I am not a farmer. What work do you think I do?"

He had come to entertain and we were keen enough to listen. We were, I felt sure, about to get all the gen. It was only a matter of asking the right questions. We proffered half a dozen answers to his poser, each of which missed the mark.

"Well, then, I will tell you. I am a policeman. I was once the policeman in the small town of Neede, some kilometres from here north. Then had I and my wife to 'dive' from the Germans. Shall I tell you of that?"

The story unfolded. He described his life of duplicity as he worked ostensibly for the Germans and in secret for his own country. He was not infrequently ordered to fetch in persons suspected of Underground allegiance for questioning. His method of preserving them was simple and yet clever. The moment he received his instructions, he would, by hook or by crook, pass them on to his wife. She would immediately cycle down to the suspect's house and give warning. Thus, when Wim arrived, the bird had always flown.

In his role of policeman he had access to documents which affected the lives of people in the area. When it was desirable and safe to do so he stole them; otherwise, he committed their contents to memory. His work took him to town-halls, burgomasters' offices and German command posts in Neede, the town of Lochem, and other administrative centres in that part. Always he kept a close watch for relevant documents and made careful mental note of the interior lay-out of buildings and the positions of safes. His sketches provided detailed information for the safe-blowers of the Movement; his stolen documents provided practice for the forgers.

An actively defecting, intelligent policeman was an invaluable asset to his accomplices. He could openly go where others could not; he was able — given Wim's undoubted abilities — to provide a flow of detailed information, which profited all but his supposed masters, the Germans. Such a life could not, however, last for ever. Suspicion fell upon the policeman who never brought in a suspect. A year or more previously he had realised the fact in time, and disappeared with his wife into the web that was the Underground. In due course they had returned covertly to the farm and had lived here ever since.

There was a pause. Wim thought for a moment, and then ploughed on.

"With Johan and Wim was it different," he said. "They had once very quickly to hide."

"With whom?"

Wim smiled.

"Yes, I give names now. Johan is the eldest brother of my wife. He and Wim once had a very bad argument with the Dutch Nazis."

The fall from grace of the two brothers had been very swift and highly dramatic.

They had for long worked openly for their father on the farm by day and covertly for the Underground by night without exciting suspicion. Suddenly, however, an unforseen event had forced them to disappear. The 'razzias' of the Dutch Nazis were always thorough and unheralded, and in one of them Baby, the youngest Underground member in the district, had been caught. It was known that the prisoners were being held temporarily at Aalten station awaiting the train that would transport them to a German concentration camp. That short period of time was fateful, for once on that train the lad would probably never be seen again, or, if he did return, it would be only as a maltreated, shattered wreck. Johan and Wim had no intention of letting that happen, for Baby was, in fact, their cousin.

There was a rough-house of the first order outside the station. Two of the armed Nazi guards were left senseless and bleeding in the gutter, others damaged. Baby was snatched from the jaws of Dachau in the very nick of time.

They did not return to the farm. The brothers knew well enough that they had been seen and recognised, so they and Baby vanished for a season into the blue. The farmhouse was, of course, quickly raided and turned inside out. Naturally, though, nothing of an incriminating nature was found.

When the shouting and the searching were over and things had quietened down, Johan and Wim II returned in secret to the farm. The affray had happened at much the same time as Wim and his wife had been forced to run to ground. The three men had spent the summer and autumn of 1944 constructing and improving hiding-places inside the farm and out. Wim now admitted to five such: three within the farmhouse and two outside.

It was a peculiar fact, as Leo had once said, that the normal German was so sure of himself once he had searched, that, provided you did not give him cause, he never bothered again. At all events, after its thorough searching, the farmhouse was left untouched.

Many things became apparent as Wim talked. Sien, his wife, had had, not surprisingly, a very bad time of it, but both she and his daughter Hannie were now doing well. Hanna, Johan's fiancée, had been the one who brought news of the hanging of the six German soldiers, for the event had occurred in the farm next to where she lived. She had rightly thought that there would be reprisals, and had cycled fast to warn the family here of impending trouble. Fortunately for them and for us the trouble had been elsewhere.

He ended his tale on a note of quiet and determined courage.

Trui had told them that when she brought us food on the Sunday midnight, her opinion was that we looked very tired. In that opinion she was absolutely right, for the lack of food, the period of doubt, and the dashing of our hopes when the worst seemed over had brought Geoff and I pretty close to despair. The problem for three successive nights had been to get our basket of food across the yard undetected under the very noses of the German cavalry. That depended entirely upon their being asleep.

"So," said Wim. "Each night late went Trui to the barn to see if they slept, for only she could so do, and she was most earnest that you should have something to eat."

"And if they had not been asleep?" I asked.

"She is a young girl. She has played, what I think is said, the part of the beautiful spy. She was not quite alone, though, for Wim stood always in the shadows."

"Armed by any chance?"

"Oh yes, he had a gun."

That concluded the revelations, but as he turned to leave Wim made one final observation.

"Much have I told you, but now I must go. Possible is it that a Dutchman can also have what you call a feeling. I feel it most strong that in one week we shall all be free men."

When he had gone, we felt a surge of real, clearly defined hope. An early release stared us in the face. He was a conservative by nature. If he said the British would be here in a week, it would probably be less. It had been pleasant to be let into a few secrets; pleasanter still was the prospect of freedom.

"Spare a thought, Cheesey," I said. "In a fortnight you could be taking a gentle saunter with some popsie or other through the hopyards of Kent."

"Wizard idea, mate. But fancy old Wim being a policeman. I should never have guessed it."

Neither, even remotely, would I. Though it did perhaps explain the disciplinary part of his approach. He had just admitted to being a defecting policeman, but nothing, in reality, could have been further from the truth. Rarely had I known a man so loyal and dependable, nor, in many ways, one so assiduous. Although by force of habit we spoke aircrew lingo to him half of the time, his English had in less than two months improved out of recognition. I particularly liked his reference to Trui, the beautiful spy. Quite the Mata Hari touch, I thought.

Sleep did not come easily to me that night. I found my mind preoccupied with thought. A series of recent experiences trooped in silent procession through consciousness and kept me awake. I had not, to the best of my knowledge, even so much as met one Dutch person until a few weeks ago. But in the interim I had met many, and I knew by instinct that the acquaintanceship would not be short. Things had gone a little too deeply for that. Those who spoke English maintained that they owed us much. I could not see that at all, for to me the boot was absolutely on the other foot.

Perhaps it was all summed up in the bravery of the Dutch girl who for three nights had resolutely gone across that dark and gloomy farmyard, prepared to vamp her way along with four Germans in order that we might be fed. That touched a particular apex of sensation in me and, in a mysterious way, brought me back to reality. I felt I had much to repay.

I found a flicker of feeling steal into my mind and stay there. During the sightless, seemingly hopeless days, there had been no spark of emotion in me. Home was unattainable, therefore — perhaps it was a subconscious defence — I never thought clearly of it, and had no sentiment for it. I simply soldiered on. Feeling now revived. I saw quite clearly the girl to whom I had become engaged two weeks before the crash. I found it beyond belief that I had been away for little more than two months. It felt like at least two years.

One other memory riveted my attention. There had once been a bomber crew stooging quietly homewards in a Lancaster after a raid on a canal. Of its scattered members I was sanguine about the fate of all but one. That we had heard nothing of Copley and Young was hardly surprising. The Underground here did not play it that way. Chuck and Johnny, the two Australians, might be anywhere, but I was sure they were safe. It was upon Norman Levick that my attention centred. Over the intercom that night had come that unmistakable, drawn-out groan of pain which now rang in my ears. Everything to do with Norman remained an enigma, and the undertones were ominous.

In a moment I was back in that billet at RAF Swinderby on a Sunday morning in late October when the billet was empty except for Levick and myself. It was a few days after a defective Stirling had almost been the end of Chuck Fowler and his crew.

The Stirling bomber had had a short and inglorious operational career. Quickly it had been relegated to secondary roles, such as the conversion course at Swinderby, where a large proportion of No 5 Group aircrew accustomed themselves to really heavy aircraft. Inevitably the drudgery of continual circuits and bumps mixed with long navigational exercises told. The aircraft here were in a very anaemic state; the aircrew almost equally so at the thought of flying the wretched things. The aircrew, particularly the pilots, had much of a blasphemous nature to say on the subject, but accepted the fact that there was a war on and that every available Lancaster was needed in the front line.

Returning one night over the English Channel, we found our way to the north-west baulked by a towering mass of cumulo-nimbus cloud. Chuck Fowler tried to climb above it, but the Stirling was an old tub more fit for the knacker's yard than for flying. All it gave him was a niggardly 16,000 feet, which was not much more than half enough. We spiralled downwards and tried to creep under the cloud. That was no use. Its base was too low.

"No joy at all here, mates," said Chuck, scrubbing the exercise we were on. "Let's stop dicing and go home!"

I gave him a course, we left the thunder cloud to dice and swirl about by itself, sailed serenely up the middle of England and arrived over base within the hour.

"Red-perch, D-dog to Control. May I pancake?" sang out Fowler.

"OK D-dog. Pancake!" Control replied.

Round the circuit in fine fettle went Chuck. Everything seemed right. In the funnels, I began to call out the airspeeds; he began to throttle back. Suddenly the aircraft slipped violently away to port with all the venom of a mean mustang.

"Christ!" said the pilot, opening up his throttles and roaring away. "We nearly took the flipping control tower with us that time."

"Try again, mate," said the navigator hopefully, when he'd detached himself from the aircraft's roof.

This went on. Round the circuit we repeatedly went, but every time he began to close his motors for the final approach that diabolical Stirling slipped violently and uncontrollably to port. Then fog began to creep across the airfield. The equation was impossible. Chuck gave up trying to solve it.

"I'm sorry chaps, but I cannot land this aircraft," he said, flatly but decisively. "Get your parachutes in readiness!"

"Go to Fulbeck, and try again!" ordered Control immediately.

The Operational Controller there listened as Fowler explained the predicament. There was a moment's pause, and then he presented us with an idea which made the equation not quite impossible.

His opinion was that the only chance we had of landing was to fly in long and low with the engines full on.

"Take her well down wind, stooge around for five minutes, and I'll have the end of the runway marked," he said.

Chuck observed that five minutes was stretching it, for we had by now a maximum of fifteen minutes fuel left.

We stooged.

Abruptly the marker glittered redly in the night.

"Now, take it steady old chap and fly at that," came the Controller's voice encouragingly. "The field's all yours, but if you can't make it take her straight up to 2,000 feet, point her out to sea and bale out!"

Fowler's interpretation of long and low was a height of one hundred feet from six miles back. I put the thought of what would happen if this lousy aircraft sideslipped again out of my mind and called airspeeds; Levick, in the rear turret, complained of the tops of tall trees and church steeples flashing past him; Chuck flew straight at the red marker.

We landed at 155mph — 60mph above the odds. Mercifully the tyres held. Fowler rammed the nose down, cut the motors dead and braked as hard as he dared. The kite's natural desire to take off again was obviated. We pulled up, after a series of see-sawing pitches, at the runway's end with just the odd gallon or two of petrol left in the tanks.

We spent a few minutes in the control tower drinking hot tea, and then rolled back to Swinderby in a station wagon in the small hours. Chuck, it was agreed, had done a great job.

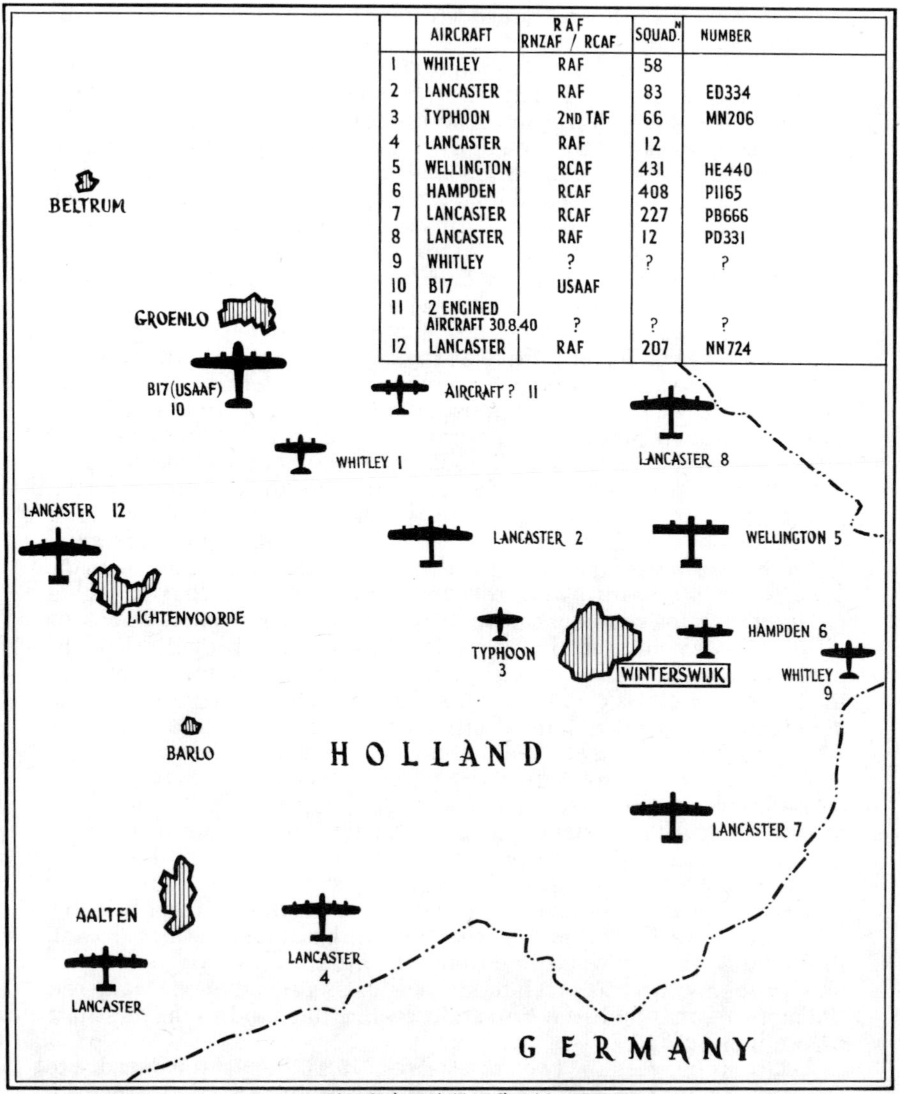

	AIRCRAFT	RAF RNZAF / RCAF	SQUAD.N	NUMBER
1	WHITLEY	RAF	58	
2	LANCASTER	RAF	83	ED334
3	TYPHOON	2ND TAF	66	MN206
4	LANCASTER	RAF	12	
5	WELLINGTON	RCAF	431	HE440
6	HAMPDEN	RCAF	408	P1165
7	LANCASTER	RCAF	227	PB666
8	LANCASTER	RAF	12	PD331
9	WHITLEY	?	?	?
10	B17	USAAF		
11	2 ENGINED AIRCRAFT 30.8.40	?	?	?
12	LANCASTER	RAF	207	NN724

CRASHED AIRCRAFT IN THE ACHTERHOEK

The chart prepared by Mr B. W. C. van Albeslo, of Winterswijk, shows that the five mile radius centring on Winterswijk and largely enclosed by the German border was the scene of many an RAF crash.

The same is true of the whole Achterhoek, for it lay on the route frequently used to the Ruhr Valley — the northernmost towns of which are less than thirty miles to the south — and was often crossed on the way to targets in northern Germany.

Many of the aircrew lie in its churchyards: 23 in Lichtenvoorde and 33 in Winterswijk to the author's knowledge.

That same afternoon a friend of mine asked me if I would go with him to fetch another of those damned Stirlings back from RAF Winthorpe where it had landed.

I was not in the least in the mood for flying, and the word Stirling was anathema to me at that moment. But, being Bob, I went. We rolled over to neighbouring Winthorpe in yet another station wagon, picked up the aircraft and flew it gently back to its home. Throughout the succeeding week Fowler's ensemble did a few odds and ends of trips to complete their course, and on Saturday night we saw Bob and his crew off on their final effort. Then we had a few drinks and went to bed.

I had known this particular pilot for several months, and in that time we had become extremely close friends. Not entirely by accident, Norman Levick and I shared a billet with him and most of his crew. Bob and I possessed a common and incurable tendency to argue and philosophise. The technicalities of the bomber game apart, we spent many a slack hour debating the morals of the offensive in which we would soon be engaged. We supposed that there would come a day when some wiseacre or other, talking from the comfort of his study and at a safe distance of years, would look back upon the whole thing as murderous, which indeed, to a degree, it was. But the question, we said, lay with the alternative. What other way than blasting the cities had been open — given the technical limitations of night bombing until recently — for the crushing of the monstrosity that was the Third Reich? If, in the process, civilian heads had to roll, they had to roll, and that was that.

We argued, of course, academically, for it was only later, when one of us actually became involved in the business proper, that the practicalities of a many-sided truth became clear. Such, for example, as the fact that with flak up your tail and night fighters harrying, you did not concern yourself with the civilians below, or even think about them. The human mind being as finite as it is, the immediate battle in the sky was enough to absorb the energies of any normal man. This we did not really know, but we had a very fair idea of the general score, were prepared to take our chances, and unprepared to slide out from under any of the ethical blame. At all events, we debated quite a lot.

We were strictly non-establishment types who eschewed 'bull' like the plague, had a predisposition to be late for everything except briefing, and were invariably the last two in for breakfast. Which meant, incidentally, that by wheedling round the mess staff, we started the day with probably twice as much food inside us as anybody else. Many was the morning that had seen Bob and I cycling like mad to the mess just before it closed.

Relations between the two crews were cordial. In part this was due to the fact that they had a very thin Australian wireless operator nicknamed Spider who was the most off-beat character any of us had ever met. He had, among his eccentricities, an aversion to English pennies and, when he awoke, he would fumble in the pocket of the tunic which hung beside his bed, and hurl every offending penny he could find to the furthest ends of the billet, cursing in a peculiar, quiet, dirging sort of way as he did so. On occasions there was a minor fortune in coppers to be found about the floor.

We had located a pub in the village of Norton Disney which suited our tastes. It had a large, barn-like room, in which the lighting was afforded by guttering candles stuck in the necks of bottles, and it possessed a piano. Chuck would troll out his small but adequate repertoire; anything up to the full complement of the two crews would bawl out songs until their throats were dry and in need of further lubrication. There was a glorious haze of alcohol fumes and tobacco smoke. "September in the Rain" was invariably our penultimate piece. And then, inevitably, would come "The Maori's Farewell".

"Now is the hour when we must say goodbye," we would carol out. And, no doubt, the locals were glad of it. It was a great life.

My friend had an easy-going sort of nature. He often found it necessary to look after Spider like a mother, for the thin wireless operator's sleeping capacity was phenomenal. When even we had eventually arrived back in the billet after breakfast, we should still find him fast asleep. If there was a flap on Bob would haul him to his feet and set him going; if not, his view was laconic. "I think I'll leave Spider to sleep it off. What the hell?" he would casually say.

Bob was a tall, rather drawly Australian, likeable in the extreme and endowed with a certain quiet charisma. It was this, I supposed, that had brought about his love affair with a girl he had met at a dance in London. Knowing him, I thought it unlikely that it was a flirtation on either side. But she came from the very top end of the English social scale, and the fact worried him.

An autumnal sun glittering brightly through the billet windows woke me that Sunday morning. Not a bad day, I thought, for going on leave. I was vaguely aware that Norman Levick, who slept in the next bed to mine, was sitting up.

"Are you awake, Stan?" he queried, quietly.

"Yes," I muttered, ungenerously.

"Then I have some bad news for you."

"Give over, Levick. Leave's not cancelled, surely."

"Worse than that. Just sit up and look around."

I did so. I expected to see the billet filled with sleeping forms after their night flight. But there were none. Neither were there any kit bags, suitcases, or other aircrew impedimenta to be seen. Blankets, sheets, everything but the bedsteads and the three 'biscuits' which formed the mattresses were gone. There was not a human soul other than Norman and I in that woebegone billet.

"You wouldn't know this, for you slept like a log," Norman continued. "But the SPs were in in the night. They took all their gear away."

"God above! You don't mean . . ."

"I'm afraid I do. Bob's dead. He and all his crew. They crashed in the night."

Levick and I could not face breakfast. Instead we trooped off glumly to the control tower to see if the service police had exaggerated. They had not. A very upset WAAF, just finishing her spell of duty, told us the score.

Two hours after take-off, Bob had reappeared on the circuit with his port inner engine out of action, asking for an emergency landing. Permission had at once been given, but in the instant of acknowledging it his voice had been interrupted by an agitated shout. "The port outer's going as well, skip'," was all the voice had said. He was a good pilot, but his engineer's warning was not enough. The loss of all power on his port wing had beaten him. One of those clapped-out Stirlings — they were replaced by Lancasters a month later — had got him. He lost her. The rest was silence.

When I left the billet for the last time I could not get those lines of a minor poet out of my head:

They told me, Heraclitus, they told me you were dead,
They brought me bitter news to hear and bitter tears to shed.
I wept as I remembered how often you and I
Had tired the sun with talking, and sent him down the sky.

It was an epitaph that might almost have been written for an Australian who had left his native land to come to the other side of the earth and fight in a cause he believed in, and who, his lengthy training almost finished, had died early that morning without striking a single blow.

My friendship with Norman Levick had been of a different order, but no less deep. We were easily the most sports-addicted members of the crew and, apart from our daily badminton sessions, we had rarely missed a game of cricket or soccer when there had been one going.

His practical bent had solved many a problem for me. My mechanical abilities were so poor that the technicalities of the wheelbarrow foxed me. Therefore, when my bike broke down, or any practical job arose, Norman either fixed it or told me how to.

There were, it was true, marked differences in outlook. His view of life tended to be down to earth and realistic, while mine frequently dribbled into the obscure and romantic. He liked beer, but stuck adamantly to a couple of pints when the rest of us drank three or four times that amount. There was one occasion when, after a binge the night before, I had such a hangover that I could not see straight enough to pack my kit the following morning for an unexpected posting. Good-naturedly he had even done that.

This was the point. He was good-tempered to a fault, level-headed and sensible, when I was frequently none of those things. Sometimes I wondered how on earth he put up with me. Possibly the final catalyst was stubbornness. It was perhaps no great virtue, but we both possessed more than a fair share of that.

Bob and all his crew were dead. A detail of men had pulled their bodies either from the upturned, shattered aircraft or from the waters of the Lincolnshire dyke three miles from the airfield into which it had finally crashed. Norman's fate was less certain. And yet that damned groan among the babble of voices on the intercom still rang in my ears. All I could do was hope for the best. It had been a revealing week. I, for my part, had to admit that I was at heart a sentimentalist. I knew one thing. I wanted like hell not to be the sole survivor of that RAF billet.

The time for remembering passed. The storm burst with unexpected speed.

On Thursday evening March 29th, Wim was in, giving us warning of impending battle. Things, he implied, were shortly about to happen.

On the next day they did. He arrived early on that particular morning. It chanced that it was Good Friday. But there was the devil in his eyes and warfare crashing noisily through the haystack wall.

"Eat breakfast quickly, boys, and then come please with me. You can help us!" he said.

15

The Awakening

We ate, and then followed him. Across the yard and into the cattle-byre we went. Unjustifiably we had supposed, and often said, that nothing more about this place could surprise us. How wrong could you get? The scene that confronted us shook us rigid. The byre was full of Dutchmen — each with an orange armband on the sleeve of his coat — and the pace was hectic. They were zealously pulling a great mound of hay to one side, and, as we watched, stout wooden crates emerged into the light of day. The crates were forced open. Lee-Enfield rifles, Sten guns, ammunition boxes, hand grenades, with, as a pièce de résistance, two Bren-guns, were laid carefully across the floor in rows.

"Hells bells, Wim, you crafty devil," I said. "You told us a few days ago that you were armed. But I never thought you owned a bloody arsenal. There's enough stuff here to equip a platoon of infantry handsomely."

Wim smiled his most enigmatic smile and did not reply directly.

"It is perhaps now humour, that the German horse-soldiers came at first into this cows-house, and would stay here. They began to pull the hay from over the weapons to feed their horses. Lucky is it that my wife's father is an intelligent man. He told them that it was poor hay and that he could give better. So were they led to the new barn."

There were not many men I would have judged cool enough and sufficiently quick-witted to have got away with that one. But our stoical farmer was just the man to have done it.

"But where the hell did all this stuff come from?" asked Geoff.

"From your RAF."

"You mean that Leo's arms-drop was made and we knew nothing about it?"

"No. I mean that not. Never has that 'drop' come, because it was thought that the place of dropping was too near a road. While the Underground looked to find a new place, the British have crossed the Rhine. These weapons were dropped in the last September."

"Near the farm?"

"Some kilometres away was it. Johan has brought them here in the farm cart. He is what you call a crack-shot and shall have one of the Bren-guns. It is with those that we are not sure how to fix them."

There was a cleaning, loading and assembling job to be done. We set about it. Upwards of a dozen Dutchmen and two Englishmen worked with a will. I was no great hand at the game, but at least I knew how to clean and load a rifle; Cheeseman, as a gunner, was in his element and worked away on the Brens. The Dutchmen were by no means strangers to the work. The arms were rapidly put into working order, and, as each man had his allotted piece of equipment made available, he trooped out across the fields to wherever the rendezvous-point was. There was a great coming and going. Other men arrived, brought information, grabbed a rifle or Sten, and went. The air was replete with rapidly spoken Dutch, with just an occasional English curse — when something went wrong — as a counterpoint. The farm had awoken. The indistinct vision I had once had was realised in fact. I had long felt it, but had never had the faintest clue what form it would take. The substance of the dream came as a complete shock.

By mid-morning all was complete, the last man departed. The loud murmur of the conflict to the south had become less general. Mere rumble and roar had been sharpened by the distinguishable and more immediate crack of mortars. Things were approaching a climax.

"What do you want us to do now, Wim?" asked a sweating Cheeseman.

"I want that you shall go once more to your haystack, and there remain until all is over."

"Aren't you going out with the other men?"

"No. Neither shall you. The haystack is your home, and to it must you go."

As we meandered back to base, a German scout car beetled smartly northwards along the sandroad a hundred yards away.

"The Germans retreat," said Wim. "Very good for the eyes to see, is it not so?"

I observed, as we passed through the sheep-fold, that the sheep were missing. While we had worked in the armoury, the farmer had removed his livestock to a place of safety in the farm buildings. Fifteen scared and marauding sheep trapped in a pen might well, in a very non-comical sense, have brought the house down. Whatever was coming we were to ride it out alone. Our neighbours, the sheep, were gone.

We entered the haystack, bolted the door by habit and awaited events.

"Tell you what," said Geoff. "We've never had a look behind this ruddy great curtain at the back of the staging. Let's see what's hidden there. One thing for sure. It's not guns."

We had, properly we thought, never breached the privacy of the small area behind the drape. But now that the chances of forcedly giving away a carefully hidden secret seemed remote, curiosity should be satisfied at the eleventh hour.

We looked. The result of our prying only proved one thing: that the Dutch are the industrious and thrifty Dutch. They had not wasted the space that the haystack offered. Behind the curtain, on the shelves of a second, much taller staging than the one on which the light stood, rested jar upon jar of preserves and jam.

"Would you bloody credit it?" I asked. "To think we nearly flaked out the other day for lack of grub, and all the time this lot was here."

"At least we'll have a few jam jars between us and the blast when the storm breaks."

It was early afternoon before the show came. It had been a noisy morning, but around midday things had quietened. A hiatus seemed to have set in. Then the quiet before the storm snapped and all hell broke loose. Out of the comparative silence there came a sound resembling a swarm of gigantic, irritated wasps. The noise of the low-flying aircraft dinned into the haystack deafeningly. They buzzed straight at us. Almost abreast of us their sting was released. A stream of cannon shells and machine-gun bullets ploughed into the fields outside. And then the fighters were gone, pursuing their prey northwards.

"Christ!" hollered Cheeseman. "Too close for comfort. If that's going to be the form, let's have the door unbolted."

That made sense. A three-foot thick shell of dry hay constituted a splendid hiding-place. But it would stop nothing of consequence in the way of flying metal, and, if that metal was in an incendiary state when it struck, the haystack would flare like a torch. Of the various fears that plagued the aircrew mind in unguarded moments, the worst, in nine cases out of ten, was the thought of being trapped in a crashed aircraft and burned alive. Incineration here was no more pleasant an idea. The ritual with the door was foregone. The escape-hatch was unbolted.

The first wave of fighters was merely the hors d'oeuvre. Singly, but mainly in flights, they swooped on the area, spewing metal in concentrated streams. The noise, in spite of the muffling effect of the hay walls, was ear-shattering. We threw ourselves flat on our stomachs and kept our heads down. The solid beams to either side of us afforded the only tangible protection, and in those beams we had to trust. The weather we knew to be ideal for the purpose, and 2nd TAF were obviously intent upon a birthday. On and on came the fighters. The zip, zip, zip of rockets as they left their parent Typhoons mingled with the cannon of the Spitfires and Tempests. The whole was a peculiarly frightening, exhausting form of bedlam.

When a pause at length occurred, Geoff propped himself up on his elbows and gave vent to a thought.

"I can't understand it," he said. "All those fighters are coming from the south and strafing as they come. There's not a single Jerry fighter up. 2nd TAF have got the sky to themselves."

There was no doubt of it. We could not see a thing, but the pattern was clear enough. Those fighters had all come persisently, almost arrogantly, at low level from that one direction. There had been none of the whining, snarling changes of engine note that would have occurred in dogfighting as pilots climbed and dived for purposes of position and evasion. The firing had all been strictly air to ground. They were unopposed. It was puzzling.

We had heard rockets zipping close by, and that argued that the Germans were withdrawing armour along the sandroad a hundred yards away and, at least in part, eschewing the main Aalten to Lichtenvoorde road. It sounded as if the German front in our region had broken and that, therefore, the flood-gates to Hamburg and the North German Plain were opening wide. 2nd TAF were masters of the sky above us, and that was not utterly surprising. But that the Wehrmacht in its moment of dire distress should entirely lack for air cover was almost incredible. The Luftwaffe was absent. It was Dunkirk in reverse.

The pause was not of long duration. The tumultuous roar of powerful aircraft engines at full bore, the crash of cannon fire and the petrifying zip of rockets resumed violently and unabatedly. A new factor in the form of the fragmentation bomb began to crack down on the fields around us. There was a spattering of expended bomb fragments on the outside walls of the barn that surrounded us. The high point came when something whizzed through one wall of the haystack itself and out of another. But that was above our heads, and it caused neither damage nor fire. The indisputable point was that Jerry was on the run, and that his air force was useless to him because, at least at the moment, it was non-existent.

Strafing was about the most demoralising business I knew. A little over two years previously I had been caught up in an incident at the Initial Training Wing at Paignton, where a couple of Focke-Wulf 190s had suddenly scudded over the wavetops and raked the front with cannon. Our flight of cadets on the march had broken and dived for the shelter of a bramble patch behind the wall of the Hydro Hotel. No-one had been hurt, but the feeling remained. Brief though it was, the adjacency and noise of the aircraft and the sense that a carpet of hot lead was sweeping inexorably towards one was not funny. I had a marked antipathy toward strafing.

The tumult outside went on. A miscellany of German infantry ran across the flat fields; German armour hastened northwards along the sandroad to Lichtenvoorde. The whole mass was being driven before a proximate, mobile, airborne artillery, like corn before a thresher's flail. But the flail was an instrument of exploding, splintering metal, and the thresher was an RAF pilot with his tail up. I could almost have found it in my heart to feel pity for those poor devils who ran by; had I not, at that moment, felt distinctly more sympathy for two other poor sods who lay prone on their bellies in the hay and hoped that the RAF, of all people, would not provide them with their proverbial 'packet' by default.

It was not in the nature of things that events could continue at that pace endlessly. A further pause ensued and endured. I felt an irrepressible desire to see what I could of the matter.

"I'm going out into the sheep-pen to see the score," I said.

"You're crazy. There's Germans all around."

"Not crazy. Just curious."

"Curiosity killed the cat."

There was truth in what he implied. The Germans who were around would be angry, strafed Germans, on the run and in no mood for asking questions. Nevertheless, it seemed a momentous point in time. Jerry was about to be thrown out of Holland on his neck and remorselessly thrust into his own backyard. I was damned if I would not have a five minute peer at the process.

I stole quietly into the sheep-fold. The door to the yard was closed, and relatively speaking, silence prevailed. For the second time in all those long seven weeks I pressed my eye to the widest crack in the rough boarding and surveyed the long green field that ended in a copse. It was upon the copse that my eye rested. Drawn up amongst the trees was a group of the Wehrmacht at something approaching company strength. They did not stand, as soldiers are supposed to do, but, with one exception, they sat. They were in full marching order, their packs upon their backs, their uniforms merging to a degree with the winter grey of the trees against which they rested. Not a few of their heads seemed bowed forward listlessly. From my viewing point, almost two hundred yards away, I would have said that they looked shattered, that their morale was low. One figure alone, possibly their officer or NCO, seemed to scorn the chance of rest. He stood with his back against a tree and looked down the field with apparent equanimity. I mentally doffed my cap.

That scene was one of inactivity and exhaustion, and not, to my mind, in any way remarkable. But to the left of the copse, and half as far away, I was aware of animation and movement. The view that met my eye as it traversed on to the sandroad caused the eyebrow above it to lift in surprise. I was late-war aircrew, trained to think that men and machines waged war, and that a yeomanry regiment was motorised. Horses in battle were to me as old-hat as battering rams. When Wim had told us of the four German cavalry who had occupied the new barn, I had goggled a touch at the thought. Now, however, the proof of that sort of pudding stared me in the face. A mixed bag of mechanical and horse-drawn vehicles threaded their way frantically northwards. The road was not the escape route of the heavy tank; rather was it the armoured car that plunged along it. But the pace of the car was restricted by the horse-drawn wagon that preceded it. The drivers were standing on the shafts, whipping and cursing at the sweating horses as they strove to get the last ounce out of them. It was like a scene from a Wild West movie. Except that the drivers cursed in German, and what they had to fear was not the odd slug from a rifle or six-shooter, but a spraying with 20mm cannon. I saw perhaps two dozen vehicles go by in a few minutes, and fully half of those were drawn by horses. The observation was merely a vignette, but, to my mind, a fairly conclusive and abundantly satisfying one. There came the sound of aircraft once more approaching from the south. I left horses, armoured cars and soldiers to sort it out for themselves. I retired to the hay.

Battle ensued once more, but it was not to last. A flight or two of RAF fighters sprayed the area with more bullets and cannon shells as a last, almost perfunctory gesture. And then the strafing was over. The tumult faded; the lads in the Tempests and Typhoons departed for a well-earned meal in the mess; for a long time silence reigned supreme in the haystack.

For three hours we had lain prone on our bellies, intermittently holding our breath. Slowly we recovered it.

"Quite a show," said Cheeseman. "Pity we couldn't see it."

I sat in the hay, puffed quietly at my oaken pipe, and thought.

"Well, I did see a bit of it, Cheesey, you clot, and I'll hazard a guess."

"Oh?"

"I think they've had it. The Germans I mean. Persistent pranging of the oil targets has paid off. If they're so short of fuel that they've got horses pulling their transport, and can't put a fighter in the sky at the break-out point, then they've no chance. Hitler and his lousy Third Reich are done for, boy."

"You could be right. It's a known fact they've kept their day and night fighters going all this winter at the expense of everything else. No Luftwaffe, no fuel. No fuel, no nothing."

"They've had their chips, I bet."

The lull after the hubbub was pleasant enough. We just sat talking.

"Well, we're all right, Jack," I said, at length. "But I wonder how the farmhouse went on in that lot? We can hardly afford to push our noses out and have a look though, can we?"

"Not on your Nellie. We sit tight till Wim comes, mate. The farm will be all right."

I hoped so. We sat tight.

The waiting was of short duration. Wim came, tapped his V sign on the door, found that it yielded to his touch, and came in. He remonstrated against the break in tradition.

"Why is it that the door is not properly closed, boys?" he asked.

"Fire risk," we said.

"Well, perhaps that was correct. Yet, is it not, however, safe to come out. Your British soldiers are not here, and some Germans are there still about in the fields and near farms. It is for them that the Underground men look. They will take prisoners. For the moment, therefore, is it wise to be careful."

The high spirits that he really felt asserted themselves. He cocked his head on one side and regarded us quizzically.

"But how is it with you, boys? Have you liked the shooting?"

"Not much, but we're all right now," Cheeseman replied. "Those fighter boys gave us a sticky three hours or so, sod 'em!"

Wim fell silent for a while, and then began almost to muse aloud.

"So that was your RAF, that part that you call 2nd TAF. It was magnificent. The Germans have run all over the fields by the farm, and have hid themselves among trees and in the near of buildings. For long have I seen the German only as a man of power in my country. It is beautiful that he now should be made to run from it. For five years have I waited for such a day."

"Bully for the 2nd Tactical Air Force," I said. "But what of the farmhouse, Wim? Was that hit?"

"No, no damage is done there. Your pilots were most careful, and all is very well."

Because we consisted of two not particularly effusive Englishmen and a very level-headed Dutchman, there was no actual slapping of backs. But we came very near to it. The Anglo-Dutch 'cordiale' bloomed well in the sweet smell of success.

Wim turned to go. He offered a final piece of gen.

"The British are Brenning in Bredevoort," he said, as a Parthian shot.

I liked the unconscious alliteration a lot; but I savoured the implication still more. Bredevoort was a mere three miles away. The aerial scythe had swept through the area and done what it could; it was the turn now of the Armoured Corps. And they were closing in rapidly by the sound of it if Bren-gun carriers were operating so close at hand.

"What now, then?" asked Cheeseman, hopefully.

"Pardon?"

"I mean, what is the next move? What do we do now?"

"You do nothing. There is food in the basket and oil in the lamp. Johan and Wim are out with the Underground men. Therefore is it so that I, because I have a young baby and its mother and two RAF men to look after, am left to guard the farm. So I think it will be most safe that you stop one night more in the haystack with the door locked. Tomorrow shall all be well."

It was vintage Wim. He never bilked at a risk if it was necessary, but the unessential one he abhorred like the plague. That was undoubtedly the way to conduct Underground business.

When he had gone we settled down, we hoped for the last time, to our bread and butter, boiled egg and ersatz coffee. Afterwards we sprawled in the hay, at peace with the world. I smoked; we both talked. The place felt suddenly as comfortable and secure as the 'snug' in The George at Spilsby: except that there was no beer. I cut the forty-eighth notch in the bowl of my pipe and added another for the morrow. It looked as if we should miss our half century by one.

As the night lengthened an artillery duel began. The shells sped their parabolic way over our heads in each direction, whistling as they went. But the explosions, as they hit the earth, seemed a comfortable distance away. The Germans were using a proportion of the so-called 'Moaning Minnie' type of shell which screeched and sobbed its way along its arc. I found myself lying there, detachedly gazing at the roof of the haystack, imagining those symmetrical parabolas and wondering about speed, height and direction.

"Odd, that," observed Cheeseman, late on.

"What is?"

"That Wim should avoid asking us into the farmhouse. I hinted broadly enough I thought, but he didn't bite. Equally strange that we should have to stick out that damned strafing in here. The thought of all this dry hay gave me the willies. They might have asked us in."

"True enough. Sheep went in, we stayed out. Must think us pretty hardened types."

"You never really get to the bottom of this place, do you? Who'd have supposed that the cow-house was an arsenal?"

"Not I, Geoff. Never gave it a thought."

"No. Full of surprises they are. Jam in the haystack, guns in the byre. Anything else do you think?"

"I shouldn't think there can be. We've reached the end of the line now, matey."

"I wonder."

Cheeseman yawned. "I'm tired," he said. "As far as I'm concerned those bloody gunners can keep that up all night. After that flaming strafing this is just peanuts. I'm going to sleep."

I finished the pipe I was smoking, finally put out the light, and fell asleep listening to the whining of the shells.

In the morning I awoke with a start. Someone was banging noisily on the entrance door. My somnolent state did not preclude the realisation that the haystack was in pitch darkness and that Geoff still slept peacefully. I hit him a smart crack in the ribs with my elbow.

"Here, Cheesey," I said, and gave him the matches. "Light that flipping lamp and I'll go and open the shop. That's Wim out there, and he's banging out the V sign full bore. We're free, my boy. And just on this very morning we've overslept."

I fumbled my way down the length of the haystack while Geoff got the light going.

Wim's face, when I admitted him, bore a grin as broad as that of a Cheshire cat.

"Good morning, boys. Have you, then, very well slept?" he asked, in his droll fashion.

"Like a top."

"Ah! I thought that it was so, for I have knocked much. 'RAF sleepers, wake!' I have said as I have knocked. But it was long before my prayer was answered. It is a lovely morning, is it not?"

"Is it?"

"Oh yes. The sun is shining and all Germans are gone. Come with me and have breakfast on the farm!"

Spring *had* come. Everything had awoken. Yesterday in the morning the farm had cast off its inhibitions and disclosed itself as the local arsenal; and then, in the afternoon, 2nd TAF had come swooping through the area with the abandon, if not the delicacy, of spring lambs. Today we had awoken belatedly — but all trammels were shed. We had awoken to freedom!

Breakfast on the farm! The idea brimmed with allure. A celebratory breakfast, no doubt. A bottle or two of wine perhaps, carefully preserved for the occasion.

"OK, Cheesey, let's go!" I said.

The bidding was superfluous. We slipped on our clogs and followed Wim. Across the yard we went, and into the house.

16

The Farm's Last Secret

The celebratory breakfast took place in the farm kitchen and held the final element of surprise. Our knowledge of the house was limited. We had, for example, long been acquainted with the byre, but the kitchen was not within our repertoire.

It was not, however, the kitchen itself which occasioned surprise, it was its occupants. We had supposed as we walked across that we should sit down to a festive meal as lone guests among whichever of the family happened to be around, but, in the event, we were, as ever, wrong. Half a dozen men sat at a long table that stood in the centre of the room, and of these we knew only the farmer who sat at their head. The remainder were complete strangers and their appearance was arresting. They were as ill-dressed as Cheeseman and I, their facial characteristics ranged from the aquiline Semitic to the broadly Dutch, and, with one exception, their faces bore the tell-tale marks of close confinement, for they were, like us, ashen-faced. The exception was a once burly man who had neither shaved nor suffered a haircut in many weeks, and from whose frame at the very least two stones in weight had dropped. He looked haggard. And yet there was, I noticed, fresh colour showing beneath the unkempt stubble that covered his sunken cheeks. Most of this strange assembly turned as they heard us enter. One proffered a few words which I did not understand, a couple of them waved a welcome, another even smiled. But the large, hairy man merely sat and stared in front of him. He seemed in a daze.

We had paused a little way inside the room in surprise.

"Who are these men, Wim?" I queried.

"They are men like you who have hidden from the Germans."

"You mean that they are Underground men?"

"No, I mean that not. Two are Jews, others are, as you say, slave labourers. They have worked for the Germans on the Rhine and are escaped. For most is their health not good."

"And do you mean that all these have been hiding in the farm while we were in the haystack?"

"Not all. The poor man who stares so have we found walking on the road this morning. He talks little, but that little is, to us, not understood. Some think that it is perhaps the language of a Russian or a Pole."

"Well, I'll go to the foot of our bloody stairs!"

"What of your bloody stairs, please?"

"Scrub it, Wim. Just English idiom. It means I am very surprised."

That was the understatement of the year. The thought that we had come and sat in all innocence in the living-room of the farm, talking and smoking on many a night, while four or five of these poor devils slept in the roof (or wherever else they had hidden them) was the final straw. How dim could you get? We had suspected neither the presence of the arms in the cow-house nor yet that of the men in the roof. The stately Catholic homes of England with their priest holes had nothing on this place. I felt now that if a pink elephant sauntered through the door, sat down, and began to partake of the breakfast, I would not bat an eyelid.

It explained much, though. We knew, because Wim had said so, that there were hiding-places within the house. Therefore, we had latterly wondered why they had kept us at arm's length all that time in the gloom of the haystack, and, more particularly once, in the harrowing discomfort of a distant pile of hay. Above all, the riding out of that savage strafing in our highly inflammable home when we might have been behind bricks and mortar had struck us as a trifle Spartan. The answer to our banishment was now as plain as a pikestaff. The men who sat to the table were east and we were west. Never, until the moment of freedom, had the twain been allowed to meet or even to suspect each other's presence. That way there could never in any circumstances have been a spilling of beans. Militarily it was admirable.

"Stan!" said a voice. I realised with a start that the farmer was calling me. It seemed strange, for he had never used my name before. He smiled and pointed to an empty chair next to the one Geoff had occupied. I snapped out of my reverie and sat down, shamefaced at having been caught off my guard.

Wim stood at the farmer's right shoulder. He opened the large, old bible he held. Slowly and deliberately he began to read aloud a not over-short extract. We had not been in Holland for nigh on two months absolutely for nothing. Here and there a word registered. It was a psalm that he read: a psalm of praise and thanksgiving. At length he finished and, at a sign from the farmer, the meal commenced.

Any ideas I had had of a fairly riotous champagne breakfast receded quickly. Food and drink were on the table for the taking; but we drank ersatz coffee and the mood was devout. I was both amazed and intrigued at the situation I found myself in. Around me sat half a dozen men, two at least of whom, but for our farmer, would not have been eating anything anywhere. They would, in all probability, have been by now mere desiccated bones in the charnel-houses that rejoiced in euphonic names like Buchenwald, Ravensbrück and Auschwitz. As it was, they all ate quite well.

I retired involuntarily into the privacy of my own mind. I was, as a navigator, accustomed to think geometrically, and particularly in terms of triangles. The Dutch version of the eternal triangle filled me with the deepest admiration. The people of the farm had sat for years on a time-bomb which, if any one of them made a mistake, was liable to explode in their faces. There could not, however, ever have been a time when that was so likely to happen as in the earlier part of the present week. During that four day period an incredible little drama had been enacted within an equilateral triangle whose sides were no more than thirty yards long. The play, whilst basically tragedy, had about it aspects of sheer burlesque; the stage, being triangular, was a fraction unorthodox in shape. At the apex stood the farmhouse, which contained: three young

Dutchmen of the Underground Movement who were proscribed by the Germans, a child a few days old whose mother could not afford to be seen for fear of throwing suspicion upon the whereabouts of her husband, a cache of arms sufficient to have equipped a platoon of regular infantry admirably, and a group of displaced persons, who were hidden away and aware only of such parts of the story as they had been allowed to know. Thirty yards away, in the phoney haystack which formed the left-hand angle, dwelt two RAF aircrew who really knew very little. Living in a barn, and constituting the right-hand angle, were four German cavalrymen who remained in as blissful ignorance of almost everything as did the steeds they rode. The theme of the play and the proximity of the actors had me spell-bound.

My attention moved from my own thought to the farmer. Circumstances had dictated that he should play the leading role in the piece. One had not for a moment to discount the parts played by the others, but the very nature of the drama had made certain that the lead should be his. He was a very accomplished actor who over a long period had pandered seemingly benignly to the German soldiers who came to his door demanding his produce. When, however, four cavalry had arrived last Sunday, taken a fancy to the cattle-byre, and begun to pull hay for their horses from over the very weapons themselves, the game had been almost up. Even so, he had successfully duped them into taking up other quarters, when he had, apart from the arms, aircrew in his haystack and displaced persons in his loft. It was a superb performance.

Now, as I watched him from the corner of my eye, I realised that his impassivity was a mask. He was, in fact, watching us very closely. His guests, without exception, were eating well, and that pleased him. He sat like a wise shepherd presiding over a singularly ragged flock.

It could not be said that the meal was in any way hilarious. The season of hilarity was not yet upon any of us. I had often dreamt of the moment when I could sit to a table and eat a meal in which I could use a knife and fork and see the food I ate. Now that that moment had come I felt no sudden upsurge in spirits, and neither, seemingly, did the others. But the point was that we ate.

At a certain despondent moment in time, Cheeseman and I, with the precision of timing of a pair of Siamese twins, had both gone off our food together. There was nothing much physically wrong with us: the lack of appetite stemmed from despair. I learned, as I watched, a fundamental if unromantic truth. In the last analysis a man is reduced to the instinct of self-preservation. That pre-eminently requires fuel. If a physically healthy man has no desire to eat, then he is full of trouble and as good as dead; if he has the wish to eat, he will survive and the rest will follow. Even the staring man who sat opposite me ate. The farmer in his wisdom was well pleased. That he was a deeply religious man there was not the slightest doubt; that his courage was ineffable there was not the slightest question. But his Christianity was of the practical type that recognises that a fundamental part of the Lord's Prayer has to do with the obtaining of one's daily bread. That essential he had provided for many a poor wretch. In reality, though, he had furnished much more. His unswerving faith had kept alight a torch in a dark world.

It was strange that the last secret of this enigmatic farmhouse should have been a humanitarian one. Strange and, somehow, singularly appropriate. I, for my part, felt extraordinarily humble. I knew that I sat in the presence of a man who would never appear in the history books, and yet had more right to be there than many a celebrity.

He was a man in his late sixties, and he had done a wonderful job with superb aplomb. And yet there was no whit of pride in the man. The majestic prose of the Book of Ecclesiastès drifted into my mind and took on a living meaning. To everything there was indeed a season, and a time for every purpose under Heaven. But, "Vanity, vanity, *all* is vanity," the Preacher had railed. I doubted that. I saw no vanity in the little man who sat at the head of our table, and certainly no vainness in the work he had done. Doubt, the arbiter, led, however, to fuller comprehension. "In the end," the preacher had said, in effect, "there is nothing better for a man than that he should eat and drink and rejoice in the good of his own works." That was it and that was neither vain nor in vain. That was precisely what our farmer now did, quietly. He could have been as proud as a peacock about his achievements, and I would still have respected him; as it was, I honoured him. Now that I thought about the concept deeply, I could have wept. In fact, I did not; I merely reached for another piece of bread.

"Well, *are* you coming?" Cheeseman's voice echoing into my brain, held both amusement and asperity in its tones.

"Coming where?"

"Wim's asked you twice to go and meet British troops on the main road, but you didn't seem to hear."

The meal, I realised suddenly, was finished. I alone was still eating.

"Whatever you say, Wim," I answered, mechanically.

"Then let us go. The farmer says he has now much work to do. It is proper that you now walk to meet some British soldiers. Many tanks and lorries stand now on the road."

It was clearly the thing to do, XXX Corps stood now, not in my dreams but in fact, on the Aalten-Lichtenvoorde road. We set off without particular haste down the sandroad that led to the main highway. It seemed unconscionably strange to be walking along in broad daylight. The sun shone beautifully and made me blink. It was a splendid early spring morning, but the sun did not enliven me. I could not explain how I felt. I had no aches or pains, and yet it seemed as if a lead weight pressed upon me. Reaction sat upon my shoulder like a black crow. Thought told me that it was reaction, but, having told me that, provided no panacea. I had little interest in what I was doing. Gunfire cracked and rumbled in the direction of Lichtenvoorde without raising so much as a flicker of interest in me. We passed the rectangular block of hay in which we had once hidden, and I gave it but a cursory glance. Some noise of idling internal-combustion engines came through the line of trees flanking the road and, in a moment, we stepped out among the vehicles of war.

By the roadside, at the point where we emerged, sat a despatch rider at ease, his legs straddling his motor-cycle. We stood for a moment, hesitantly.

"Go on!" said Wim. "Talk with him!"

Cheeseman took the initiative.

"Excuse me, mate," he ventured. "We're a couple of shot-down aircrew and we've been hiding round here for two months. We're looking to you chaps for help. What's the form?"

The DR gazed at us in utter astonishment. It was a few seconds before he spoke, but when he did his voice proclaimed both his disbelief and the fact that he had, for a substantial part of his life, been no stranger to the sound of Bow Bells.

"You're what?" he queried.

"Two aircrew. A navigator and a gunner, to be exact."

"Cor blimey, you could've fooled me. You look more like a pair of flippin' tramps. But what 'ave yer got on yer feet?"

"Clogs of course," we answered in unison, surprised that so inane a question should have been asked.

"Well, so 'elp me, I've seen it all now. I never thought I'd live to see the day. Aircrew in clogs!"

The thought set him off roaring with laughter. Our appearance had obviously made his day. The conversation developed rapidly. Wim stood a little to one side and tried desperately to hang on to the flood of quickly spoken English. We told the rough gist of our tale; the Cockney acknowledged that the sudden descent upon him of two tramp-like figures speaking idiomatic English in a foreign land had shaken him rigid. After a while he cooled off suddenly as a thought struck him.

"Arf a minute," he said. "I'm taking you two at face value. You'd better come and see my officer."

He left his motor-cycle standing, and led us down the line of vehicles to where a large, square, closed-in tender stood. Two officers were conversing outside it. The DR approached them, saluted, and gave the younger of the two his account of the story. The subaltern turned his attention to us and heard our version. He seemed in no way to doubt us.

"You've come to the right part of the column," he said. "This is the signals section, and if you like I could send a message home for you. Your people would appreciate it, don't you think? Hang on a minute!"

He disappeared into the wireless truck, and re-emerged with message pad and pencil.

"Just write your names, ranks and numbers followed by your addresses and a short message. I'll see it gets back."

This was, I thought, very civil. Here we were in the middle of a major land battle sending a telegram home to mother.

"Thanks very much," I said, as I wrote. "This is fine. But what do we do now?"

"I'm not sure what to tell you to do. The big boys up front are stuck at the moment, but we're likely to be on the move again soon. I'd suggest you go back with your friend to the farm and await the infantry. Keep clear of the verges, by the way. They may be mined."

He turned and went with our messages into the wireless truck.

Several soldiers were standing interestedly nearby. Geoff became engrossed in a conversation-piece with them, but I felt in no mood for talking. I wandered off up the road to have a look around, avoiding the verges like the plague.

Certainly the British show of power was impressive. As far as the eye could see, an array of military vehicles stretched in each direction along the straight road. This was not the area of the heavy tank, for that was making its ponderous presence known by ominous cracks and bangs which rent the air three miles away at the approaches to Lichtenvoorde and thundered back down the column. This was the realm of the troop-carrying lorry, the despatch rider and the ration truck. The banging up front continued, a couple of flights of Typhoons whooped low over our heads making the earth shudder with their roar. Most impressive, I thought.

And then I realised that one solitary remnant of the German might of yesterday remained, like jetsam washed up on a hostile shore. I noticed that the line of vehicles detoured at one point from the left to the right of the road. The cause was immediately apparent. There, lying in a heap, with holes in its side and belly, and with its legs twisted at incredible angles, lay a horse. Behind it, the two-wheel cart it had been pulling had broken at the shafts and tipped backwards, spilling its wares all over the road. Tins of jam, loaves, sausages and potatoes lay scattered about, and, in the middle of this mass of food, stood the remains of a German helmet. I sought the driver, and I found him drooped over the opposite verge, with his feet dangling over the lip of the ditch and his head on the very edge of the road.

I looked for the first time at close quarters on the face of the enemy. That is, I looked in reality on half a face. He lay on his back gazing toward the heavens with one sightless eye. The bottom half of his body appeared superficially undamaged, for there was no blood, and his legs were stretched out normally in front of him as if he had jumped from the cart and fallen over backwards. But the upper part of him was smashed. Whatever had hit him had struck his shoulders and head, particularly on the left-hand side. That shoulder was in part shot away, and the arm seemed only to remain attached to him because his greatcoat still hung together. His head had been severed almost precisely in two longitudinally, so that, distinguishable through the dried blood and the blackness that came from scorching, were the remains of a nose, half a mouth and one eye. Blood had gushed down the front of his grey service greatcoat and he was covered with a dusting of grit from the road. With his arms outstretched as they were, he looked like a scarecrow that had been damaged and fallen from its pole.

I stood staring down at him because, unlike the soldiers who occupied the road, I had never seen his like before. I gazed down with the silence and detachment of an undertaker's mute. What, precisely, had shorn his head in two I could not tell, but I felt no speck of pity for the man who had been out provisioning with his horse and cart, and certainly no satisfaction in the death of an enemy. My mind was clinically active but emotionally dead.

Suddenly I was aware that Wim was standing by my side. He looked at me and then down at the corpse. When he spoke his voice was as devoid of emotion as were my thoughts.

"He is very dead," he said.

"Yes, very dead," I answered, automatically.

But speaking brought me to life. Mooning about here was not the slightest damn good. I moved across to where Geoff was still conversing with a couple of soldiers.

"Come on, Cheeseman," I said. "Let's get home!"

"Back to the farm?"

"Naturally. Where the hell else? We're doing no bloody good hanging about here. Come on!"

"So you must spend more time on the farm, eh?" queried Wim, as we trod the homeward sandway.

"Looks like it, Wim, if you'll have us," I answered, briefly.

"But that is not perhaps so bad, is it?"

"Not at all."

Wim sensed the moodiness in me.

"I think," he said, "that I shall now show to you my daughter, for you have not ever seen her. Then, of course, shall you see the hiding-places in the house." — There came that little sideways cock of the head when he was half joking and half in earnest. "Best of all for you however is it, that you can now shave with hot water!"

Geoff and I fingered our beards and grimaced.

There was still trouble around. Hardly had we re-entered the farm's living-room, when the farmer's wife bustled in with beakers of hot milk for us. It was almost as if she had expected our return, and she smiled a welcome. But while we drank she talked agitatedly to Wim. He translated.

"It is about that poor man we found walking on the road this morning. He is not well. Shall we go and talk with him?"

We found the man seated on a chair in the kitchen as we had left him, still staring abstractedly in front of him.

Very gently Wim tried him with easy phrases in Dutch, English, German and French, asking simply his name and nationality. The poor fellow did at least respond, which was something, but his reply was broken, unhealthily agitated, and in a tongue that was wholly unfamiliar. I doubted whether he was coherent, and said as much.

"Yes, perhaps that is true," said Wim. "It is not good that his mind should so be. He is, I think, a Russian, and the Germans have treated him badly, as they do for those peoples. I shall in the afternoon bring him a doctor."

Cheeseman and I went to the haystack and brought in all our gear, including our flying-boot bottoms. We restored those mildewed objects to our feet and discarded our clogs. In a way it was like parting with faithful friends. The change made, we washed and prepared for dinner.

The meal began at midday. The farmer, his wife and Trui sat down with us to table. Wim said, by way of conversation, that he expected to move back to his police job in Neede within a week or two, and that Johan and Wim II would be co-opted into the 1st Canadian Army. We were about half-way through the meal when there came an interruption.

Brisk footsteps sounded on the concrete outside the window. A sharp knock on the door followed immediately. A squat, swarthy man with a Sten gun on his shoulder and the orange armband of the Resistance on his sleeve was admitted. We recognised one of the two men who had brought us down here on a Sunday evening seven weeks ago.

"This man is named Pietje," said Wim. "He has come to take you to a friend in Lichtenvoorde who will official make you known to the British. Pietje wishes that you should quickly eat and then follow him."

There was an urgency. We had our marching orders. The remainder of our food was eaten rapidly.

"And do we know this man in Lichtenvoorde?" asked Geoff, academically.

"Oh yes, you know him. Piet says his name is Leo. But now you must quickly go."

There was yet a secret that I intended to prise out. I asked Wim for names.

For a moment he was hesitant. Secrecy in that respect was a years-long habit. Then he shrugged, fished a couple of pieces of paper out of a drawer, and wrote:

D. H. te Lindert,
Huize Boschman,
Barlo 58,
Gelderland,
The Netherlands.

"Thank you, that is the farmer's name, I think," said Geoff. "Now — what is yours?"

"I," replied Wim slowly, "am Wim Lensink."

Then there was a final flash of his puckish brand of humour.

"Wim Lensink has deceived you," he said, gravely.

"Really?"

"Yes, really. The name of the little dog who did tricks for you is not Skippy. It is Roely."

There was no following that.

We made our farewells to them as best we could. Words were totally inadequate to express what we felt. There was a tear in Mevrouw te Lindert's eye, Trui looked downcast, Meneer te Lindert and Wim Lensink pressed our hands heartily. We turned and followed Piet out. We left the farm without seeing Wim's wife or daughter; the hiding-places remained a mystery. The evasion was at an end. We were off to see Leo and be handed over. All our troubles were over — at least, we thought they were.

17

The Irish Guards

Down the sandway to Lichtenvoorde as if we owned it we strode. Piet, who brought up the right, seemed as happy as a linnet, and although his exact meanings as he quipped away in Dutch were not clear, his elation was infectious. Even I, as I trooped along on the left, felt the high spirits, and shed a portion of my melancholy. And then, within ten minutes of leaving the te Lindert's, the German sprang out. We were passing a farmhouse which bordered the way, when suddenly he appeared slap in front of me. I heard his final movements as he came round the farm wall in the same instant that Piet raised his Sten gun. I realised in the split second that he stood before me that over his grey uniform he wore a kind of apron that had once been white. I looked, with the speed of light, first at him and then at the ditch towards which I was beginning evasively to move. The dive into the nettles was never made. In the instant before making a complete ass of myself I grasped the absurd truth. This was not one of the paratroopers in which the area had recently abounded. Far from being armed to the teeth, he was a medical man equipped with nothing more lethal than a set of glass phials. A kind of wooden tray, three inches wide, was fixed over the dirty white surcoat which ran from shoulders to waist, and in this tray six or eight bottles containing liquids of various hues stood upright in circular holes. The absurdity of the situation lay not in the man's trade, but in the fact that he was our prisoner. He stood there with his hands up, and he was extremely and obviously tired. Never had I seen a man so washed-up. His eyelids repeatedly drooped over his eyes as he endeavoured to say something or other, and he rocked on his feet. He was, to all intents and purposes, out standing up. It seemed a shame, in boxing parlance, to let the fight continue. Nevertheless, Piet motioned him forward with his gun and, ironically, we proceeded into Lichtenvoorde complete with prisoner.

The streets of the old town teemed with life. The armoured column wound through those streets like an enormous snake. The tail jutted backwards in a southerly direction on to the Aalten — Lichtenvoorde road, the body stretched sinuously through its main thoroughfares past the town square, the head stood firmly ensconced to the north on the road to Groenlo. The tank, the armoured car, the heavy military lorry, all were there. To the north, and not particularly distant, thunderclaps proclaimed that the head of the snake was striking out; but, temporarily, the bulk of the column was at rest within the borough, and the whole population had turned out to see the show. Citizens of both sexes and all ages stood in excited groups talking and staring at the flood of steel which had that day liberated them. The civilians occupied in the main the left-hand side of the thoroughfares. The other side belonged at the moment to the Army, for the soldiers, in typically British fashion, had hopped out of their tanks and were brewing up tea on small spirit stoves on the right-hand pavements.

Our little group of four threaded its way through the troops, the German prisoner at our head. He was so quiescent that Piet scarcely bothered to cover him, but merely grunted the odd instruction from time to time and used his gun to point the way. We passed the town square, on which a cluster of tanks were drawn up, and had gone perhaps a hundred yards or so further along the column when we were stopped.

An officer was leaning out of the turret of a tank, languidly surveying the scene. As we drew abreast, he stared down at us closely and asked a question.

"Are you the two aircrew?" he queried.

Dressed as we were, his powers of observation staggered us, but we answered in the affirmative.

"What was your pilot's name?"

"Fowler. Flying Officer Fowler, to be exact," I replied.

"That checks. Though I'm afraid I have to tell you that he may be dead."

The captain who addressed us was quick and decisive of speech, and seemed to have perceptive powers bordering on the clairvoyant. I remembered that we had once given our names, ranks and numbers to Wim, and that the man we were on our way to meet had said that he knew exactly who we were. Presumably our chat this morning with the signals officer had confirmed something that was already known. Nevertheless, although this chap's performance was remarkably adroit, I doubted whether his crystal ball was right where Chuck Fowler was concerned. It did not gell at all with the information that had seeped to us along the Underground grapevine in early February. I believed Chuck was a prisoner, and said so.

"You may be right," the captain replied. "There's no certainty in my information there. In fact it's a touch confused. But do you see those tanks drawn up on the square?"

We looked back along the column and acknowledged that we did.

"They are the Irish Guards. Report to them and tell them I sent you. I'm the Field Security Officer, by the way."

Pietje had been waiting patiently with his prisoner. He had not understood a word of the conversation, and now looked at us enquiringly.

We conveyed in sign language that he should proceed without us. Half the quartet moved off one way, we went the other. The handing over was already done; we were reporting to the Irish Guards; our meeting with Leo was off.

I reflected as we walked back to the town square that our acceptance by the Army was proving much more of a piece of cake than we had a right to expect.

That reflection was quickly proved wrong. The guardsman with whom we made contact eyed our appearance and listened to our speech with as much trust as a middle-aged maiden lady of impeccable virtue bestows in a circumstance where she is suddenly left alone with a known rake.

"Wait here a minute and I'll fetch someone," he said, gruffly.

He returned with an exceptionally tall, rangy man of about thirty, who bore the markings of a company sergeant-major on his sleeve and the ribbon of the Military Medal on his chest. His attitude was belligerent from the start.

"What's all this about?" he snapped, in an accent that spoke more of Liverpool than of the Emerald Isle.

Geoff explained who we were and who had sent us. The sergeant-major was by no means impressed.

"A couple of more unlikely looking aircrew I've not yet seen. What proof of identity have you got?"

The card designed by the Air Ministry pundit did not do the trick. A ten-week growth of hair flowing over our collars, grimy stubble on our pasty cheeks, and tatty clothes on our bodies impressed a CSM of the Guards much more — unfavourably!

He waxed irate as he picked on me. His interrogative style was brisk, and developed to the crunch question quickly.

"Are you English?"

"Yes."

"Are you interested in football?"

"Yes."

"Then who won the FA Cup in 1937?"

For the life of me I could not think. Given another time and place, the answer would probably have come, but here and now it did not. If he had chosen 1931 there would have been no problem, for West Bromwich Albion won it then. But 1937? — I had no idea.

"Poor," said the CSM. "Where do you come from?"

"Birmingham."

He then embroiled me in a questionnaire about New Street Station, the Queen's Hotel, and various other institutions in the centre of the city. I, in turn, waxed gradually shirty.

"I haven't the remotest bloody clue," I said, slowly and deliberately insolently, in answer to one of his questions.

Cheeseman, who had so far remained relatively unscathed, asked him why, if he would not accept us, he did not get in touch with the Field Security Officer who already had. To the reply that he proposed to settle us two himself, Geoff then said that possibly a new-fangled device known as radio might be a useful piece of equipment for the Guards Armoured Division to install in its tanks.

The taunt did nothing to remedy the situation. Quite a shindig began to blow up in Lichtenvoorde town square. And then I realised that, whilst a slanging match might be great fun for the soldiers gathered around, we were on a hiding to nothing. The impasse called for a touch of low cunning.

"We demand that you take us to see your CO," I said.

He thrust his face forward belligerently to within a foot from mine; his glare would have wiped the inscrutable smile from the face of the Sphinx.

"*Demand*?" he thundered.

"Yes, *demand*. You see, it's obvious from your questions that you haven't the ghost of an idea who we really are. If the FSO could accept us, why can't you? For all you know we could have some valuable military gen tucked up our sleeves. We ought to see your CO, don't you think?"

He thought about that for a moment. Then he turned to a nearby guardsman. "If I'm wanted I shall be with the major," he said.

He stalked down the main street at a brisk pace with us in his train. He spoke not a word, nor gave us so much as a glance. Our first brush with the Guards had been rough. We hoped now for better things.

The CSM entered the grounds of a large house that stood back from the road. Through the front door, down a long, once sumptious hall we went, until, at the last door on the right, he paused and knocked.

A voice bade him enter. Without a word he motioned us in, and we preceded him into the room.

The place was large, and barely furnished. At the far end, three officers were standing round a table, poring over a military map. We remained near the door; they looked up in some surprise.

"I'm busy, sergeant-major," said the senior of the three, rather abruptly. "What's the problem?"

"These two men are the problem, sir. They claim to be RAF aircrew."

"Good lord above! And what do you think?"

The CSM gave a brief resumé of the confrontation. In answer to the major's question, he did not absolutely damn us, but said that there was room for doubt.

"So the ball's in my court, eh?"

"I'm afraid so, sir."

The tactical discussion had evidently concluded at the moment of our arrival. The two subalterns trooped off, casting slightly incredulous looks in our direction; the major sat down, I thought a trifle wearily. The floor was ours. Except that the sergeant-major stood starchily by and listened as the cross-examination began.

The style was civil, but the questions sharp. I sensed no easy passage as we told our tale from the raid on the Dortmund-Ems Canal to the row in Lichtenvoorde town square.

"And what is this valuable military information the sergeant-major says you may have tucked up your sleeves?" the major asked, when we had finished.

That, we had to admit, was largely myth: though we did of course know that the area had once been the haunt of Germans from the searchlight battalions, and, more latterly, that their paratroopers had been thick on the ground.

"Then why demand to see me on the strength of stuff that is well known and by now academic?"

We said that since we could not convince the sergeant-major, the suggestion of the possession of prime gen seemed the surest way of reaching top authority. Particularly as the CSM couldn't possibly know whether we were telling the truth or not.

"Subtle," said the major. "But go on! You couldn't convince him. How do you propose to satisfy me?"

We put our identity cards and escape-kits before him on the table, demonstrated the fact that beneath our shirts the two asbestos discs with our names, numbers and religions hung on the usual pieces of string from our necks, pointed out that the shirts themselves, although exceptionally dirty, were undeniably RAF issue, and showed that our filthy shoes were, in fact, fur-lined flying-boot bottoms.

It was not enough.

"I'm sorry," he said. "I'm very much inclined to believe you. You sound right to me. But all this stuff could so easily be counterfeit. I can't afford to take risks."

Despondency hit me again with the smothering force of a wet blanket. Shades of a prison-house overflowing with Kraut POWs for company loomed ominously in my mind.

"What else can we possibly do to convince you, sir?" Geoff asked, in desperation.

"Tell me one thing that you alone could know if you were genuine. It needs to be something that I also would know from my own experience, and it needs to be quick. This armoured column is likely to be on the move again at any moment."

The table he sat at proved, on closer examination, to be a desk. There was a filing tray on one corner and a blotter in the middle. The room itself was austere. The walls lacked pictures, the wallpaper was beginning to sag in some places and to peel off in others, the carpet had worn threadbare with the repeated passage of heavy-booted feet. Ironic, I thought, that a British officer sat behind that desk and questioned us when yesterday the questioner would have been German. Particularly ironic since our immediate destination looked like being the same — prison.

Geoff and I put our heads together; the instinct of self-preservation begot a useful thought. Between us we recounted the raid by eight hundred bombers that had taken place on the towns of Goch, Kalcar and Cleve, and was designed as the curtain-raiser for the Armoured Corps to launch its attack from the Maas. Precise time and date were given.

Things changed in the twinkling of an eye. The major threw his head back and laughed. "OK, chaps, you're on," he said, encouragingly. "I happened to be around Cleve at the time."

"Thank God for that!" said Cheeseman, relief oozing.

The upshot was that we were recommended to go back into harness for a while. There would, the major said, be a vacuum for a time when the column pulled out, because the infantry had by now been left well behind. Therefore, he suggested, our best bet for a speedy return to England was to go up with the armour, and, when they bivouacked for the night, come back on a lorry of the supply echelon.

Cavorting northwards had not exactly been the line of escape we had envisaged. But the youngish senior officer who recommended rather than ordered had about him all the attributes of a good RAF squadron commander. We took his point.

"Thank you, sir," I said. "We'll go with the tanks."

He told our erstwhile foe to install us with the regimental sergeant-major, and told us, jokingly, to buzz off.

We had not gone more than ten yards from the gate of the house when the CSM checked his long stride, turned to us and spoke.

"Rumour has it, and it could well be right, that I can be a bastard," he began. "But at least I'm a bastard who'll own up when he's wrong. I admit that I was suspicious of you blokes. We've learned a few hard lessons this winter on the Maas. Not only escaping Dutchmen came over that river in boats. We can't be too careful. However, I was wrong. You are RAF without a doubt, and I'll now do anything I can to help you. No hard feelings?"

Well, perhaps there was. The injustice of being suspected for a spy still rankled. But I sensed the type of man with whom we dealt. The Guards Armoured Division did not fight by shuffling papers any more than we did. Aircrew tempers tended often to be quick; quarrels, thank God, direct and in the open. The same was doubtless true of ultra front-line ground troops. I felt a kinship. In any case, his apology was so blunt and off-beat that it could not be other than genuine.

"No hard feelings, sergeant-major," Cheeseman replied, forestalling me by a split second.

The hatchet was quickly buried, and not in anybody's skull. We walked back to the town square as amicably as blood brothers. He took us to the ration truck. A young guardsman stood outside that holy of holies.

"Look lively there, lad. Turn out your luxury wares for the two airmen," the sergeant-major snapped. "Anything they want they can have — tobacco, chocolate, fags — anything at all and as much as they want."

We came away with the pockets of our scarecrow jackets and corduroy trousers bulging comfortably. I particularly relished the fact that I had a couple of two-ounce tins of my favourite tobacco on me.

The tanks of the Irish Guards still occupied the square, but the column along the main street had changed somewhat in consistency. There were more lorries and less tanks. Observed more closely, it was not stationary. There was a constant deployment on. A tank would pull away and head up the road northwards, and a lorry full of infantry would take its place. Three miles or so in the operative direction, surges of strident sound came crashing back. Amid the dissonance the church clock struck two. We had been in the town an hour.

A Daimler Scout Car rested by the kerbside, positioned in almost the exact spot where our initial confrontation with the Field Security Officer had taken place. By its side stood the regimental sergeant-major, engaged in conversation with his driver. He was older than the CSM by at least a decade, stockier of build and, although a tall man, at least three inches shorter. At that moment he wore no cap, and grey locks showed in his hair. The hand-over was quickly effected; the company sergeant-major took his leave.

"Well, I'm away now, lads," he said. "I'll wish you a safe run with us and a quick return to England."

Off he stalked in his rangy manner. We watched his tall figure disappear among the tanks in the square.

The RSM went off on his rounds; we manoeuvred inside the car; the driver remained seated at the wheel. The afternoon sun was warm. We took advantage of the fact that the roof was open, shed our old coats, and stood upright basking in the sunlight and surveying the scene. Along the Groenlo road the battle still rumbled.

"A fair hold-up you're having," Cheeseman hazarded. "What's in the way — tanks?"

"Not so much tanks," the driver replied. "There's a couple of nests of German self-propelled guns operating. They're causing a bit of trouble up front."

The driver was a man of relatively few words. But he picked those words with care, and gradually proved to be a mine of information. The Guards Armoured had, the previous morning at five o'clock, crossed the Bailey Bridge over the Rhine at Rees, passed through the bridgehead secured by the 51st (Highland) Division, and had been going hell-for-leather ever since. Aalten had presented some difficulty due to a series of large craters on the approach road and a blown bridge over the river. The town had been taken by a night attack, and then, early this morning, they had set forth once more on their drive northwards.

"Hamburg and Bremen, that'll be our lot," said the driver, knowingly. For myself, I'd sooner have a look at Liverpool again."

We spoke of the quick-tempered nature of the CSM, and were bluntly told that, whilst true, he was a damn good soldier.

"He's certainly not the grudge-bearing type," I said. "We started off at each other's throats but finished up as close as three peas in a pod. He ladled us out with tobacco, chocolate and oranges on the grand scale. Does that prove something?"

"It proves that once he knew for sure you were RAF he intended to look after you. We'll all do that."

It seemed that the partnership between the Army and 2nd TAF had been going great guns. In particular, the rocket-carrying Typhoon was regarded very favourably by the Armoured Corps, for it helped combat that massive thorn in the flesh known as the German Tiger Tank.

It was nice to feel the fighter boys' popularity slop over on to us. That couldn't be bad.

The sun continued to beam down. A lorry loaded with motorised infantry drew in behind us, its troops pouring on to the pavement and brewing tea on a primus the moment the wheels stopped turning. Two Typhoons, line abreast, shot low over the housetops heading north. A variety of Germans were marched in ones and twos up the middle of the road at the end either of British bayonets or Dutch Sten guns.

"Your friends of the Resistance are having quite a day," observed the driver.

And then we became aware of a persistent, soft hissing. Unobtrusively, a small crowd, composed largely of young women, had surrounded the car as we stood talking, and were regarding us with venom in their eyes and a sibilant sound issuing through their clenched teeth.

"God almighty, what's this?" asked Geoff in amazement. "Why the bloody hell should they hiss us?"

It remained a peculiarly depressing puzzle, until our thoughtful friend the driver hit on the answer.

"It's your blue-grey shirts they don't like," he said. "To them the British wear khaki. They think you're a couple of captured Jerries."

We did the only thing possible. We indulged in a tripartite shaking of hands, clapping of backs and passing round of fags. It was ostentatious burlesque, but it worked. The Dutch girls departed with painful bewilderment written on their faces. To be hissed out of Lichtenvoorde would have been supreme irony.

Quite suddenly the primus stoves disappeared from the pavement. The regimental sergeant-major returned to his car. The hatches were battened down. "Lead on, driver!" ordered the RSM. At something after half past two on the afternoon of Saturday March 31st we began our tank drive.

I sat in the left-hand seat, watching the road ahead through a slit in the front of the armoured car. Behind me, on a raised seat, sat Geoff Cheeseman, his knees pressed into my back just below the shoulder blades. The sergeant-major stood, crouching because of limited headroom, behind and slightly to the left of his driver. He wore a headset, and pattered out a commentary from time to time as we drove. The car was designed for at most three people. At the moment it was crowded.

The driver sat, erect and expressionless, at the wheel; the car ploughed steadily on. We covered the first couple of miles or more towards Groenlo without incident. Shells were exploding sporadically ahead and across the fields to our left, but they were too far away to give undue bother. Encased as we were in steel, I found the old feeling of immortality that sustained me on bombing trips returning. It was a comforting defence mechanism that permeated aircrew minds and kept them sane. The impression that shells were intended always for someone else and never for you was the best morale retainer in the world, and I found that it applied equally well on the ground as in the air. We proceeded, then, in the company of a powerful armoured column that thrust slowly but inexorably forward.

As the road ahead bent to the left, some Sherman tanks in front were visible through the lines of bare trees. Somewhere further ahead stood the source of those explosions, and feeding the guns that originated them were men in Wehrmacht grey, sweating as they rammed in the shells. Close to them other tanks were deploying as they sought their destruction, for we could hear the rapid mutter of their guns. We rode always towards the storm, and that was all.

The rumbling in front increased in intensity. Above the noise of the engine, it cracked and drummed through the air. Dutch horizons seem, because of the flatness of the land, always to be close; and our western sky-line flickered vividly in shades of red and yellow. The column slowed down. With the decrease in engine noise, the din of the guns was sharpened. Of air activity there seemed a complete lack. The battle was essentially landlocked; we were entirely in a foreign element, like fish flung up on a pebble beach in a storm.

Momentarily the defence mechanism snapped. I felt a strong urge to leap out of the slowly moving car and hare it back to Lichtenvoorde. Funk is, however, never pretty and rarely prudent. Pride refused to allow the impulse its head. I wished, though, that I had a job to do. The useless passenger had an unoccupied mind. And he paid for it by being slightly petrified.

We crawled round a crater in the road. The column picked up speed again. We were quickly across a railway line, and there, side by side, resembling shattered sentinels still guarding the line, stood the remains of two self-propelled guns of the 88mm class. The shooting that had destroyed them had been precise. In one case the gun was no more than a jagged stub ending just above the breach; in the other the slim length of the barrel was apparent, but the upper couple of feet hung by a thread of metal with the muzzle pointing forlornly at the ground. An outstretched bundle in Wehrmacht grey lay face downwards at the base of the guns. Two more were spreadeagled in the field twenty yards away. I admired those German gunners. They had, without any real cover to shield them, held up an armoured column and paid for it with their lives. The driver took a more practical view.

"Lovely shooting, that," he said, leaning across for a moment. "Slap down the bloody barrels."

We moved on towards our goal. Over the fields to the left the sky remained agitated. The lurid reds and yellows showed now through a canopy of black smoke. Low over the tanks ahead a flight of Tempests swooped across our line of direction and vanished westwards. Slow and stop began now to characterise our progress once more. We crept, snail-like, past another crater. A knocked-out British tank lay solitarily to one side of the way. The hammering towards Groenlo began again in earnest. I concentrated my gaze on the road in front as if the focusing of my attention on that would absolve me from all the rest.

The RSM listened to and relayed messages unceasingly. He gave his findings in a military jargon that was unfamiliar to me and was, in any case, largely lost in the roar of the engine and the crash of the guns. But to whom he listened and to whom he spoke I had no clue. One phrase alone registered, because it was repeated often enough. "Our big brothers," was the term he used. But, in the bedlam, I failed always to find out what our brothers were doing or where they were going or even who they were.

The car drew to a complete halt. The sergeant-major removed his headset, ran the back of his hand across his brow, and stood for a moment in thought.

"I'd better go back and see what he wants to do, driver," he said.

He stepped quietly out of the car, and moved off as casually as if he were at home and slipping round the corner to the local for a drink. Who 'he' was, and why the RSM had to leave his car in the middle of a pitched battle to talk to him when radio was available, was a mystery. However, he had gone, the car stood still, and that was that.

"Where's he sloped off to?" I asked.

"He's gone to talk to the CO."

"Well, who are 'our big brothers' when they're at home, then?"

"The Grenadiers. They're in the lead today. That's why you're with us and not them. I'll lay any odds we change over tomorrow."

"I shan't be with you to see it."

"Some people get all the luck. The Mobile Artillery's coming up nicely though," he observed, jerking his thumb to the left.

That, I thought, was evident enough. The wait continued.

Suddenly Geoff Cheeseman behind me announced that he intended to get out. I thought for a second that he'd gone raving mad, and then realised that, unlike me, he'd seen nothing since we started. A view limited to the inside of a lurching armoured car involved in a tank battle had, I suspected, resulted in claustrophobia. I began to open the car door, but the driver objected. "It's my job to tell you to stay where you are," he said, doggedly.

"No dice. We're going out," I answered.

"Then keep off the verges for Christ's sake!"

We stood on the road by the side of the scout car. The air we sniffed was tinged with the stink of cordite; the noise, now that we were in the open, seemed to be multiplied by at least two. It was continuous, harsh, abrasive noise, as if a malevolent giant were frenziedly running a huge stick persistently across an enormous corrugated-iron roof without any intention ever of stopping. It rolled over the car in staccato waves of thunder that threatened to submerge it. I felt an urge to duck and stay ducking, but, instead, walked across to the far verge and looked down the column. The tanks stood battened down like immobile leviathans, a wall of steel divided into individual units. Geoff and I were the only human beings visible on that straight stretch of road.

"Come on, Cheesey, let's get back!" I said. He did not demur. We clambered back inside and resumed our places in silence. The driver, I felt, was not particularly pleased with us.

"A very thorough man, your RSM, I should think," I said, to break the human silence.

"Very thorough, very fair, and very regimental," he replied, almost primly.

That, I supposed, was reasonable praise for any sergeant-major.

The halt continued; so did the firing. Nothing exploded absolutely in our vicinity, but the feeling persisted that it probably would. I hated this business of sitting here being shot at. It was a peculiar advantage of the Lancaster that the deafening roar of its Merlin engines was so loud that you never really heard the flak. Only the stuff that was close enough to buffet reminded the navigator in his cabin of its presence. Then again, once airborne, there was no stopping. In bomber work there was no delay while somebody cleared the guns away. It was short and sharp for the most part. This game we were involved in went on and on. I was sick of those damned guns. The noise of them pounded on my ears until my head ached. For Christ's sake let's get mobile!

Abruptly the sergeant-major was re-entering the car and putting on his headset. "Be ready to move off, driver!" he ordered. "We're going for Eibergen."

We ran steadily into Groenlo. At the point where the river flowed under the road stood the remains of field-guns, lined up on the far bank. The road was heavily cratered; the going consequently slow. A couple of German tanks stood in shattered silence near the bridge. Remarkably, they were connected by a chain.

"Tigers?" I queried, leaning across.

"No. Panthers. Not quite so big as the Tiger, but lethal enough," the driver replied.

"Why the towing chain?"

For a moment his immobile face creased into a grin. "Lack of petrol," he said.

It was pitch dark when we entered Eibergen. The six miles from

Groenlo had been covered I knew not how. That it had been a long drawn out process was beyond doubt, for the afternoon had not been all that far advanced when we passed through Groenlo. I did not believe that I had actually fallen asleep during the later stages of the drive, but I might as well have done. The constant hammering of guns and the lassitude that stemmed from reaction had induced a sort of waking coma in which I saw nothing with exactitude and heard nothing other than a continuous rumbling, alternately near and farther away, that had somehow begun to resemble the sound of waves on a wild sea shore. The whole had swallowed me up and lulled me. I had observed nothing and would, therefore, remember nothing. In the gradually fading light the world had become a chimera of wheels turning, of guns banging, of a heavy internal-combustion engine roaring, and of one man carefully and silently driving an armoured car while another spoke cryptic messages into a microphone. There had been a long wait in the dark, and then, quite suddenly, we had sailed quickly and smoothly forward and there were houses all round us. All it needed was a man in a dark uniform to have appeared by the car shouting, "Eibergen! Eibergen!" and I would have stepped sleepily off the train.

"I'll go now and see to the billeting arrangements, driver," said the RSM when the car had stopped. "Fix the two airmen up with the best place you can find!"

He wished us good-bye and, without fuss or effusion, went about his business. A thorough-going, reliable man, I thought, and one to whom 'flap' and long speeches were equally anathema.

I lay flat on my back on the top section of a double-decker bunk and considered the ceiling above me. Geoff Cheeseman sat on the edge of the bunk below, chatting with some of the dozen or so guardsmen who were with us. The billet the driver had found was snug enough; the bunk, in a room in which there were not bunks for everyone, had been generously awarded to us so that we could rest a while before the supply echelon came up and took us back with them.

This place had, I imagined, once been a school, for we had passed through what still retained an aura of an assembly hall, and the room we rested in could easily once have been a small classroom. That, however, had been a time since. Schooling had not been the order of the day here in the recent past.

The shooting war seemed at last to have come to an end, for all was peaceful outside; the camp-fire tale of evasion that Geoff was telling had an attentive audience; I continued to stare at the ceiling. I felt abominably tired, and yet utterly unable to sleep. My mind was still going with the tanks, still involved in an argument with a sergeant-major of the Guards, still intrigued as to what manner of man the German was who had slept in this bunk last night — assuming he had any sleep.

The soldiers below began to turn in; deliberately I asked a question.

"Have any of you seen or heard of two other aircrew round here?"

The answer was, as I had expected, completely negative. That melancholy black crow of reaction still sat firmly on my shoulder and niggled discouragingly. Copley and Young ought to be in this region somewhere, but no-one had heard of them. Perhaps the news about

Chuck Fowler had been right after all.

Sleep was the order of the hour for all bar one soldier. He sat on a wooden chair, his rifle between his knees; the remainder, I noticed, had their rifles close at hand. The British occupation of the town was but an hour or two old. There was a telephone on the wall outside our door. I had the feeling that if it rang and was answered the voice on the other end would be German.

The single, blue-painted light bulb which illuminated the place cast a dim, almost funereal light over the scene. After the clamour of the day the calm was oppressive. The area seemed enveloped in it and sleep. And yet I could not succumb to either.

The dingy light burned on; the silence continued. I began, as a kind of mental exercise, to review the events of the last two months in as careful detail as possible. The game of evasion I thus dwelt on had been rich in its lessons of humanity and cool courage. These I was proud to have witnessed, and would, I felt, never forget. Until today, however, the affair had been markedly unglamorous with a basic keynote of passivity. Yet we were here, at the very crest of an armoured assault that had battered a dent thirty miles deep into the German defences in little more than the same number of hours. We had had the singular honour of operating with the Guards Armoured Division (albeit as passengers) at the start of a break-out on to the North German Plain that augured of the sensational. Shortly we should be on our way back and available to resume our part of the fight. Therefore, the evasion had succeeded. The credit belonged, not to us, but entirely to the Dutch. That happened to have been the way in which our particular cookie had crumbled.

I had a yen to be moving on. I looked at the silent figure who sat on the chair.

"When are those blasted petrol lorries coming up then, old lad?" I asked.

"They should be here any time now," he replied.

"Thanks. I can't sleep, so I'd sooner be on the move."

Suddenly there was a hand on my shoulder and a voice in my ear.

"Come on, then! Wakey! Wakey!" said the voice. "You're on your way home."

18

The Road Back

We bumped out of Eibergen in the darkness that precedes the dawn. The time was in fact four o'clock of Sunday, April 1st: a combination of Easter Day and All Fools Day.

The dawn was a cold one and came but slowly. Long before its first faint grey fingers had begun to spread a lighter smear across the east I was shivering in my threadbare coat. When the supply echelon drew to its first complete halt, the driver, a large, seemingly taciturn man, slipped off his greatcoat and passed it without a word across the cab.

For the first time in two months the partnership between Geoff Cheeseman and I was, in a sense, broken, for he sat in the mate's seat of one lorry, I in that of another as we journeyed slowly southwards.

As the sun came up, the route we had traversed a few hours ago in the opposite direction became increasingly visible. The landscape was attractive in a flat sort of way. There was a hint of spring about it, and the battle of yesterday had not left grievous scars. It was true that there were craters in the lush fields and, here and there, in the road itself. But the tide of war had swept swiftly over it, so that, apart from the occasional splintered tree by the roadside, I felt that its evidence would be gone in a few weeks.

Kaleidoscopically, impressions registered: a flight of Typhoons which roared low over our heads flying north; a troop of tanks rumbling over a crossroad heading east; signs which had appeared as if by magic announcing that the verges of the road were clear of mines; an absence of gunfire; the omnipresence of the British; a feeling that the shooting war was a thing of the past.

The morning was still young when the convoy stopped outside a long, low building surrounded by a concrete yard. The driver, who had gradually thawed into a blunt, expletive-studded style of speech as the day lengthened, suggested I might like to stretch my legs.

"You might even get some bloody breakfast if you're lucky," he said as I walked away.

Geoff came up the road towards me, resplendent in army greatcoat.

"Breakfast soon," he said. "What do you make of the caper so far?"

"Pretty easy, I'd say."

The place was a supply depot in the process of being set up. When we came away we could not grumble. We had food inside us, army berets on our heads and shaving gear in our pockets.

"Still no sign of the Luftwaffe," said Geoff, as we wandered back to our lorries. "I wonder why?"

"I couldn't care less. Perhaps Jerry's flat on his Teutonic back and I hope he stays there."

The sudden sight of several hundred Germans arrested my attention as we approached a small town. Harmless, dejected Germans they were, bundled together inside a brand new wire cage by the roadside. So full was it that it looked as if a fresh injection of prisoners would burst it at the seams. The handful of British soldiers and Dutch Resistance men on guard gave us a wave as we went past. The pace of the take-over was fascinating.

The sun flickered fitfully as we entered the frontier village of Dinxperlo. The border-line split it plumb down the middle, for along the edge of one pavement of the main street a high wire fence had been erected, so that the street and one pavement were evidently in Holland while the other pavement was in Germany. Behind the fence dozens of German children had gathered to watch the convoy go by. Their more fortunate Dutch contemporaries were being showered with sweets and chocolates from the slow-moving lorries, but there was nothing for the luckless children of the collapsing Third Reich.

"Prospective vicious Hitler Youth among those brats," observed my blunt friend, as if reading a touch of sentiment stir in my mind. We pressed on into Germany.

Shortly after we had crossed the border there came an example of living off the land. An elderly, bull-necked German farmer gesticulated fervently as the soldiers of the halted supply column demanded his produce. But it was no use. His larder was rapidly emptied. I could have had qualms, had I not remembered how often over many years my Dutch friends had been forced to do the same thing.

"Sod all Krauts!" said the driver, as we left with some eggs.

The countryside began to take on an increasingly battle-scarred look. In Isselburg there was devastation. The convoy drew to a halt. I hopped out of the lorry to stretch my legs again, and stood between it and the gutted remains of what had once been a house on a street corner. The pavement was narrow; I daydreamed in the morning sun. A small, wispy, elderly woman dressed in black had crossed the street and stood oscillating nervously to and fro before me.

"Entschuldigen Sie bitte, Herr Soldat," she said, plucking up courage.

I stood back and let her pass through the narrow gap, half pleased with myself at being taken for a military type again and half ashamed that an old lady should have to ask me to let her walk along her own street.

I watched her dejected, slight figure as she moved on up that shattered street. Her head drooped; she exuded despair. She was a symbol of the ultimate tragedy of war: an elderly, lonely, doubtless sensitive survivor left stranded among the rubble that had once been home.

We rolled into Rees as the morning was ending.

"So long, then. Glad to have had your company," said the driver as I got out of his lorry.

"Thanks very much. Same here. You'll want your greatcoat back."

"Not I, lad. You keep it. I'll easily get another bugger."

I hoped he was right. I'd grown to like the rough diamond who drove that petrol truck.

The captain in charge of the forward echelon handed us over with the words — "You'll never believe this, old chap, but these two are RAF aircrew. Orders are to expedite their return to England. I'll leave them with you. Cheerio!"

The man he addressed was a young, dark-haired officer whose tanned face suggested a love of the open air. He was, of all things, assiduously digging the front garden of a large house. Though whether he regarded it as a recreation or had been burying something was not clear. He immediately laid aside his spade and led us round the back of the building and into a cowshed.

Geoff found it necessary to disappear into one of the empty stalls, and while we waited the army type thrust a hip flask into my hand and told me to have a good swig. I choked for a moment, but the fire in the whisky gave me new life.

"That's better," he said, regarding me studiously. "Actually, you look groggy, but you'd be wiser pressing straight on. The Bailey Bridge here ought to be a prime target for the Luftwaffe, but since all his airfields were knocked out ten days ago Jerry hasn't made a move."

That explained a great deal.

When he said press on, this particular army officer meant it. He installed us on a convoy heading for Gennep, on the Maas, within half an hour.

"Aim for Eindhoven!" he advised, as we left.

The lorries ran for a short distance along the east bank of the Rhine. The road had been hastily repaired, but the fields were cratered beyond description. Cattle still lay where they had fallen, tangled, pulpy masses of decomposition. The sickly sweet smell of death and rotting flesh hung over the area like a pall. Not for nothing had three thousand heavy guns roared in continuous salvo along a short front for hours on end from the far bank.

We came to the bridge and commenced the crossing. Objectively it looked to be half a mile of Bailey and pontoon. But the grey, dismal-looking river lashing hard against the pontoons made the pitching bridge seem longer. However, in a few minutes we were over it. The elusive Rhine had at last been crossed. We were really on our way home.

The land between the rivers was joyless. The fighting in this northernmost tip of the Siegfried Line had been bitter and protracted: the countryside and the towns proclaimed as much. Kalkar was a sorry mess; Goch was an absolute shambles. It was useless to compare either with anything I had yet seen, stupid to think in terms of mere damage. The cumulative effect of bombing and shelling had resulted in utter decimation. We were halted for a while on the road through Goch. The town was a mountain of rubble in which nothing stood upright — a huge heap of shattered brick through which bulldozers had hacked a track. One felt enclosed between the towering mounds to either side. What lay beneath the debris, being invisible, was a matter for the imagination. But for the second time that afternoon I sensed the unpleasant odour of death. It was overpoweringly sombre and depressing.

We drove through the southern fringes of the Reichswald and reached Gennep in the late afternoon. The broad Maas flowed elegantly under its bridge as Cheeseman and I thought out our next move. The supply column had dropped us within sight of the bridge and gone about its business. What we had to do was thumb a lift to Eindhoven, but we were not too certain of the most effective method of doing that.

"The direct way's the best," said Geoff. "Let's ask this MP type."

A corporal of the military police stood directing the traffic at the eastern end of the bridge. Dressed as we were in guardsmens' greatcoats a couple of sizes too big for us, Dutch farmer's breeches and collarless RAF shirts, it seemed to be courting trouble. I foresaw another round of arguments and interrogations. But there was nothing else for it. We approached him and put our case. He was a thin, wizened man with only one serviceable eye, for the other was closed up. It was soon transparently clear that he was an Irishman.

"Well, glory be, boys! You look as if you've had a rough time. I'll help yuh. I'll stop a lorry and get yuh to Eindhoven," he said.

Glory be for trusting folk in a mistrustful world, I thought. This one could have had a medal on the spot for my money.

This driver had a date with a girl to keep; the road was a godforsaken effort made worse by heavy military usage. We bounced and bucked over it like bats out of hell, and were alternately airborne and chairborne until our backsides ached. Nevertheless, it had been dark for some time when we reached our goal.

We were deposited at the headquarters of the RAF service police. The place was large, solid and possessed of an air of dignity.

Easter Sunday still had a couple of hours left to run as we sat on a bench in a corridor and waited to be called, though I felt that we had been mobile for a week. The cumulative effects of an armoured car, military lorries and negligible sleep had shattered me. Listlessly I wondered what our re-entry into the RAF would be like. It chanced that I was first on stage. Into the unknown of the interrogation-room I went.

At a desk in the centre of the room sat a rather small RAF officer. He motioned me to sit opposite him. His voice, when he spoke, held the soft, lilting quality of the east coast Scot.

"Put your identity card in front of me and then tell me your name, rank and number," he said, coolly.

I was on my guard quickly. His manner was suave, but faintly nettling. I sensed a hint of hostility in him.

"1582306, Flight Sergeant Hanson, S.E." I replied, reeling it off parrot-fashion.

"You are aircrew?"

"Yes."

"And what do you say your aircrew trade is?"

The question could have been phrased differently. The implication that he intended to doubt whatever I answered needled me. Nevertheless, I replied to a precise question in the vein in which it was put.

"I say that I am a navigator, sir."

"Tell me, then, your squadron, squadron commander, Group and Command."

"No 207 Squadron, No 5 Group, Bomber Command. Wing Commander Black had the squadron at the time we were shot down."

"I see."

Even the way he said those two simple words irritated, somehow. He was a precise little man and he was beginning to get on my nerves. I wanted badly to bring this to an end and get off to bed. But there was no sign of that. He wrote my answers down assiduously on a large sheet of paper.

"Where is your squadron stationed?" he continued, speeding things up a fraction.

"At Spilsby, Lincolnshire."

"And is yours the only one stationed there?"

"No. No 44 (Rhodesian) Squadron lives there, too."

"I see."

The Scotsman paused and casually lit a cigarette. How long, I wondered, would this hocus-pocus continue? And how many times would this punctilious clot say "I see"? I felt that if he repeated it too often I would still find the strength to reach across his desk and throttle him where he sat. Having had a quiet smoke and looked through his papers he came briskly back to work.

"Your squadron markings?" he queried avidly.

"EM"

"The markings of 44 Squadron?"

"KM."

"Your station call-sign?"

"Lobin."

"The type of aircraft you flew?"

"Lancaster."

"Its serial number?"

That really was the flaming end.

"I haven't a bloody clue," I said. "I don't go wandering round with the serial number of every damn Lancaster tucked away in my head."

"I see."

I felt obsessively drawn to the idea of murder. We were a hundred miles back from the front line. The Army — who were the front line — had accepted us and done us proud. Why the hell should the RAF bilk at us? I could hardly believe it, but this type was in deadly earnest. His method was plain enough. He intended interrogatively to lead me up a seemingly innocent garden path, suddenly find a great hole in it, pounce, and thrust me in, right up to the neck. He had by now a pile of information on the paper in front of him. Pretty soon, he'd be back to it, trying to trip me up.

It was as if my minor loss of temper decided him upon a change of tactics.

"Well, perhaps it was a bit much to expect you to remember the serial number of the aircraft, but what was its designatory letter?" he continued, with an approach that had suddenly become almost pally.

"The Lanc we flew that night was X. X for X-ray."

"Who, by the way, was the station commander?"

"Group Captain Harris."

"I see."

I was diverted from committing mayhem into a discussion that centred on my time in Holland, where I had been, and how by the use of various Guards Armoured Division and RASC lorries, I had managed to reach Eindhoven. He gave me a cigarette and had another himself. At last we were matey. I found myself enthusing about the Dutch and their capacity to run an Underground Movement. I half thought I had convinced him. That was a mistake.

"You said that you were 1583206 Flight Sergeant Hanson and that you flew Lancaster KM — X-ray," he said, changing the line of thought like greased lightning.

"No, I did not. You've deliberately transposed a number, and our aircraft was EM — X-ray."

Off we went again into a patter of rapid irrelevancies. But I was wary of him this time. These were 'throw-away' observations and questions. He'd soon be back to the game. All the more reason, I reckoned, in spite of the fatigue that was beginning to swamp me, to play a straight bat. He did not waste overmuch time.

"Your squadron commander, you said, was Wing Commander Harris."

It was no good. My interrogator became my tormentor. My bat became crooked; I went berserk.

"You know bloody well I didn't" I ranted. "I said that Wing Co' Black commanded the squadron, and I meant exactly that. You can try tripping me up all night if you like, but it won't succeed."

In no very quiet way I gave my opinion of men who sat on their shiny arses asking questions. That sentiment and a bit more I raved at him. Vaguely I was aware that it was asking for trouble. But I cared not a damn about that. Whatever was in his mind, there was only one operative idea in mine: I intended in the shortest possible time to let my people know in person that I was still alive and kicking.

A door at the far end of the room opened, and a burly, red-haired flight lieutenant with 'Canada' marked on the shoulder flash of his tunic entered.

"I heard voices raised. Do you need any help there?" he asked, looking at the interrogator and then glaring at me. The glaring was mutual.

The Scotsman smiled. "No, not necessary, we're doing very nicely, thanks" he said.

The game, without my realising it, was almost over. His next words tended to put the matter to bed.

"There was no need to lose your temper, flight sergeant," he said, when the Canadian had gone. "I had a job to do, I've done it and I'm satisfied. If I were not satisfied, that mumbo-jumbo, as you called it, would have gone on all night. As it is, you can go now and send your comrade in. Are you all right for tobacco, by the way?"

I replied, sulkily, that I had plenty, and left the room.

Geoff's interrogation was shorter than mine. While I waited I reflected on the Scot. He had been thorough, but eminently correct. Certainly he had not taken offence or pulled his rank when I flared off at him. Maybe he'd intended all along to make me lose my temper. Probably I had been a churl, but I still felt truculent.

Cheeseman came out and resumed his seat on the bench beside me.

"Had a row with the type in there did you?" he asked.

"Yes I did. He shouldn't have tried to make me out a liar."

"The bod was only doing his job, you clot."

"That's what he said. I'm sure you're both right."

I was spared from bunking down in the corridor by the arrival of a disgustingly healthy-looking sergeant SP who gently blethered something about the need for rest as he led us away. He seemed to look at me as if I were a creature resurrected from the grave. "Sod you for a Jeremiah!" I thought, quite unjustly, as we went to the place of rest.

The bed was warm and comfortable. Nothing of consequence disturbed the peace. In seconds I was sound asleep.

I stood for a good twenty minutes in the ablution room with brand-new razor, brush, shaving soap and unlimited hot water, and solemnly hacked every offending bristle off my face. That, when I stared in the mirror, pleased me even less than usual, for it now possessed the smooth chalky whiteness of the Siberian Plain in mid-winter. Every vestige of colour had ebbed away. Nevertheless, the morning found me feeling immeasurably better. Conversely it was Geoff's turn to feel morose.

The jeep we sat in crossed the Belgian border in the early afternoon of Monday, April 2nd. I enjoyed the feel of the air on my face as we travelled. Geoff was very quiet. We arrived at length at an army camp. It had a deserted air as we passed the lines of brick-built barracks and the extensive parade ground. Quite a place, but, so far as I could see, empty.

A medical was the first thing on the agenda. There was a small bonus given, for, the normal thorough checking done, we were dusted with powder to settle the hash of non-existent lice.

"You'll do, my lad," sang out the MO, jovially. "A few weeks leave and you'll be as fit as a fiddle."

Yesterday I would have judged that a platitude; today I felt he could be right.

The CO of the camp had a chat with us. He said that the place was almost in readiness to receive some of the thousands of prisoners of war who would be released in the Allied advance. He was very pleased to see us, for we were his first customers.

To our observation that we badly needed a bath, he told us to get the priorities right.

"What you really need, lads, is a good meal followed by a long sleep. Then in the morning you can have the finest shower you can think of. This is a prewar Belgian army camp and you'll find the baths palatial."

He dismissed us courteously. He was a kindly sort.

As we followed the orderly round the edge of the parade ground in search of the good tea the colonel had promised, a jeep pulled up on the opposite side. The driver went into a building; two men remained motionless in the rear seats.

I could only really see the nearer of the two. But something about him was familiar. He was a hundred yards distant and disguised in an army greatcoat. And yet I knew I could not be mistaken. The yellow hair and the cut of the head made me certain. The nearer figure in that jeep was Eric Copley. Therefore the other must be Ron Young.

"Christ! Cheesey," I said. "That's Yorick and von Kluge over there. I'm off."

I ran across the parade square as fast as my out-of-form legs would carry me, and stood puffing and panting at the side of the jeep. At closer quarters Copley's disguise was accentuated. He had grown a luxurious moustache.

"Look, von Kluge! Here's Mrs Hanson's son," said Yorick, with the usual touch of deprecatory banter. "The lad's run like a hare to get here, but he looks a bit white round the gills. How did you manage to get a colour like that?"

"A long story, Yorick. I'll tell it you sometime. But here's the driver coming back, so I'll leave you to get deloused."

"Deloused?"

"Naturally. A very painful process. See you later. We're just off for a meal."

The colonel was right: the tea was excellent. After it Cheeseman and I retired to our billet. There was no conversation. It was as if a sense of anticlimax had drained us, particularly Geoff. And yet, in a way, my spirits had never been higher. We had two of the crew back with us for sure. I went to sleep as the evening drew in and knew nothing till morning.

We were moved on quickly. There was just time for a shower after breakfast. It was sheer delight to soak under a stream of hot water, apply some soap, and watch the dirt and muck of two months gurgle down the plug-hole. That done, we were off for Brussels.

The imposing building of the RAF Headquarters Unit stood in the rue du Congrès. Up its broad flight of steps went our driver; down, a few moments later, bounded an energetic-looking group captain. His smile was infectious as he airily waved aside our somewhat ragged attempts to salute him.

"Where exactly have you come from, chaps?" he asked.

"From Gelderland, sir."

"You've escaped, I believe."

We acknowledged that it could be put like that.

"Well done! Well done!" he said, and shook us all cordially by the hand.

This was red-carpet stuff, and very flattering, coming as it did from 'top brass'. It seemed somehow to make the whole thing worthwhile.

He took us to a room which he said was reserved for distressed aircrew. There were bottles of beer in a locker, sandwiches made available, magazines to read and armchairs to loll in. In five minutes we felt completely at home.

"Would it be a good idea if I sent my sergeant up at eight o'clock tonight to take you round the clubs?" he asked as he left us.

"Marvellous, sir," we replied.

The wares of the locker were tried gently for size.

"They bred some wizard sorts in the old RFC," said von Kluge, sprawling languidly with a glass in his hand. "Great type that Groupy!"

Amen to that, I thought, as the ale gurgled down.

It was not only stray airmen who used the distressed aircrew room. For of the two other occupants already in residence, one was a corporal of the Airborne Regiment who had been captured at Arnhem. He and the RAF wireless operator — shot down over Denmark in 1940 — who was with him had escaped from a POW camp in a manner that was both slick and illuminating.

Their Stalag stood in an area that had been the subject of persistent bombardment from the air. One recent day when the American

Fortressed rode once again immaculate and high across the heavens, the 'goons' had panicked and left a motor-cycle adjacent to the unguarded gate. The two had seized their chance and zoomed out of captivity on the transport kindly provided. That it could have happened at all spoke volumes for the collapsing morale of Jerry.

In the late afternoon our numbers increased to seven. It was not in the least probable that the dress of the six incumbents would have delighted even a lenient adjutant, but at that point in time a Canadian entered who put us all to shame. He had somehow avoided the acquisition of so much as one scrap of army equipment and appeared before us in an ungodly ensemble of rags and tatters. He looked about as resplendent as the local rag and bone man, and seemed not unproud of the fact.

He was, in reality, a fighter pilot who swore that he had shot himself down by running into the ricochets of his own cannon shells whilst strafing a road near Enschede, and near that town he had remained in hiding ever since. Three months previously he had had his own squadron of Typhoons.

In the evening the sergeant took us out to savour the night life of the city. The lights shone brightly as we meandered round on a Belgian pub-crawl. The clubs were full, the life gay. Nobody gave a damn any more about the prospect of German bombing — that was a thing of the past. The beer flowed wherever we went; we were in our oiltots immediately, and slipped progressively into our cups. There was, however, one peculiarity about our pub-crawling session. Not infrequently as we ambled round the centre of the city, our little group would find itself short of a member.

"Where's he gone now?" the corporal from Arnhem would ask.

More than once we retraced our steps to find the wireless operator standing on a street corner, just staring at the lights of the town. The long-term Kriegie (Kriegsgefangene) who had seen nothing but barbed-wire and the dismal grey of a German Stalag for five years was attracted by those street-lamps as surely as a moth to a candle. He was all right, but, for the moment, dazzled.

On the stroke of midnight we returned to 10 rue du Congrès. The bulk of the party went straight to bed; Copley and I, having had too much to drink, sat on the stairs to clear our heads. We were by no means paralytic. What we really wanted to do was to swap tales, a thing which up to now we had, somehow, not managed to get round to.

"What's the gen?" queried Yorick.

I told him our story, ending with the news about Chuck Fowler. He was basically as disinclined to believe that as I was, but the only evidence we had to the contrary was the statement long ago by Karl that one of the crew had been caught in Lichtenvoorde and the construction we had put on it.

"Ironic," said Copley. "All along I've worried about Norman. Now you tell me it's Chuck."

I found I had grave doubts about both. It was inevitable that the mask one wore to conceal the innermost feelings should sometimes slip. But there was no good purpose served by letting the slide continue.

"Come on, Yorick!" I said. "Tell us about the great escape!"

"Escape? How do you do that sitting in a room for two months on end?"

"A room with a view?"
"Well, yes, at least there was that."
The room they had lived in stood in the centre of the town of Groenlo. It was, in fact, the attic of a bank. To this room Copley and Young had been led by dead of night, after Cheeseman and I had left them in the hen-coop.
There was a peculiarity about this particular bank, for, at the time in question, it no longer fulfilled its normal function. A German infantry division was at rest in the town and, as luck would have it, had commandeered the building as a home for its Pay Corps. Thus, daily, the ground floor was used to calculate the wages of the Wehrmacht; van Eisen, the out of work bank manager, and his family occupied the first floor; and the RAF the attic.
"Comic set-up, eh?" queried Yorick, a flicker of amusement beginning to dawn in his eye.
"Too funny for words. I marvel you got away with it."
The view they enjoyed was afforded by the attic window, which looked directly out upon the town square. A parade was held each morning, and the RAF representatives in the area spent many an hour peeping furtively out and awarding marks for the German division's drill.
The attic was barely furnished, for it contained no more than a chair, a single bed, and a wardrobe.
There had been a little yellow haired hunchback named Sjeffie, the son of the burgomaster, who had undertaken to act as travelling librarian. He was so frail-looking that nobody ever suspected him as he cycled round with enough English books in his saddlebag for swapping to keep even the insatiable Copley happy in that respect.
There was also a priest who had twice been put in concentration camps for his sins and gone slightly crazed as a consequence. He had been let, perhaps unwisely, into the secret of their presence and had gone round the district in his dog-cart, knocking on doors and loudly demanding cigarettes for the two English airmen. A merciful Providence had worked hard on their behalf, for they had continued to get away with it.
"I still can't believe it could have worked," I interposed, at this point. "Wasn't the area ever searched?"
"Too damn right it was. Those lousy sods of Dutch Nazis searched often, because they knew there were 'divers' and Jews hidden away in the town. But we were always warned when they were coming, and in any case we could see them strutting about in their uniforms when they got close. Then, of course, we used the escape route and disappeared from the scene faster then the vanishing lady."
Yorick warmed to his tale. There had, he said, been a moment of high drama when Leny had come flying up the stairs to warn them that the German Pay Corps officer was unexpectedly coming aloft to visit the family. It was early evening, and the pair had been busy at the time in the kitchen below peeling potatoes for dinner. In the mad panic to get back to the attic, the bucket they were using was knocked over, and the visitor waded through a spud-bestrewn kitchen to knock on the living-room door a moment after they reached the safety of their den.

"Leny? A girl in your bank, Copley?"

"Two, actually. Van Eisen's daughters played a leading role. Shall I tell you about Leny?"

"Do!"

"Well, she's about eighteen, slim, and quite a dish. The German officer I spoke about was a stolid, chunky Kraut in his forties, but to string Jerry along Leny affected an attachment for him. Therefore he used to come back to the bank some evenings and stand singing "Gebundene Hände" and all those dripping-with-sentiment type old German love songs in the room below, while she accompanied. You can imagine von Kluge's comments as the strains wafted up."

It did not stretch the imagination to breaking point to see Ron Young and Eric sitting in the attic howling — quietly of course — at the amorous Kraut singing love songs beneath their floorboards. However, on the theme of the slender but devious Dutch maiden and the portly, duped German officer Copley's thumb-nail sketch came to its close.

The tale he told had not been fundamentally an amusing one. In fact, the tensions and tedium for the aircrew and the appalling risks run by the Dutch made it a combination of the gallant and the hair-raising. And yet, the way Yorick told it, it was in parts more than funny: facets of it were plain bloody hilarious.

"Come on Cop'! It's getting late," I said.

Our heads having cleared somewhat, we rose from our cold perch on the stairs and staggered quietly off to bed.

In the morning we were issued with a small amount of money and let loose on the streets of Brussels with a guide. I bought a bottle of perfume for my intended and a pipe for myself. The effort cost me all the cash I had, and I felt that I'd been rooked. Still, blewing a fiver was a marvellous feeling.

After lunch we moved off for Waterloo Airport. The Group Captain commanding in Brussels was, as Ron Young had observed, a great type. He would have none of our travelling in jeeps. He put his limousine at our disposal, and we rolled the few miles to Waterloo in great style.

The guard on the gate saluted the car with due deference, but peered at the occupants incredulously. There was no braid or 'scrambled-egg' inside. Just odd bods in ill-fitting army greatcoats and tatty old clothes.

"Not to worry," said Yorick. "He probably thinks it's the flaming Chinese General Staff arriving."

Arrived we had. In no time we were aboard an aircraft of Transport Command and airborne. There was opportunity for a quick look at the bomb-battered landscape of the Pas de Calais. And then we were stooging across the Channel. Over the south coast of England we flew. The Dakota's wheels touched the concrete of an English runway. We landed at RAF Down Ampney, in Cotswold country, just in time for tea.

Epilogue

On the morning following our return to England we were whisked smartly off by train to Military Intelligence in London. There were no half measures. The door of the compartment was solemnly locked behind us; the whole thing possessed an atmosphere of cloak and dagger. 'Abandon hope all ye who enter here', was not actually written above the portals of that pearl of the Establishment, but there were times when I felt it ought to have been. However, there came a moment when all interrogations were at an end and all that remained was to collect a travel warrant.

There followed a long leave, during the course of which Eric Copley and I visited Norman's parents in Nottinghamshire. They looked to us for news, but we had, of course, nothing to offer. It was a difficult business explaining how it was possible for their son, our rear gunner, to disappear without our hearing so much as a word from him. The groan each of us had heard over the intercom was not mentioned, but almost three months had gone by since the crash, and absolutely nothing had been heard of him. The matter was not improved by the fact that the gen about Chuck Fowler was palpably duff. He and Johnny Eaton, the wireless operator, were known to be prisoners of war. But the crew's baby seemed to have vanished into thin air. Things looked black.

The war in the west had actually ended when news came. At the other end of the telephone Mr Levick strove very hard to be calm that Saturday night. He told me that Norman had been reported alive and back in England. RAF Cosford had been turned very largely into a hospital and rehabilitation unit for returning sick and disabled POWs. Among them was his son.

Cosford was no great distance away. I took an early train for Wolverhampton the following day and reached the hospital while the morning was yet young. As I walked along the corridors my mind was plagued with doubt. There were some very sick and some severely disabled people in RAF Cosford. In what shape should I find him?

The anticipatory doubt was worse than the reality. As I entered the ward I was aware that someone was sitting up in the bed facing the door, waving like mad to attract my attention. He had recognised me on the instant, and after a second's pause, I recognised him. It was undoubtedly Norman Levick. But it was a very thin-looking Levick, and his face was as yellow as a Chinaman's. Certainly he looked more than nineteen years old.

"Great to see you, Norman! You look fine!" I lied.

"Oh, I'm not so bad now, apart from this flaming jaundice."

"How did you manage that?"

The tale unfolded and solved all problems, bar one. Why we had failed to hear from him during the fighter attack became immediately clear. Odd creatures known as gremlins had been known to interest themselves, frequently disastrously, in the affairs of RAF aircrew for years. Most often they played hell with aircraft equipment. Such had been our fate. Norman had been bawling manoeuvring instructions into a dead intercom as the Junkers attacked. The result had inevitably been that we had flown on as straight and level as a duck on a placid pond, and paid the penalty. That the attack had not been persisted with had undoubtedly been due to an element of tit for tat, for the Junkers broke away through the cloud below us with a fire blossoming nicely on his starboard wing. Still, we were finished; the gremlins had won.

A very late exit from the aircraft, with flames streaming well past his turret, had followed; a characteristically dour performance before a German interrogator at Dulag Luft had brought about a Teutonic loss of temper and an assurance that the Red Cross would never be told that he was a prisoner of war; forced marching on very little food as the Germans drove their prisoners deeper into the Fatherland in front of the Allied advance had weakened him to the extent where he had lost three stones in weight; jaundice had finally laid him low.

There was no point in asking whether he had been hurt in the attack, for clearly he had not. The groan we had heard, and come to the wrong conclusion about, was not his. A dead intercom precluded the possibility. That puzzle would remain unsolved for ever. But why worry? The whole crew had baled out and all seven were alive to tell the tale. That was all that mattered.

Before that morning session ended he'd begun to make a crack or two in good style. There was no doubt he'd soon be well. No news had become good news in the end. Come to that, the outcome of the entire business was almost too good to be true. I wondered who the clot was who'd said the age of miracles was past.

Hostilities over, we inevitably went our separate ways. There was a pretty riotous party at the Levick's house in the summer of 1945. There the crew met for one last fling, and then that was that — or almost so. Yorick, who combines his job as chief engineer in charge of the complicated machinery of a hosiery factory with an absorbing interest in the Leicester Air Training Corps, Norman, who breeds pigs and runs a transport concern in Beckingham, Notts, and I, never lost touch. To the excellent memories of Mr E.H. Copley and Mr N.S. Levick I owe much in the writing of this book.

Not long ago that ace researcher of the Lancaster, M.A. Garbett, presented me with an address in Melbourne, and I was able to re-establish contact with Chuck Fowler, who had in the meantime become a lawyer.

On the Dutch side of the coin I was lucky enough early on to strike up a correspondence with Wim Lensink and Henk Hulshof. Wim had gone back to his job in the police force, and remains in it still. Ironically, he returned in recent years to Neede — once the scene of his defecting activities against the Germans — as chief of police. Via their agencies it has been my good fortune to meet again virtually everyone who helped me along the way. And that was not always so easy as it sounds, for the superb Dutch capacity to be tight-lipped when they chose, whilst ideal in the running of an Underground Movement, posed problems of re-discovery later. Still, there was always a welcome when we did find them. And what more can you ask for than that?

The old farmer, who had once numbered a hollow haystack among his possessions, lived on to the grand old age of eighty-eight. Many a time in the after-war years I was to sit and smoke a quiet pipe with him. A very undemonstrative but deeply human man, Meneer te Lindert carried through to the end the traditions of hard work and application that have, within the last century, turned the sandy, basically unhelpful soil of Gelderland into the rich farming province it now is. His wife — as kind a person as I ever met — having died, the management of the farm was increasingly left to Johan, the elder son, and his wife Hanna. The old place has been to some extent modernised in recent years, but it still somehow retains an aura of the time when it was farm, arsenal and place of refuge rolled into one.

It is a fact that, so far as I was concerned, the spring of 1945 came late. In the darkness of the haystack it seemed to approach with the excruciating slowness of a lumbago-ridden snail. But finally it came, and the compensations have been more than ample. I haven't a clue what I've done to deserve it, but Johan, 'Leo', Norman, Wim and 'Yorick' are still my close friends to this day. Come to think of it, I wouldn't have missed that spell in the dark for the world.